CHILDREN'S HEARINGS

'*I hope my drawing will help people to understand how children feel at hearings.*'

Karen (15 years)
Dr. Guthrie's Girls' School, Edinburgh

CHILDREN'S HEARINGS

Edited by

F. M. MARTIN and
KATHLEEN MURRAY

with a Foreword by
LORD KILBRANDON

1976

SCOTTISH ACADEMIC PRESS

Published by
Scottish Academic Press Ltd,
33 Montgomery Street
Edinburgh EH7 5JX

SBN 7073 0128 8

Printed in Great Britain by
R. & R. Clark Ltd, Edinburgh

CONTENTS

FOREWORD

by Lord Kilbrandon

IT HAS THE APPEARANCE of unusually expeditious social reform: a Departmental Committee set up in 1961 with instructions to examine a highly controversial subject on which opinions have always been as diverse as the interests concerned: a Report (unanimous) in 1964: Legislation giving effect to its fundamental conclusions in 1968. No-one can be held blameworthy for the fact that the machinery sanctioned by Parliament took three years to set up. It was quite a feat that the elaborate, and in some ways revolutionary, system was evolved and brought into action so soon. Now, after 5 years of actual operation, it is in every sense appropriate that the new system be examined by impartial experts, the principles upon which it is found re-examined, and the practical efficacy of the reforms evaluated. Five years is not too short a time; social changes have come upon us since 1971 at a faster rate than peace-time has ever brought us, and in any case 5 years is a long time in the life of a child. The 'children' we studied are now, I suppose, 'young persons', and the young persons will, many of them, be parents themselves.

After reading this magisterial work, I find some of my own rather uninstructed impressions confirmed. First, I do not regret that the Committee's idea of attaching the children's panels, and the supporting field organisation, to the education authorities was rejected in favour of the Social Work system as we know it. I do not mean that intellectually or fundamentally we were wrong, but rather that the organisational difficulties would have led to much opposition and frustration. On that aspect, I would like to pay a particular tribute to the unselfish public spirit of the probation service. Their loss of identity must have grieved them, yet I remember, at a very early date, hearing the late Frank Dawtry, whose memory so many cherish, saying to the Cambridge Institute of Criminology that he thought the change was right.

Second, I have misgivings at the number of cases in which children, on Crown Office instructions, are tried in the criminal courts. This may be a concession partly to a public opinion which is not yet sufficiently familiar with the new system to be able to understand the principles behind it, and partly to the innate distrust of change common among those learned in the law. The fact of *trial* in the criminal court is of comparatively minor importance, provided that after a finding of guilt the accused is remitted to the children's hearing for the appropriate treatment to be assessed. There is, I believe, something to be said for making this mandatory instead of discretionary. It could well be that the interaction between the Crown court jurisdiction and the powers of the hearings requires reconsideration in all its aspects; the key consideration, which ought to govern them, is that the control and review of the hearings are part of the civil, not the criminal, functions of the Queen's courts.

Third, the inadequacy, arising from malnutrition, of the supporting field organisation can give occasion only for regretful acknowledgement. It is, however, important to emphasise the fact, not infrequently ignored, that the available resources would be equally inadequate were they deployed by the criminal enforcement agencies.

Lastly, there is this for the Scottish social work services to be proud of. My connection with the working out of the new principles has for many years been less than tenuous. Nevertheless, merely because my name is fortuitously associated with the plan, I am in constant touch with learned and devoted foreigners, especially from the United States and from European countries, who are anxious to know more about what they regard as an important contribution, for which Scotland should take credit, to the problem of making it easier for the young to enjoy and to make the most of their youth. This book will meet a large international demand.

16th July 1976   Kilbrandon

THE CONTRIBUTORS

<table>
<tr><td>GEOFF APLIN</td><td>Lecturer in the Department of Social Administration and Social Work,
University of Glasgow.</td></tr>
<tr><td>RICHARD W. BETT</td><td>Staff Officer to H.M. Chief Inspector of Constabulary for Scotland.</td></tr>
<tr><td>DOUGLAS A. F. CONOCHIE</td><td>Depute Regional Educational Psychologist,
Grampian Regional Council.</td></tr>
<tr><td>MARGARET DOBIE</td><td>Regional Chairman,
Dumfries and Galloway Children's Panel.</td></tr>
<tr><td>ALAN FINLAYSON</td><td>Regional Reporter to Lothian Children's Panel.</td></tr>
<tr><td>A. RUSSELL FORREST</td><td>Principal Psychologist,
East of Scotland List D Schools.</td></tr>
<tr><td>SANFORD J. FOX</td><td>Professor of Law,
Boston College Law School, Massachusetts, U.S.A.</td></tr>
<tr><td>CARYL GODWIN</td><td>Legal Apprentice,
Strathclyde Regional Council.</td></tr>
<tr><td>GERALD GORDON</td><td>Professor of Scots Law,
University of Edinburgh.</td></tr>
<tr><td>JOHN P. GRANT</td><td>Senior Lecturer in the Department of Public International Law,
University of Glasgow.
Member of Strathclyde Regional Children's Panel.</td></tr>
<tr><td>JANET HASSAN</td><td>Psychologist.
Formerly Principal Psychologist,
East of Scotland List D Schools.</td></tr>
<tr><td>VERA HIDDLESTON</td><td>Principal Lecturer in Social Work,
Jordanhill College of Education.
Member of Strathclyde Regional Children's Panel.</td></tr>
<tr><td>MAEVE McDONALD</td><td>Member of Strathclyde Regional Children's Panel.</td></tr>
<tr><td>F. M. MARTIN</td><td>Professor of Social Administration and Dean of the Faculty of Social Sciences, University of Glasgow.</td></tr>
</table>

GEORGE J. MURRAY — Assistant Secretary,
Social Work Services Group,
Scottish Office.

KATHLEEN MURRAY — Lecturer (Children's Panel Training) in the Department of Extra-Mural and Adult Education,
University of Glasgow.

SUE SPALTON — Training Officer,
Grampian Regional Social Work Department.

PATRICIA THOMAS — Head Teacher,
James Gillespie's High School, Edinburgh.
Formerly Member of West Lothian Children's Panel.

KEITH WARDROP — Consultant Forensic Psychiatrist,
The Douglas Inch Centre, Glasgow.

DAVID WATSON — Lecturer in the Department of Moral Philosophy,
University of Glasgow.
Member of Strathclyde Regional Children's Panel.

INTRODUCTION

IN SUCH FIELDS as health and welfare, education and local government, Scottish legislation is enacted separately from that for England and Wales. Characteristically, Scottish Bills go through Parliament about one year after their English counterparts and differ in many matters of detail though rarely in general scope and intent. One striking exception to the common practice was the Social Work (Scotland) Act, which antedated by two years its nearest equivalent, the Local Authority Social Services Act 1970. The departure from the customary pattern was not merely in terms of priority in time, but also in the significantly broader and more ambitious range of the Scottish Act. In particular, the latter established a wholly new system of juvenile justice, which was not to be replicated for England and Wales either as a part of the reorganisation of social services or as an alternative to the reform of juvenile court procedure outlined in the Children and Young Persons Act 1969. The Scottish system of 'children's hearings' has now been in operation for exactly five years, and it is with that system that this book is concerned. Our contributors and we as editors have tried to present an account of the history and development of juvenile justice reform in Scotland, of the present structure of the system and the mode of operation of its component parts, as well as to offer some examination of the critical issues raised by the new system.

The book as a whole has been designed to serve several different purposes, and it will be clear that not all its chapters are directed towards the same objectives. A central feature of the Scottish system is the work of some 1,600 volunteers who form 'Children's Panels', and our first purpose – first in terms of its rôle in the evolution of the book and in terms of the importance we attach to it – was to provide a text which would be of value in the training of panel members. We believed too that both inside and outwith Scotland there were sufficient professional people and concerned laymen with an interest in young people in trouble to justify the production of a volume containing a detailed review of a new and distinctive mode of provision. Finally, we thought it important that the experience of participants in the Scottish system should be articulated and the views of some observers of that system be defined and given public expression at the present time; not because it is yet possible to pass some definitive judgement, but rather in the spirit of an interim statement, one of whose principal purposes it is to stimulate interest in the possibilities of further observation, commentary and research. The lessons to be learned from the Scottish system of juvenile justice are not relevant only to that system. In its philosophical and operational complexities are reflected issues encountered in greater or lesser degree by any attempt to respond to law-breaking in terms other than the merely deterrent and retributive. The very explicitness of the underlying principles of Part III of the Social Work (Scotland) Act makes it impossible to conceal tensions and conflicts which elsewhere may be less open to scrutiny, but are no less significant.

Many of our contributors have been closely identified with the development of the hearings system, having worked within it either as panel members or as associated professionals, and several others have become involved through contributing to the training of panel members. They represent a wide range of backgrounds, as we have deliberately tried to bring together laymen and professionals, practitioners and academics who have either directly experienced or studied the operation of the system, so as to share their observations and interpretations. We have also tried, though with rather limited success, to draw upon experience acquired in as many as possible of the regions of Scotland. There are of course vast differences in population structure, environmental conditions and prevailing life-styles and value-systems, so that the experience of Glasgow may have little relevance in Orkney. Perhaps inevitably, however, the great majority of our contributors are drawn from the Strathclyde and Lothian Regions, which between them contain about 70% of the population of Scotland.

The chapters of this book have been grouped into five sections, and since many readers will be seeking to satisfy specific interests it may be helpful briefly to indicate the scope of each of these sections. The first deals with the historical origins of the hearings system, its objectives and formal structure, its relationship with the established judicial system, and with some quantitative aspects of its operation. In section II are brought together accounts of the principal elements of the new system: the rôles and functions of the children's panels; of the reporters who administer panel business and make critical decisions concerning referrals; of the police who are the source of most referrals; and of the social work departments of the regional authorities, responsible for the provision of essential reports and for carrying out supervision orders. The third section is perhaps more heterogeneous. Its central concern is the hearing, the heart of the system, and it includes consideration both of theoretical principles and of their practical application. Problems of assessment, of interviewing and of evaluation of reports are discussed together with the rules of procedure; a review of theories of delinquency gives panel members an opportunity to examine the assumptions which may underlie their own reactions to young offenders. In the following section contributors outline and comment on the services provided by a number of agencies upon whose resources the children's hearings may draw, whether based on the social work service, on the educational system or on medicine. In addition, particular attention is given in this section to the uses of intermediate treatment and residential services. The last major section of the book introduces some critical and comparative perspectives. Underlying philosophical and legal issues are discussed; children's hearings are considered in an international context as a distinctive system of juvenile justice, and panel membership is examined in the light of experience. In a final chapter, we attempt an overall assessment of the strengths and weaknesses of the hearings system, drawing partly on the material provided in the foregoing chapters, partly on the findings of research, and largely on our own judgement.

The cover design and frontispiece were chosen from a range of fine drawings submitted by children in List D schools who had been invited to convey their impressions of a children's hearing. We should like to thank the children for their interest and in particular Joseph (12 years) of St. Ninian's School, Gartmore and Karen (15 years) of Dr. Guthrie's Girls' School, Edinburgh for their imaginative contributions.

A number of friends and colleagues, in addition to the named authors, have contributed to the compilation of this book. We should like in particular to thank Mrs E. W. Grant for her invaluable help in editing many manuscripts, Mrs J. Banks, Mrs M. Clubb and Miss E. Dunbar who typed successive drafts of chapters. We are grateful also to the Children's Panel Training Group convened by the Social Work Services Group of the Scottish Office, for their encouragement and advice. Their moral support however does not confer any official status upon this book; it remains a collection of individual statements for which only the respective authors and we as editors bear any responsibility.

F. M. MARTIN
KATHLEEN MURRAY

Section I

A NEW SYSTEM

BY THE LATE 1950's it had become unmistakeably clear that many of the expectations which had been placed on the social and economic reforms of the post-war years had not been realised. In spite of a major legislative programme that had created a new national pattern of welfare provision, in spite of advances in material standards of living and the maintenance of high levels of employment, a whole range of social problems showed no sign of diminishing; many, indeed – and not least among them the problems of crime and delinquency – appeared to be steadily increasing. From this recognition of continuing social malaise flowed a variety of intellectual and political consequences. Among other things, there followed a decade of eponymous reports. Successive Governments set up a series of committees to look into such matters as the problems of youth, the management of delinquency, the need for personal social services. One such committee, in Scotland, was concerned particularly with the possibilities of using more creatively the machinery of juvenile justice. Its recommendations, in general implemented, though in an organisational context quite different from that anticipated by the committee, proposed the transfer of responsibility for dealing with children and young people in trouble from the courts to a new and largely welfare-oriented system.

After five years of operation the new system of children's hearings, with its interaction of lay and professional participants, has acquired a distinctive and in most respects an independent identity. Yet it is not and cannot be wholly insulated from the court-based judicial system. Apart from appeals and denials of grounds of referral, a substantial minority of young people continues to be prosecuted, for a variety of reasons, by traditional court procedures. This overlap of two modes of response to the young offender, embodying contrasting and on the face of it conflicting assumptions both about causation and responsibility and about the objectives of 'disposals' and 'sentences', raises important issues concerning the internal consistency of the values and attitudes underlying current practices.

Disputes over values cannot be settled by recourse to arithmetic; however, information couched in statistical form can throw light on the working of a decision-making system and by relating intentions to outcomes assess the validity of its claims. As yet, the consequences of disposals by children's hearings have not been analysed systematically. In the meantime it is possible to assemble a simple framework of descriptive statistics which gives some indication of the scale of the work in different parts of the country and prepares the way for future evaluative studies and for further analysis of patterns of delinquency in the community.

I

JUVENILE JUSTICE REFORM

GEORGE MURRAY

THE ESTABLISHMENT of children's hearings in Scotland has been the most recent of a series of reforms of juvenile justice ranging over some sixty years. The creation of juvenile courts in 1908 had in its time been a very important measure of reform, involving the recognition that children should be treated separately and that the sheriff, burgh and JP court arrangements for children should differ from those for adults. A new concern for education, training and reform began to supplant the traditional emphasis on punishment. Subsequently Scottish legislation in the 1930's recommended a specific transfer of jurisdiction for children and young offenders to specially constituted JP juvenile courts, with specially suitable justices. Only four Scottish authorities however introduced these arrangements. One major difficulty remained implicit in the system: the juvenile courts did not differ fundamentally from the adult courts even though they employed a different range of disposals. The sheriff, bailies or justices of the peace were still concerned with the establishment of guilt or innocence in the formal court setting. They had to decide upon a sentence which would be appropriate in the context of the normal working assumptions of a court of justice, while at the same time relating this to the welfare of the child, which was now a clear requirement both of the statutes and of enlightened public opinion.

POST-WAR REFORMS

While the juvenile courts were grappling with these problems, the very unsatisfactory and complex arrangements for dealing with children in public care led to the setting up of the Curtis Committee[1] in England and the Clyde Committee[2] in Scotland. These resulted in the Children Act 1948 which produced local authority children's departments with an obligation to consider the needs and abilities of children in their care. The growth of a specialised child care service was followed by an increasing realisation that if children were to be able to remain within their own homes, more preventive action would be needed in relation to the whole family situation. The work of the Ingleby[3] and

McBoyle[4] Committees was followed by the Children and Young Persons Act 1963 which empowered local authorities to give positive help to families though on account of shortage of staff and funds the progress has been limited.

The Ingleby Committee in England and Wales also suggested changes in the juvenile court system which would diminish the emphasis on crime and punishment. Apart from raising the age of criminal responsibility to 10, the 1963 Act did little to modify the court process. A subsequent ambitious White Paper, 'The Child, the Family and the Young Offender',[5] proposed replacing juvenile courts with family courts and provoked such a flood of controversy that the suggestion was abandoned. The Government later produced a new White Paper, 'Children in Trouble',[6] which advocated a new form of procedure for young offenders and led in 1969 to the Children and Young Persons Act for England and Wales.

The Kilbrandon Committee

In 1961 the Secretary of State for Scotland appointed a Committee under the chairmanship of Lord Kilbrandon: *to consider the provision of the law of Scotland relating to the treatment of juvenile delinquents and juveniles in need of care or protection or beyond parental control and, in particular, the constitution, powers, and procedure of the courts dealing with such juveniles and to report.* The findings were published in 1964.[7] Its analysis was that children appearing before the courts, whether for offences or as being in need of care and protection, showed a basic similarity in a failure of the upbringing process, and had a common need for special measures of education and training. These would involve working closely with the parents, and required the formation in each area of a locally based treatment authority. The existing juvenile court arrangements did not make this easy with their emphasis on guilt or innocence and punishment of the guilty. The Committee was clear that there must be a separation of the fact-finding part of the process from the consideration of treatment; and that this could hardly be done under the existing system.

The Committee's solution was to take juveniles under the age of sixteen out of the criminal system except for the gravest cases; to replace the juvenile courts by juvenile panels; to have cases referred to the panel only by an official called the reporter; and to set up a matching fieldwork agency to provide background reports and recommendations for treatment. The panels could act only when the facts were admitted. Disputed grounds would be determined by the sheriff, as would appeals against panel decisions.

The White Paper

Two years later, in October 1966, the Government set out its policy intentions in the White Paper 'Social Work and the Community'.[8] There had been widespread consultations with professional bodies as well as advice given by a joint working group which the Government had set up with the local authority association, engaging the help of three social work consultants – Professor Richard Titmuss, Megan Browne and Kay Carmichael.

The White Paper accepted the principle of the new system of children's panels as well as most of the Kilbrandon Committee's detailed recommendations on machinery with the exception of making the sheriff responsible for appointing panel members. The main area of discussion and dispute was concentrated on the organisation of the matching fieldwork department, its precise structure and the range of its responsibilities. The Government came out in favour of a separate social work department rather than the 'social education department' proposed by Kilbrandon. The new department was to be given very wide powers and while not without opposition, its responsibilities were to include the probation and mental health services. Read in retrospect the White Paper may be taken as an indication of the faithfulness of the present arrangements to the policy decisions taken in 1966. Such a reading however may also lead to the conclusion that the time has come for some modest changes in the light of experience.

The Social Work (Scotland) Act 1968

The White Paper proposals were enacted in the Social Work (Scotland) Act 1968. In the end, the only major changes from the White Paper were the success of the large burghs in securing that they should have social work functions as well as the counties and cities and the introduction into the legislation of the very important section 12. The latter gave local authorities a duty *to promote social welfare by making available advice, guidance and assistance on such a scale as may be appropriate for their area, and in that behalf to make arrangements and to provide or secure the provision of such facilities (including the provision or arranging for the provision of residential and other establishments) as they may consider suitable and adequate.* These comprehensive powers gave local authorities a wide positive rôle in meeting and indeed searching out the needs of and in encouraging individuals, families and groups to help solve problems with their own resources or with the aid of resources available within the community.

The new social work departments were to come into being on 17 November 1969 but the introduction of the system of children's hearings was left until later. The intention was to allow the departments time to settle down and prepare for the new obligations associated with providing services for the new system. Time was also required for the preparation of procedural regulations, for the appointment of appropriate officials and for the setting up and training of the children's panels, the body of lay people from which hearings are constituted. The system commenced operations on 15 April 1971.

Part III of the 1968 Act is the legal framework on which the system of children's hearings rests. The statute law is all to be found in Part III, in which a few amendments have been incorporated by subsequent legislation: the Children and Young Persons Act 1969, the Local Government (Scotland) Act 1973 and the Children Act 1973. Information about subordinate legislation is contained in Annex C.

THE STRUCTURE OF THE SYSTEM

The essential elements of the system are arranged within a local stucture which leaves certain checks and balances to central government but gives operational independence to the children's panel and the reporter.

Children's Panel Advisory Committee

Each regional and island authority is required to appoint a Children's Panel Advisory Committee (CPAC). This local authority committee, normally serviced by an identified clerk, includes two members nominated by the local authority. These are not always elected members, but are usually the convenor and vice-convenor of the Social Work Committee. It has also three members including the chairman nominated by the Secretary of State and these are virtually never elected members of the local authority. At the time of local government reorganisation the committees were given the power, which most have exercised, to set up sub-committees to cover areas within the region.

The primary function of the CPAC is to submit names of possible panel members to the Secretary of State. The committees were given guidance by the Secretary of State on the desirable characteristics of panel members. This guidance has underlain the various circulars and consultative arrangements for CPACs in subsequent years and ran as follows:

> Essential to the success of the system of children's panels and hearings is the finding of sufficient suitable members of the community to serve on them. They should have knowledge and experience in dealing with children and families and should be drawn from a wide range of occupation, neighbourhood, age group and income group. They require the right personal qualities, including the absence of bias and prejudice, and a genuine interest in the needs of children in trouble and their relationship to the community. Moreover, the success of the children's hearings will depend to a large extent on the ability of their members to get through to the children and their parents; and a capacity to communicate with them, and an understanding of their feelings and reactions so that they gain their confidence will be of a great importance. It is hoped that the new system will attract suitable people whose occupations or circumstances have hitherto prevented them from taking a formal part in helping and advising young people or who might not have previously thought of themselves as candidates for public service.[9]

At the same time the committees were given the following advice about selection procedure:

> Persons who appear to be eligible for consideration should generally be invited to attend an initial interview, with the dual purpose of giving information about what panel membership involves and of enabling a preliminary view to be obtained of a person's capabilities. A single inter-

view would not normally be sufficient for this purpose, however, and it is therefore important that the persons considered appropriate by the Children's Panel Advisory Committee should thereafter attend a fuller session of interviews and group discussions designed to give a clearer picture of the implications of panel membership and of the suitability of individuals for it. Generally speaking, the Secretary of State would intend to appoint as panel members only those who have been recommended by the Advisory Committee after going through a procedure broadly of this kind.

The implications of these guidelines are discussed briefly in a later section in this chapter on changes from the previous system, and in much more detail in chapter 6. Achieving a blend of panel members with the right personal characteristics and the proper mix of community representation is a continuous task. The degree of success and the extent to which this is fundamental are ongoing questions.

The CPACs were also given the task of advising the Secretary of State on certain matters relating to the general administration of panels. The Secretary of State has in fact referred the following matters for their advice:

1. the volume of work which may be expected to fall on each panel;
2. the number of members to be appointed to the panel;
3. the action to be taken in any circumstances which may cast doubt on the fitness of a panel member to serve;
4. the extent to which further training for panel members may be needed.

Apart from their obligation to advise the Secretary of State on questions he may refer to them, it is open to the CPACs to consider other matters relating to the work of the hearings; for example, relations with the general public, proposals for research or general questions on which the chairman of the panel wishes consultation. Consideration of the cases of individual children is of course completely the responsibility of the hearings and not the function of CPACs.

Children's panels

The Secretary of State is required to appoint a children's panel for each regional and island authority, with a chairman and deputy chairman. The size of each panel changes according to the recommendations from time to time of each CPAC. There are currently 1,500–1,600 panel members ranging from approximately 900 in Strathclyde to 10 in Orkney. Many panels in the larger regions operate through a system of informal area panels. The aim has been to achieve within each regional and island panel an approximate balance of the sexes and an age range from about 20 to a maximum of 60 (cf. chapter 6).

Broadly, children's panel members are appointed for three years at a time although some initial appointments at the beginning were for two years. Recent circulars give some indication that if suitable new members are available, children's panel members could usefully withdraw at least for a time after three terms of what is undoubtedly difficult work; and which in some areas has involved at least weekly commitments. This chapter does not attempt to assess the enormous contribution made since 1971 by the average panel member.

Children's panel members agree, in their acceptance of the office, to undertake pre-service and in-service training. Part III gives both the Secretary of State and the local authority the power to train panel members. The Secretary of State finances appointments of organisers in Glasgow, Edinburgh, Aberdeen and Dundee Universities. These organisers, working within guidelines laid down on a national basis, provide for new panel members a varied programme of lectures and other meetings and subsequently make a variety of in-service sessions available each year. At the same time meetings arranged locally are taking place with existing panel members, social workers, police, assessment centre staff and other relevant officers, and there are visits of observation to hearings, and to local facilities.

The reporter

The official with primary responsibility for the children's hearings system in each area, and with substantial responsibilities of his own, is the reporter. He and his deputies and staff are appointed by the local authority 'for the purpose of arranging children's hearings and for the performance of such other functions in relation to the children's panel or the children's hearing as may be assigned' (1968 Act, S.36(1)). The system of checks and balances operates, however, in the fact that the reporter may not be removed from office by a local authority nor be required to resign nor be employed in any other capacity, without the consent of the Secretary of State.

Apart from being the official responsible for running the system, the reporter has the fundamental and independent responsibility of receiving initial referrals of children in trouble. Those cases which appear to the reporter as being in need of compulsory measures of care are referred to children's hearings. The Secretary of State has power to prescribe qualifications for the reporter, but has not so far done so. The Secretary of State and the Lord Advocate have also power to prescribe in regulations the training, qualifications or experience necessary before a reporter or one of his staff may appear before the sheriff in certain circumstances. There are twelve regional and island reporters and about eighty deputies or assistants. An analysis of the reporter's rôle as seen by one regional reporter is contained in chapter 5.

THE OPERATION AND ARTICULATION
OF THE SYSTEM

The flow chart at Annex A and the statistics at Annex B may be
found useful when reading this section.

A child under 16 gets into the system if he is referred to the reporter by some person or agency which believes that he may be in need of compulsory measures of care. In 1974 there were over 31,000 referrals.* More than 90% of cases are referred to the reporter for having committed offences. Other grounds for referral are truancy; falling into bad associations; or suffering neglect or abuse. Referrals to the reporter may be made by the public, by the social work department, by the education authority or other agencies. The bulk of referrals however are made by the police.

The police do not refer to the reporter all children who are known to have committed offences. First offenders and those committing minor offences may be given an informal warning, or a formal warning before a superintendent. As many minor offences are not considered to merit compulsory measures of care, police warnings have increased substantially since the inception of the system. In 1974 there were over 10,000 police warnings. A number of police authorities also issue warnings at the request of the reporter.

At the other end of the spectrum a variety of more serious cases also do not come within the scope of the children's hearings system at this stage. The 1968 Act provided that children could be prosecuted in the sheriff court or in the High Court on the instructions of the Lord Advocate. The procurators fiscal have been directed by the Lord Advocate to consider such prosecution in serious cases involving offences against the person, forfeiture of weapons, and where technically necessary for proof, as in some cases where offences have been committed jointly with adults. There has been a determined effort to reduce the number of these cases brought before the sheriff court which are now under 3,000 a year, but still substantial. However, the court may, and in some cases must, remit the case to the children's hearing for advice; and may also remit the case for disposal (cf. chapter 2).

Cases referred to the reporter

When the reporter receives a referral he uses his own judgement in making initial investigations. This may involve obtaining reports from the social work department, the school, the police, or other reporters and departments in other areas. The reporter then has three main courses he may follow.

1. He may decide no further action is required. This formal decision has given rise to a lot of misunderstanding. 'No further action' may in fact cover a range of informal actions or have a variety of explanations (cf. chapter 5).
2. He may refer the case to the social work department with a view to their making voluntary arrangements for the advice, guidance and assistance of the child and his family.
3. He may bring the child before a children's hearing:
   (i) if he is satisfied that there is evidence of at least one ground for referral
   and

*These are provisional figures: final figures for these and the subsequent statistics will be found in *Scottish Social Work Statistics* 1974 HMSO.

> (ii) if it appears to him that the child is in need of compulsory measures of care.

Over 15,000 cases were referred to children's hearings in 1974. If the reporter decides a child should be referred to a hearing he will then make the necessary arrangements; obtain the background reports provided by the social work department, school, and other agencies; and ensure that the parents and the child are notified. The parents have a *duty* to attend unless excused and have also a *right* to attend.

Reporters as a whole normally bring about half their referrals before hearings. In 1974 the figures were over 15,000 out of 31,000.

The children's hearing

A children's hearing consists of three children's panel members, including a member of each sex. Its accommodation must be dissociated from police stations or courts, and is usually an ordinary not-too-large room with a fairly large table. At the hearing and round the table sit the chairman of the hearing and his two colleagues, the child and his parents, the reporter and the social worker. The hearings are private. The Press, however, may attend but rarely do and any report must not identify the child. Occasionally, the chairman allows an observer such as a panel member in training.

Before the substance of the referral can be considered, the child and his parents must accept the grounds for referral. If they do not, the hearing must either discharge the referral or have the case referred to the sheriff to establish the facts. This follows out the Kilbrandon concept that the hearing must concern itself only with the consideration of what action should be taken to help the child. The establishment of the facts is a matter for the sheriff in civil procedure in chambers but with the standards of proof appropriate to criminal charges. If the facts are established the case comes back to the hearing for consideration. Before arriving at its decision the hearing considers the grounds for referral, the report obtained from the social work department, and any other relevant information. The basis for the course of action decided upon must be *the best interests of the child*. This is the sole criterion to which the hearing is required to address itself. Throughout the proceedings the hearing has to have as full a discussion as possible with the parents and child. The aim is to be informal enough to enable a proper exchange of views to take place over a reasonable period. In practice the hearing of each case seems to be averaging about 40 minutes.

There is only a limited range of decisions open to a hearing.

1. It may decide no further action is required and discharge the referral.
2. It may require a child to be supervised in the community. Conditions may be included in the requirement; but the major use of this is to impose a condition about residence, for example, in a relative's home.
3. It may require a child to reside in a 'residential establishment'. In

effect this means a local authority or voluntary establishment. Children's hearings in 1974 discharged over 6,000 (42%); and made over 7,000 (47%) supervision requirements in the community and about 1,600 (11%) involving residence away from home in a residential establishment.

The social work department

The social work department has two main responsibilities. First, it is responsible for preparing the social background report which is the main document for consideration by the hearing; and at some stage in the process before decisions are made, it may also be responsible for residential or non-residential assessment. Once a supervision requirement is made it is the duty of the local authority, working through the social work department, to give effect to it. A child who is the subject of a supervision requirement is regarded as being in the care of the authority who have an obligation 'to exercise their powers with respect to him so as to further his best interests, and afford him opportunity for the proper development of his character and abilities' (1968 Act, S.20(1)). This responsibility applies whether the child is under supervision at home or in a residential establishment.

A supervision requirement merely requiring supervision by the local authority is usually though not always a simple document without conditions, on the grounds that it will be for the social worker with the child to work out whatever possibilities may have emerged in the hearing. In practice, facilities for what is loosely called 'intermediate treatment' are increasingly available. Intermediate treatment may be broadly defined as structured programmes of treatment falling between simple supervision and full residential care. These may include group and individual discussion of problems, and various recreational pursuits designed to widen the child's interests and increase his ability to find satisfaction in purposeful co-operation with others. Full use may be made of facilities available from other departments, and short periods of residence away from home may be involved. The nature of this treatment programme is at the discretion of the social work department, with the co-operation of the child and his parents. Any suggestion of a full-time residential programme would involve a decision by the hearing.

All supervision requirements including those with a requirement of residence in a designated establishment are supervised by social work departments. Only a small minority of such placements are currently within their own establishments, although the range of establishments available is beginning to widen. The bulk of the placements at present, however, are in schools on the Scottish Education Department's List D which are almost all run by voluntary managers with the costs shared by local authorities and central government. The range of treatment provided in these schools is discussed in chapter 14. The key points that require to be mentioned here are the extreme pressure on the schools for places and the awaited decisions on their future organisation.

The above has been an essentially skeletal account of the main statutory provisions, both organisational and procedural, and gives no real impression of the general burdens on panel members or the complexity of the reporter's administrative arrangements. It has made no mention of continuation of cases or the large number of *emergency* hearings where children have been taken to places of safety overnight by the police, having been either arrested or retrieved from situations of danger. Nor does it refer to the many hearings dealing with *warrant* cases where children have to continue to be held for defined periods, until the hearings are in a position to deal with their cases. More important, nothing has been said about *reviews*. There is a requirement to have a full review of a supervision requirement by a hearing every year, or more frequently at the request of parents or child. A review may vary as well as discharge the supervision requirement and in its flexibility it is one of the most useful and envied powers of a children's hearing. A fuller account of the procedural provisions, a note of an appropriate booklet and details of the statutory rules are given in Annex C.

THE REALITY OF THE CHANGES

The new system would certainly seem to have brought about major changes. These might be listed as:

1. the removal of children from the courts and the separation of trial and treatment;
2. the creation of a new lay body to deal with children in a more informal way and with a greater input of consideration and information;
3. the setting of new objectives in the process of dealing with the child in trouble;
4. the recognition of the need for a wider range of treatment resources, with greater flexibility in their development.

The question is how far there is reality behind these changes. How far did the previous system, whatever its formal structure, act in a way resembling the new position? And how far are the new names and arrangements masking a process and results not very different from the previous situation?

1. *Removal of children from court system and separation of trial and treatment.* The great majority of children in trouble are now clearly removed from the court system. They are dealt with in an informal situation, where the children's hearing is concerned only with the action that should be taken and not with detailed establishment of guilt in a trial situation. The Kilbrandon Committee took the view that 95% of those in the juvenile court plead guilty and that simple acceptance of the facts at the children's hearing would enable the vast bulk of cases to proceed. This has been borne out. In only about 10% of the cases that come before a children's hearing are the facts not accepted and the case brought before the sheriff for establishment of the facts, and then returned to the hearing. There are, however, still around 3,000 cases taken in the sheriff court under the direction of the Lord Advocate, because of the nature of the offences or because

they are jointly charged, and only a small proportion of these are currently referred to the children's hearings for disposal. This figure of 3,000 is roughly one fifth of the number of cases heard by the hearings. Research is said to be showing that the children dealt with by the courts differ very little, if at all, in characteristics from the children who appear before children's hearings. A question that has been raised in a consultative document issued on behalf of the Secretary of State is whether it is desirable or possible to bring children who have been dealt with by the courts, within the panel system to be dealt with after conviction. Another complication is that hearings may deal with children between 16 and 18 who are already under supervision requirements. Some children's panels feel it would be helpful for a number of these cases to be referred by the hearing to the sheriff court.

2. *The new lay body and the new informal style.* Chapter 6 demonstrates clearly the fact that the lay body *is* of a new kind. It is the product of a very considerable response to open advertisement, careful selection and of continuing preparation. There is and has always been a virtually equal and intended balance of the sexes. With an age range of 20–60 and a median of the early 40s it is much younger than other public bodies.[10] Similarly, the way children's panel members conduct hearings has very considerable underlying resemblance throughout the country in its new basic informal approaches, as is illustrated at various points in section III. This is not to say that some of the special juvenile courts were not conducted in this way, or that some English juvenile courts may not bear a fairly close resemblance to hearings in style. But the comprehensive adoption of the new style, and its novelty in a Scottish setting where JP courts had not achieved the same importance as in the south, marks out the approach as new. Observers from other countries have been impressed with the informality of the style, and with its humanity, and flexibility.* The question remains as to how fully it does and should reflect the community balance and real community involvement.

3. *The setting of new objectives.* The informality of children's hearings is not without its problems, which are perhaps appropriately discussed here in relation to the extent to which the children's hearings system has been set new objectives in dealing with children. It is too simplistic just to say that the children's hearing is required only to act in the best interests of the child, and that the juvenile court was concerned with guilt and punishment. The very creation of the juvenile court indicated that children were being specially considered. The sheriffs and magistrates did have regard to the child's welfare in their decisions; as well as to the other components of decisions in criminal cases. An important study of the new system by Allison Morris and Mary McIsaac concludes that it is 'an empirical amalgam of welfare, due process and control'.† It seems most likely that, seen in historical perspective, the children's hearings system is not so

---

*For example see chapter 21 even with its qualifications; and Task Force on Child Care Services: Interim Report: Eire Parl. 4915, 1975.

†In final drafting stage: Morris and McIsaac, *Juvenile Justice*. A major study of the children's hearings system drawing on detailed research carried out in a Scottish city and county.

much an entirely radical step in the direction of treatment for the individual child as simply a clearly perceptible move in that direction along the 'spectrum' or 'balance' of the treatment of children and for that matter offenders. The new system represents a perceptible shift as a result of its dual requirement: action by the children's hearings must not only be in the child's best interests, but should be taken first by the reporter and then by the hearing only when a child is in need of 'compulsory measures of care'.

The statistical evidence indicates that criminal behaviour is particularly common in youth and declines markedly and quite quickly thereafter. There is a growing view therefore that we should try to minimise any risk of confirming young people in a criminal identity by the over-liberal use of judicial processes. Instead, it is argued that we should wherever possible aim to 'divert' delinquents from the criminal process. An example of 'diversion' is the drunk who is charged but then passed on for medical treatment (detoxification) rather than sent to prison. There may be something of a related process in the children's hearings system. In percentage terms the police warnings filter off about 25%; the reporter decides not to bring another 40% to the hearing. The hearing discharges about 16% of the remaining 40%, which means that 1 in 4 or 5 have a formal treatment disposal by the hearing.

If children's hearings represent a move along the spectrum away from a court system, they are also likely to be moving away from some of the formalised protections built into that system. Chapters 2 and 20 consider these points and sometimes take differing views. Protections are built into the system in the establishment of the facts by the sheriff if this is required, and in the right of appeal to the sheriff, used only in a handful of cases. The Children Act 1975 envisages separate representation for children in particular circumstances. The informal procedure can sometimes present problems and the challenge is to improve it without destroying its essence. Chapters 2 and 20 make suggestions. The arguments for more legislation are quite finely balanced and some court decisions on appeal may be necessary before the issues become sufficiently clarified for any specific legislative action either way.

4. *Disposals and the range of resources.* The reality of the new system should ideally be examined through its 'success' rates if these could be defined, and if comparisons were possible with earlier procedures. This kind of approach has tended to flatter to deceive. Detailed statistical evidence is only now becoming available for proper study. The most that can be said is that there are some reasonably encouraging figures in particular areas. Children stopped short of children's hearings by the various methods at earlier stages, have in the substantial majority of cases not reappeared in the system within the year; and the same applies to children whose supervision requirements have been removed. If the 'output' is difficult to measure we are forced back to 'input'; and resources are examined in detail in section IV. The question to be considered in studying section IV is how far the treatment resources have improved or are improving under the new system; and how far they are developing in range. If their range expands then the effective range of the hearings' disposals also develops. The pressures on list D schools and on supervision are, however, well known. Less

well known are the build up of assessment places and resources, which are somewhat disguised by the holding function necessary with the shortage of residential places; and the recent developments in 'intermediate treatment'. Just as children are diverted from the hearings' disposals, so a feeling is beginning to emerge that it is desirable for children who have appeared before a hearing to be kept within the community, and diverted from full-time residential care except where clearly necessary. Section IV may perhaps demonstrate the possibilities that are developing under the impetus of the new system, rather than showing as yet a system which in all cases is providing treatment resources of a different order from those previously available. Such a view, while reflecting accurately the frustrations of panel members, might perhaps not reflect fully the new approach of the social work departments to the continuing and changing limits of care that are available under the review system; their interest in the whole family situation; and in spite of difficulties their greater quantitative and qualitative interest at the report and assessment stage. Be that as it may, the current situation in 1976 is such as to focus attention on the possibility of giving children's panels extra powers, and the Secretary of State has issued a consultative document containing some modest suggestions for discussion. These include the power to remit cases of over 16s to the sheriff; the power to forfeit weapons and to disqualify from driving; the power to require security for good behaviour; and the power to take formal note of conduct when there are new offences, even if there is no desire to change an existing residential disposal. The question of fining is also canvassed. None of these is seen however as a real substitute for the imaginative development of the range of resources.

ANNEX A
PROCEDURE FOR BRINGING COMPLAINT TO HEARING

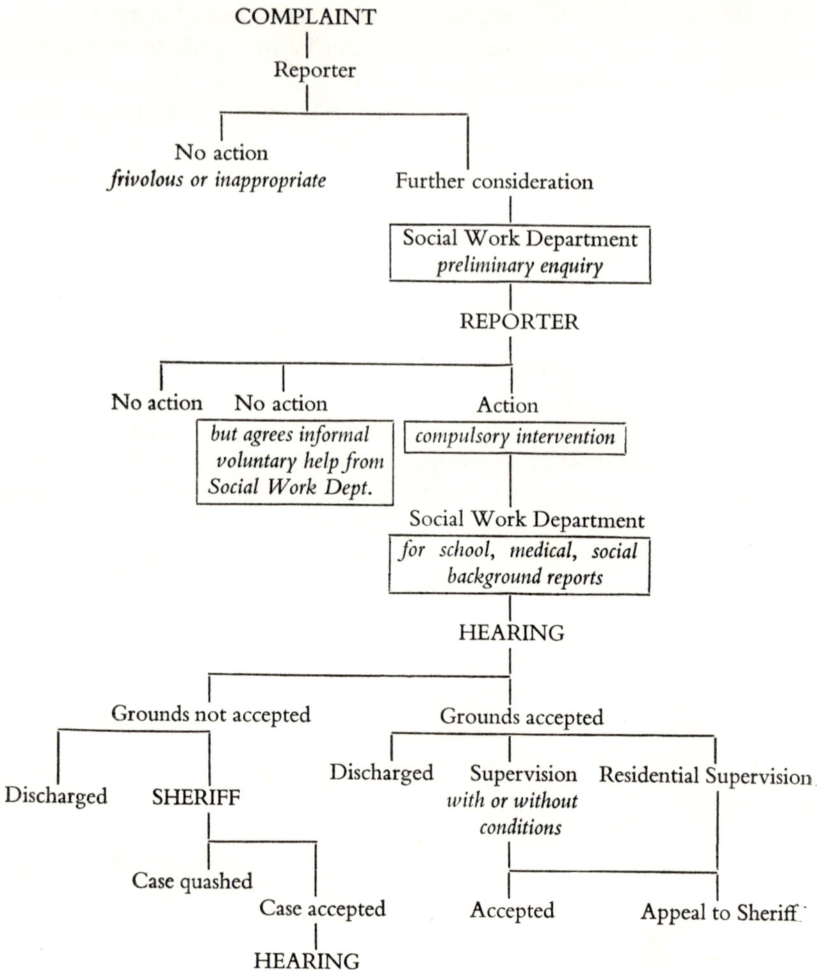

ANNEX B

STATISTICS

Since 1971 there has been a substantial increase in the work of hearings and in the number of referrals to the reporter. Figures are contained below together with some decisions in respect of children appearing before a children's hearing. Detailed statistics are contained in the annual HMSO publication 'Scottish Social Work Statistics'.

	1971 15.4.71–31.12.71	1972	1973	1974
Offences by children under 16	18,495	29,626	35,932	38,993
Police warnings	7,516	9,167	9,824	10,716
Juvenile liaison scheme	*	599	740	758
Proceedings taken in all courts	1,664	2,390	3,192	2,900
Reports to reporters (including non-offence cases)	13,417	24,219	29,384	31,524
Reports referred to hearings	6,712	12,519	14,961	15,108
Disposal of reports referred to hearings:				
No supervision requirement	1,890 (28·2%)	4,502 (36·0%)	6,155 (41·1%)	6,335 (41·9%)
Non-residential supervision	3,720 (55·4%)	6,209 (49·6%)	7,069 (47·2%)	7,181 (47·5%)
Residential supervision requirement	1,102 (16·4%)	1,808 (14·4%)	1,737 (11·7%)	1,592 (10·6%)

* part year figure not available.

ANNEX C

PROCEDURAL ASPECTS OF THE CHILDREN'S HEARINGS SYSTEM

1. A general account of the workings of the system is contained in Children's Hearings: Social Work Services Group: Scottish Education Department: HMSO (revised 1976).

2. The main statutory instruments are:

The Children's Hearings (Scotland) Rules	1971 No. 492 (S.60)
The Reporter's Duties Rules	1971 No. 525 (S.72)

They require to be read along with Part III of the Social Work (Scotland) Act 1968

REFERENCES

1. Report of the Care of Children Committee (1946), Cmnd. 6922 HMSO.
2. Report of the Committee on Homeless Children (1946), Cmnd. 6911 HMSO.
3. Report of the Committee on Children and Young Persons (1960), Cmnd. 1191 HMSO.
4. Prevention of Neglect of Children (1963), Cmnd. 1966 HMSO.
5. The Child, the Family and the Young Offender (1965), Cmnd. 2742 HMSO.
6. Children in Trouble (1968), Cmnd. 3601 HMSO.
7. Report of Committee on Children and Young Persons Scotland (1964), Cmnd. 2306 HMSO. (Kilbrandon Report).
8. Social Work and the Community (1966), Cmnd. 3065 HMSO. (White Paper).
9. Social Work Services Group Circular, No. SW7/1969.
10. Murray, G. and Rowe, A. (1973), Children's Panels: Implications for the Future. *Policy and Politics*, Vol. 1 No. 4.

2

THE ROLE OF THE COURTS

GERALD GORDON

ALTHOUGH the main purpose and effect of the Social Work (Scotland) Act 1968 was to remove juvenile offenders and their problems from the courts, the courts are still involved in a number of cases. This involvement is of three kinds, each of which occurs at a different stage in the proceedings. The first is where a child is prosecuted in a criminal court instead of being dealt with under the Act. In this case the child, initially, is not 'put into' the hearing system, although as we shall see he may in the end find his way into it. The second is where, in terms of the Act, a case brought before a hearing, on any ground, is referred to the sheriff because the child or his parents are unable or unwilling to admit the ground of referral on which he has been brought before the hearing. This recourse to the courts is not a form of prosecution – it is indeed, at least in name and in law, a referral to a civil, i.e. a non-criminal, court even where the ground of referral is an offence – but an integral part of the hearings system; some, indeed, would say that it was the element which gave the system its special character. The third kind of court involvement is where there is an appeal to the court – again always a civil court – against a decision made by a hearing. The appeal court cannot itself make any supervision requirement – it is limited to two courses of action: the discharge of the child, or a remit back to the hearing.

The relevant law was originally contained in the Children and Young Persons (Scotland) Act 1937, and the Social Work (Scotland) Act 1968 which we shall refer to as the 1968 Act. Some of these provisions are now to be found in the Criminal Procedure (Scotland) Act 1975 (the 1975 Act).

CHILDREN IN THE CRIMINAL COURTS

The provisions for prosecuting children may be seen either as an example of the failure of the Kilbrandon Committee to have the courage of its convictions or as a sensible concession to the realities of life. Certainly the Committee was not troubled by any question of principle that might have affected its recommendations, but seems rather to have taken over into the new system the existing power of the Lord Advocate to prosecute children (Kilbrandon Report[1] paras.

124–125). It is true, however, that Kilbrandon saw prosecution as limited to exceptional instances of serious crimes, and may not have envisaged the prosecution of children in summary courts at all. A summary sheriff court is one in which accused persons are tried by a sheriff who sits alone without a jury. More serious offences are dealt with on indictment, that is to say before either a sheriff or a High Court judge, sitting in each case with a jury.

Under the 1968 Act the police are required to report all offences by children both to the appropriate reporter and to the appropriate prosecutor, i.e. the procurator fiscal (S.38(2)). Indeed the reporter may, in theory, be entitled to deal only with those whom the procurator fiscal decides not to prosecute: the reporter has no power to stop the prosecution of any child. Nor, oddly enough, have the prosecuting authorities any power to prevent the reporter referring a child to a hearing, but in practice no child who is being prosecuted will be sent to a hearing, unless by the court after he has been found guilty. In practice it is only in a limited number of cases that children are reported by the police to the procurator fiscal, the relevant classes of case being laid down in instructions from the Lord Advocate. And even where children are reported to the procurator fiscal he may decide not to prosecute, but himself refer the case to the reporter who is then free to deal with it in the same way as with any other cases brought to his notice. It is the policy of the prosecuting authorities to maintain a close liaison with the reporters. Many of the children who are prosecuted are eventually dealt with by or on the advice of a hearing.

(In 1973, 3,192 children were proceeded against in courts: 227 were placed on probation, 854 fined, 767 admonished and 78 received absolute discharges; 359 were remitted to a hearing for disposal; the number remitted for advice is unknown. Most of the prosecutions were summary, and were for theft (1,020 including theft by housebreaking) or breach of the peace (1,103). Many of these prosecutions were probably due to the child's involvement with adults. But there are wide regional variations: very few children, for example, reach the courts in Edinburgh.)

There are, broadly speaking, two kinds of reason for prosecuting children rather than bringing them before a hearing: technical or procedural reasons, and the seriousness of the offence. These two classes correspond fairly well with summary proceedings and proceedings on indictment respectively.

Summary prosecutions

Section 31 of the 1968 Act provides that 'No child shall be prosecuted for any offence except on the instructions of the Lord Advocate or at his instance; and no court, other than the High Court of Justiciary and the sheriff court, shall have jurisdiction over a child for an offence.'

So far as summary proceedings are concerned, there are two important provisions in this section. The first is that the references to the High Court and the sheriff court mean that a child cannot be dealt with by a district court. While much of the rest of the Act is concerned to keep children away from lawyers, this section ensures that if they are to be tried at all they will be tried by

a legally qualified sheriff. The reasons for this provision were probably dissatisfaction with the old burgh and JP juvenile courts, and that in 1968 the Lord
Advocate's control of summary prosecutors did not extend beyond the sheriff
court fiscals.

The second provision is more problematic. A child can be prosecuted only
on the instructions of the Lord Advocate. It is accepted that this does not mean
that the Lord Advocate must personally approve every prosecution. But it has
been argued that it should mean that all cases in which a child is prosecuted,
like all cases in which anyone is prosecuted on indictment, should be considered
by the Crown Office in Edinburgh, which is the part of the Lord Advocate's
department concerned with his functions as public prosecutor. The High Court
has held that it is enough for the Lord Advocate to give general instructions to
procurators fiscal listing classes of cases which may be prosecuted. The procurator fiscal is then free to prosecute any case in one of the classes prescribed
(*M. v. Dean*).[2] Since then, however, the Lord Advocate has declared that proceedings are not to be taken against children under the age of 13 without
reference to Crown Office for his authority (see Secretary of State's statement
to House of Commons, 30 July 1974).

One important group of cases in which prosecutions are taken consists of
cases where a child is alleged to have committed an offence along with an
adult. Prior to the operation of the 1968 Act such cases had to be taken in the
adult court. The effect of the Act was to leave the procurator fiscal to decide
whether the circumstances indicated that prosecution was appropriate. This is
still the position, but it has been made clear that the child will be prosecuted
only where this is essential.

It must be remembered that when one speaks of children and adults in this
connection one is often speaking of persons just under and persons just over 16
respectively. Where the child proposes to admit guilt there is no problem in
leaving him to the reporter. But where he denies guilt, to deal with him
separately may mean not only inconvenience to witnesses who will have to
give evidence twice, but may also make it difficult (because of the rules of
evidence) to present the case for or against either child or adult fully, and may
be unfair to the adult. It can be argued, however, that in such a case it should
be mandatory for the child to be remitted to a hearing for disposal after guilt
has been established in the joint trial.

The other principal reason for prosecuting a child summarily is that his
offence is one for which he is liable to disqualification for driving or to have
articles forfeited. The latter consideration could apply to any offence in which
any article used in the commission of the offence had been recovered, but it is in
fact limited to cases where a statute specifically provides forfeiture, such as
poaching or the carrying of an offensive weapon. Kilbrandon mentioned road
traffic offences and suggested that they be dealt with by the hearings, who
could report the child to the procurator fiscal who could in turn report the case
to the sheriff who could order disqualification (para. 126). The 1968 Act is silent
on the matter.

The crux of the problem is that the hearings have no power to forfeit or disqualify. The reason for this is not so much practical as credal: the hearings are not to resemble courts or have power to impose anything which is describable only as punishment. At the same time weapons must be forfeited and erring drivers disqualified. So it is thought better to break the spirit of the Act by prosecuting children in such cases rather than to spoil the image of the hearing by giving it the necessary powers. The obvious solution is to prefer the real to the nominal and give the hearings the powers. Forfeiture cases may be got round by the child agreeing to give up his weapon or his salmon or tackle, and most disqualification cases by limiting the power to prosecute for this reason to 'children' over the age of 16, but these are unsatisfactory devices of limited efficacy.

Prosecution on indictment

Most summary prosecutions of children are unfortunate necessities: we do not want to prosecute but there are technical reasons which prevent resort to the hearings system. Prosecutions on indictment, on the other hand, are taken because it is thought that prosecution is the appropriate course, in the light of the seriousness of the offence. The offence must, of course, be serious enough to be indictable anyway, but where children are concerned it must be more serious than would be necessary in the case of an adult if only because no one enjoys the spectacle of a child sitting lost and bewildered at the centre of a solemn jury trial; children are prosecuted on indictment only when they have committed offences of particular gravity. Cases such as murder, rape, culpable homicide, attempted murder, assault to the danger of life, and assault and robbery with firearms, will be reported to the procurator fiscal and reported in turn by him to Crown Office, but they will not necessarily be brought to trial even if criminal proceedings are taken initially. Every effort would be made to avoid putting a child on indictment just because he was acting along with an adult who was indicted.

Yet it is difficult to reconcile even such rare prosecutions with the Kilbrandon philosophy. As Allison Morris has put it, 'If the offence is symptomatic of underlying disorder there should be no reason for referring children who commit certain types of offence to a court. Or are only minor offences symptomatic of underlying personality or family disorder?'[3] It may be that the power to indict children was just carried over from the old system as something believed to be obviously necessary. It may be that it is a concession to the public belief that the hearings are a soft option. It may be there to provide for the possibility of long periods of detention for dangerous 15-year-olds. It may be just that some offences are regarded as so serious that they demand public, formal judicial inquiry and denunciation whether or not the offender is sufficiently 'socially maladjusted' to be liable to compulsory treatment by a hearing.

Trial procedures

Since the abolition of the juvenile court by the 1968 Act a child who is prosecuted summarily is nominally prosecuted in an ordinary criminal court.

In fact the old special procedural rules for juvenile courts now apply to the summary trial of children (Act of Adjournal (Summary Proceedings) Children 1971 S.I. No. 446). As before they do not apply where the child has been charged along with an adult.

The special provisions include provisions that the court is to sit at a different place or time from that at which other courts in the building sit, that the child is to be kept away from adult offenders (other than relatives), that the trial is to be held outwith the presence of the public, and that the child's parent may assist him in his defence. The court is required to explain the substance of the charge to the child in language he can understand before asking whether he admits it. The child is also given the right, not available to adults, of electing to make a statement not on oath and not subject to cross-examination, instead of giving evidence.

The procedure in trials on indictment is the same as that in the case of an adult.

In all trials, however, there are restrictions on publicity. The reporting of the name or any identifying particulars of any person under the age of 17 who is concerned in any way in summary proceedings (other than a trial of a child charged along with an adult) is prohibited, subject only to a right in the Secretary of State to allow publication if satisfied that it is in the interests of justice to do so. In addition, any court may direct that such particulars shall not be published in relation to any trial.

The powers of the court

The sheriff summary court may deal with a child who pleads or is found guilty before it by granting him an absolute discharge, by admonishing him, by imposing a fine upon him, by placing him on probation, or by sentencing him to a fixed period of detention not exceeding two years. The latter sentence takes the form of committal 'to such place as the Secretary of State may direct for the purpose of undergoing residential training' (1975 Act, S.413). Although such a child may be sent by the Secretary of State to a List D school, the court cannot itself make a List D school order. Where, however, the court and a hearing agree that a List D school is the appropriate disposal, this result can be achieved by a remit to a hearing. A child who fails to pay a fine may be detained for up to one month in a place chosen by the local authority, if the court is satisfied that no other method of dealing with him is appropriate, and if he had been placed under supervision for the purpose of assistance and advice in paying the fine (ibid. S.400 and S.406). The powers of a court on indictment are similar to those of a summary court, save that the court may make an order detaining the child for a fixed period of any duration. A child detained on such an order may be released on licence through the Parole Board (ibid. S.206(2)).

Remits to reporter

The most significant feature of the disposal powers of the court is its power, which is in some cases a duty, to seek the advice of a children's hearing, and its power to remit the case to a hearing for disposal. Any court before which a child pleads or is found guilty of any offence other than murder may, instead of dealing directly with the child, request the reporter to arrange a children's hearing for the purpose of obtaining their advice as to the treatment of the child, or may remit the case to the reporter to arrange for its disposal by the hearing. Where the court requests advice it may, after receiving the advice, remit the case to the reporter to arrange for its disposal by a hearing. Where the child before the court is already subject to a supervision order, the court is obliged to request the reporter to arrange a hearing for the purpose of obtaining their advice; having received the advice the court is free to deal with the child itself or to remit the case to the reporter to arrange a disposal hearing. A summary court is also empowered to seek the advice of a hearing regarding a person between 16 and $17\frac{1}{2}$ years old who is not subject to a supervision order, and may after receiving such advice, remit him to the reporter for disposal by a hearing (ibid. S.373). Where a court does remit a case to a reporter to arrange for disposal, the court ceases to have jurisdiction over the child, whose case 'stands referred to a hearing' (ibid. S.173 and S.373). A certificate by the clerk of court that the child pleaded or was found guilty is conclusive evidence of the commission of the offence (1968 Act, S.56(5)).

The above provisions do not apply to children convicted of murder. In such cases, as in the case of any person convicted of a murder committed when he was under the age of 18, the child is sentenced to be detained during Her Majesty's pleasure, and is liable to be detained as and where the Secretary of State directs (1975 Act, S.206(1)).

Mentally abnormal children

Special provisions are made for children who appear to be mentally abnormal and children's hearings have no power to make an order under the mental health legislation. Where the hearing think that a child should be made the subject of an application to the sheriff for a hospital order or a guardianship order under the legislation applicable to mentally abnormal persons who have not been convicted of offences, they are required to report the matter to the appropriate mental health officer (1968 Act, S.46(1)). That officer has then to deal with the case. A child who needs to be dealt with under the 'criminal' provisions of the mental health legislation must be prosecuted, but this is unlikely to arise unless in connection with a type of serious offence which would in any event be reported to the procurator fiscal (1975 Act, S.174–178 and S.375–379).

Commentary

At first sight the two alternatives of prosecution and referral to a hearing are utterly opposed. The court is concerned to punish offenders in proportion to their responsibility for a specific offence, in order to uphold such values as social order, retribution and general deterrence. The hearing is concerned to take whatever measures are best suited to the child before it, taking account not of the specific offence but of the child's needs seen against his whole personal history and social background. The court cannot impose severe measures in respect of a trivial offence, whereas the hearings are not restricted in this way at all. The hearings cannot impose exemplary measures, or even severe measures for a serious offence, if the child can be dealt with by supervision whereas the court is entitled to punish even where the punishment is not necessary for the social welfare of the offender. Yet in practice the dichotomy is more nominal than real. Children referred to hearings under section 32(g) of the 1968 Act, who constitute the overwhelming majority of referred children, are referred because they have offended, and the nature of the offence can hardly be left entirely out of account. All courts have long been obliged when dealing with a child 'to have regard to the welfare of the child ... and in a proper case [to] take steps for removing him from undesirable surroundings' (1975 Act, S.172 and S.371). And courts, like hearings, deal with children on the basis of social workers' reports. It is true that courts do not have the 'big brother'-like review powers of the hearings, but there is not a great deal of difference between a sentence of detention under the control of and terminable by the Secretary of State (see Children and Young Persons (Scotland) Act 1937 S.58(A)(3)) and a List D school order. There is no difference between a probation order and a simple supervision order, except that as in the case of the residential treatment order, the court has to set a time-limit to the operation of the order, whereas the hearing has a continuing jurisdiction until the child is 18.

It may, indeed, be interesting to consider the points at which prosecution may be more favourable to the child than proceedings by a hearing, assuming that both procurator fiscal and reporter would treat him as in need of compulsory measures. An arrested child may be liberated on bail or on an undertaking to appear whether he is to be dealt with by court or hearing. If he is not so liberated and is dealt with by prosecution he is entitled to apply for bail when he appears in court, which will be at latest on the next day following his arrest, excluding Sundays and public holidays. But if he is not to be prosecuted he may be detained for a period up to seven days until the reporter decides not to bring him before a hearing or until a hearing sits, without any right to apply for liberation (1975 Act, S.296). Again, the child who appears in court is entitled to legal aid from the outset, and if in custody will be represented by the duty solicitor. He will thus have the opportunity of receiving legal advice before deciding whether to admit the charges against him, and a qualified and experienced person to speak for him thereafter. This avoids one of the greatest weaknesses of the hearings system which, while it does not prohibit the child having a lawyer as his representative, makes no specific provision for it, and discourages it by not providing legal aid before a hearing. As a result the child has no advice as to whether what he is prepared to admit having done constitutes the offence which forms the ground of referral, nor as to the likely consequences of admission; he is often not even aware that if he does not admit the ground of referral, the reporter will have to prove this before the sheriff.[4] It is not clear what differences if any there are between a trial before the sheriff and the hearing of an application to the sheriff for a finding whether grounds of referral under section 32(2)(g) are established. Any that exist will probably have the effect on the latter of reducing the procedural protections which would have been available if the child had been prosecuted. So far as disposal is concerned, the only point to note is that by appearing before the sheriff the child has the chance of what he may regard as the easier options of a fine or admonition. As against that, of course, he loses the advantages of the full discussion and sympathetic consideration of his position which he will receive before the hearing. The best of both worlds might be achieved – at some cost in time and trouble to the procurator fiscal and the sheriff – if the reporter sent all the section 32(2)(g) cases he thought were in need of compulsory measures to the procurator fiscal, and the sheriff returned to the hearing for disposal such of them as were eventually prosecuted and found guilty. In practice, many children who are now prosecuted have their cases sent to a hearing, at least for advice.

THE APPLICATION TO THE SHERIFF
(The 'section 42 application')

The central feature of the Kilbrandon procedural scheme was the separation of the functions of adjudication and disposal. The hearings were seen as disposal experts, while the function of adjudicating on disputed questions of fact was seen as more appropriate to adjudication experts: the courts. The reason for this division of function was, however, only partly a question of expertise, of the shoemaker sticking to his last or, perhaps of horses for courses. The recourse to the court was also seen as a protection for the child. 'If society is prepared on the proof of [offences] by juveniles to authorise fairly sustained measures of education and training . . . it is clearly of paramount importance that the initial basis for action should be established beyond doubt by stringent and testing procedures. This is precisely what criminal procedure aims to do' (Kilbrandon Report para. 70). The division between adjudication and disposal is not quite as simple as Kilbrandon suggests; it is at least arguable that the initial step of admitting or denying the ground of referral belongs to adjudication rather than disposal, and it may have been left to the hearing on grounds of convenience because of the large number of children who do not deny the charges against them. Nor is any provision made at all for determining a dispute as to statements contained in social work reports. But the main picture is clear: if the child does not or cannot admit the grounds of referral and the case is not to be dropped altogether, the hearing must refer the matter to the sheriff for adjudication.

Not all disputed referrals are referrals for alleged offences, although of course the vast majority are, if only because the vast majority of all referrals are on this ground. Perhaps partly for this reason, but probably principally because of the dogmatic determination of those who created the Social Work (Scotland) Act to avoid any suggestion of criminality or guilt, the repeated assertion of the Kilbrandon Report that the appropriate method of adjudication was that of criminal procedure has been disregarded, and the trial of an application is not one governed by criminal procedure. It is clear that what is involved is a judicial proceeding (see *McGregor v. T.*),[5] and indeed this must be so or there would be no need to have recourse to the sheriff; but it is a procedure *sui generis*, which fits neither into the ordinary idea of criminal trial nor into that of a civil proof, at any rate where what is in issue is the commission of an offence. If anything it is more civil than criminal, although when hearing an allegation of an offence the sheriff has to be satisfied that the offence has been proved beyond reasonable doubt and must apply to evidence 'the standard of proof required in criminal procedure' (1968 Act, S.42(6)). Indeed the Court of Session has held that 'whatever else this judicial proceeding is, it is not a criminal proceeding since it is not concerned with a prosecution and it can lead to no conviction' (Lord President Emslie in *McGregor v. T.* supra). One result of this is that although the child's parents are in a sense parties to the proceeding, may make unsworn statements instead of giving evidence, and may themselves call witnesses, it is open to the reporter to call them as witnesses against the child (*McGregor v. T.* supra). No reporter has yet, so far as I know, had the temerity to call the child as a witness for the reporter's case in an offence referral, and it is not clear whether he can do so, or whether he can make reference to previous offences committed by the child. The answers to these questions depend on whether the child in a section 42 application has the same protections as he would have if he were being prosecuted before the sheriff. It has been held that the 'basic rules of evidence' must be followed in applications under the Act (*Kennedy v. B*),[6] but the relevance of the special rules of criminal evidence remains undecided.

Procedure in section 42 application

An application must be heard within twenty-eight days of being lodged by the reporter, and the reporter must lodge the application within seven days of being directed to do so by the hearing. The hearing of the application must be begun by some procedures before the sheriff in the presence of the child and his parents within the twenty-eight days, but once begun it seems it may be adjourned or continued beyond the twenty-eight days. (See 1968 Act, S.42(4); Act of Sederunt (Social Work) (Sheriff Court Procedure Rules) 1971; *H. v. Mearns*[7]).

The hearing of the application takes place in private. The child and his parents may be represented by a lawyer and/or by anyone else at the hearing of the application before the sheriff, and legal aid is available to the child and his parents in much the same way as in criminal proceedings. Evidence is led in the same way as at a trial, except that the sheriff may stop the case at the end of the reporter's evidence if he does not think a *prima facie* case has been made out, and the sheriff may hear evidence in the absence of the child (but not of the child's parent or representative) if such a course is in his opinion in the child's interest. The sheriff may also exclude the parent while the child is giving evidence or making a statement, provided he gives the parent an opportunity of meeting any allegation the child makes. Neither of these powers is likely to be used in applications relating to an offence. Where an offence is alleged the sheriff may find on the facts that any offence established by the facts has been committed, even if it is not the offence named in the ground of referral.

Disposal of section 42 applications

If the sheriff finds the referral established he sends the case back to the children's hearing; if not he discharges the referral in respect of the ground brought before him.

One problem which has arisen in connection with section 42 applications (and also with appeals) on grounds other than the commssion of an offence has been the time in relation to which the grounds have to be established before the sheriff. If a child is brought before a hearing as in need of care and protection in August, and the sheriff hears an application in September, can the sheriff discharge the referral on the ground that he has heard evidence to satisfy him that by September the child was no longer in need of care and protection? The Court of Session has held that the relevant time is the time of the hearing of the application by the sheriff, treating such cases as analogous to cases on the custody of children. They have held further that where the first intimation of any change in circumstances comes in a statement made after the reporter has concluded his evidence, the sheriff should adjourn the case to allow the reporter the chance to meet this new evidence (*Kennedy v. B.*).[8]

APPEALS

In order to appreciate the position of appeals in the hearings system it is necessary to consider two separate kinds of appeal, known to lawyers as appeals on questions of law and appeals on the merits (or on questions of fact) respectively. In the context of appeals from the hearings, questions of law are likely to relate to questions of procedure, to alleged failures by the hearings to conform to the rules governing their operation; these failures may be minor and technical or may involve a breach of the principles of natural justice, i.e. involve a failure to give the child or his parent a fair hearing. An appeal on the merits will be about whether the hearings decision was the right decision. The existence of appeals to the courts on questions of law is uncontroversial and inevitable: it follows from the courts' normal function of making sure that legal rules are obeyed. That having been said, it should be noted that the total number of appeals has so far been under 20 per year. Despite the hearings' informality they are governed by some fairly detailed procedural rules, but the lack of legal representation makes it unlikely that breaches of these rules will be noticed, and the rules themselves are secreted in statutory instruments. Appeals on the merits are, however, very difficult to justify within the hearings system.

One of the strongest arguments advanced by the Kilbrandon Committee for the replacement of the juvenile court by the hearings was the lack of expertise on the part of the sheriff, another was the opportunity for informal consideration of the case in depth by the hearing. Again, the treatment of children was to be taken away from the courts because the courts were hampered by the 'crime-responsibility-punishment' model which militated against preventive action because of its restriction of the punishment to measures which fitted the crime. After all that, it is surprising to find that there is an appeal from the hearing's disposal decision to that same sheriff who has been declared unqualified to make such decisions. The question in such appeals was seen by Kilbrandon as being 'whether the measures ordered are in all the circumstances warranted in the interests of the child, or whether they amount to unjustified interference between parent and child amounting to unwarranted infringement of individual liberty' (Kilbrandon Report para. 111). The sheriff was seen as capable of determining the interests of the child, and perhaps also of applying a crime-responsibility-punishment test to determine the correctness of the hearing's decision.

What may be appealed

The child or his parent may appeal to the sheriff against any decision of a hearing, including the decision to grant a warrant. In the latter case the appeal must be heard within three days of its lodging. There is also provision for the hearing to suspend a supervision requirement pending appeal, but there are no special provisions for appealing a refusal to do so (1968 Act, S.49). A decision to direct the reporter to apply to the sheriff for a finding as to whether the grounds of referral are established instead of discharging the referral is not a decision for the purposes of appeal (*H. v. McGregor*).[9] Review decisions are appealable like any other but when the sheriff holds such an appeal to be frivolous he may direct that there shall be no appeal for twelve months against the decision to continue the supervision requirement in question (1968 Act, S.49(6)).

The reporter has no right of appeal from the hearing to the sheriff.

Procedure in appeals

The appeal is made first in writing, and the reporter is entitled to lodge written answers. The appeal is then heard orally by the sheriff in private. The child and his parent are entitled to legal aid. It is almost certain that the appeal, like a section 42 application, is a judicial proceeding. The appeal has certain elements of a rehearing. Where the appeal is on the ground of 'an alleged irregularity in the conduct of the case', the sheriff may resolve any conflict between the facts stated in the appeal and the reporter's answers, by hearing evidence on behalf of both sides (Act of Sederunt (Social Work) (Sheriff Court Procedure Rules) 1971, rule 14).

The Act empowers the sheriff to examine (in the absence of the child if he thinks this appropriate, but not in the absence of the parent or any representative) the reporter and the makers of any reports which were before the hearing, and to call for any further reports he thinks helpful (1968 Act, S.49(3)). This provision stresses the sheriff's power to make his own assessment of the needs of the child. The Act of Sederunt (supra) goes further and allows the child or his parent to lead evidence (something they cannot do at the children's hearing) regarding any information first disclosed to them in the course of the appeal.

Disposal of appeals

The sheriff's powers on appeal are negative. In an appeal against the issue of a detention warrant he may recall the warrant. In any other case, he may discharge the child from any further proceedings in relation to the grounds of the referral in question or he may remit the case with reasons for his decision to the children's hearing (1968 Act, S.49(5)). He cannot himself make any decision as to the disposal of the child, although presumably he can in his reasons indicate his views on the appropriate disposal. The hearing to which the case is remitted must then reconsider the case, and their reconsidered decision is of course again open to appeal.

Two appeals

It may be helpful to refer to two reported appeals to the sheriff which indicate the way in which at least two sheriffs regard their function. One was an appeal on the merits, and one an appeal on a question of law.

D. v. Sinclair[10]

This case is important because it is the only reported case of its kind. The sheriff allowed the appeal in question because it was conceded that the hearing had had difficulty in reaching their decision, and because the case as a whole had gone on long enough for there to have been a material change of circumstances. He accordingly remitted the case for the hearing to reconsider it in the light of up-to-date reports. What is significant, however, is what the sheriff said about the court's function in such an appeal, which he saw as much narrower than had been envisaged by Kilbrandon. He said, 'In approaching this case I had a firm view that the procedure for appeals against determinations of a children's hearing made it clear that a sheriff should not interfere with the determination simply because he felt another form of treatment might be preferable. This conclusion seems to me to follow from the fact that, although in practice a hearing had a choice between only two effective methods of supervision, a sheriff who finds one method is not justified is still not entitled to substitute the other method. Accordingly, I consider that a sheriff should not allow an appeal unless there was some flaw in the procedure adopted by the hearing or he was satisfied that the hearing had not given proper consideration to some factor in the case.'

K. v. Finlayson[11]

This was a care and protection case in which the sheriff on a section 42 application found the grounds of referral – that the child had suffered severe bruising – established. When the hearing came to consider disposal, however, they took into account information from two reports which had not been placed before the sheriff. In an appeal against their decision the sheriff held that the hearing had no jurisdiction to proceed on grounds which had not been stated as grounds of referral and which the child's parent, in this case, had had no opportunity of disputing. What the sheriff was doing here was insisting that the hearings conform to the fundamental judicial rule of not proceeding on information which has been neither admitted nor tested by the ordinary legal rules for testing evidence. This decision could have far-reaching effects on the extent to which allegations in reports considered by the hearing will require to be incorporated in the grounds of referral and so require to be proved in court if disputed.

Appeals to Court of Session

Both the child and his parent, and the reporter may appeal to the Court of Session on a point of law. Such appeals are likely in two kinds of case. An appeal may be taken against the decision of a sheriff in a section 42 application. Where the ground of referral is an offence such an appeal will often be indistinguishable from an appeal against a decision in a prosecution although in form it will be an appeal from and to a civil and not a criminal court. An appeal may also be taken against a decision by the sheriff on appeal from a hearing. The purpose of such an appeal, and of some appeals against section 42 decisions, will be to settle disputed questions of law, such as the relevant time at which the child's needs are to be determined (see *Kennedy v. B.*, supra), or whether the approaches of the sheriff in the two appeals just discussed were correct. In fact these two cases were not further appealed, so that it remains to be seen whether other sheriffs will take the same view, and whether at some subsequent stage the Court of Session will issue a binding judgement on these matters. It is not likely that that court will encourage sheriffs to substitute their own views on disposal for those of the hearing but it is likely that they will insist on strict adherence to the procedural rules governing the hearings, and on the observance of what are seen by lawyers as basic principles of fair play and individual rights such as those involved in *K. v. Finlayson.*

REFERENCES

1. Children and Young Persons. Scotland (1964), Cmnd. 2306, HMSO (Kilbrandon Report).
2. *M. v. Dean,* 1974 Scots Law Times, 229.
3. Morris, Allison (1974), Scottish Juvenile Justice: A Critique. *Crime, Criminology and Public Policy: Essays in Honour of Sir Leon Radzinowicz.* London.
4. Fox, Sanford J. (1974), Juvenile Justice Reform: Innovations in Scotland. *American Criminal Law Review* 12, 1.
5. *McGregor v. T.,* 1975 Scots Law Times, 77.
6. *Kennedy v. B.,* 1973 Scots Law Times, 38.
7. *H. v. Mearns,* 1974 Scots Law Times, 184.
8. Supra, reference 6.
9. *H. v. McGregor,* 1975 Scots Law Times, 110.
10. *D. v. Sinclair,* 1973 Scots Law Times (Sheriff Court) 47.
11. *K. v. Finlayson,* 1974 Scots Law Times (Sheriff Court) 51.

3

CHILDREN AND THE HEARINGS: SOME STATISTICAL PATTERNS

F. M. MARTIN

THE MAN IN THE STREET regards statistical data with a fair amount of suspicion; and not without good reason. Statistics are sometimes used with gross dishonesty to present, for political purposes, a deliberately misleading picture of social or economic reality. More often, statistical data have placed upon them a greater weight of interpretation than they can really support, or have inappropriate or irrelevant conclusions drawn from them. These latter misuses do not necessarily stem from any intention to defraud or confuse, but generally reflect a lack of thoughtful awareness of the nature of the data in question and of the ways in which they are constructed. It would be a mistake however to conclude that the honest man would do well to wash his hands of statistics. If figures can mislead, by design or by accident, so too – and no less powerfully – can words, or indeed any means of human communication. But it is incumbent upon the consumer to use information thoughtfully and critically, with a due sense of its limitations and possible biases.

The statistics relating to children's hearings provide a good example of these problems of interpretation. As we shall see, the number of children referred to reporters varies quite considerably from year to year and from district to district. The danger we must avoid is that of interpreting these variations as direct evidence of changes over time in the level of delinquency, or as true measures of the levels of delinquency prevailing in different parts of the country. We know, after all, that many offences are committed which are not reported to the police; that some offences known to the police cannot be laid at anyone's door; and that in still other cases the likely offender is known, but for one reason or another is not brought to the notice of the reporter. Even if we leave aside, therefore, the discretionary aspect of the reporter's own work, it remains the case that the frequency with which he receives reports depends a good deal on police activity and on police decision-making, and not merely on the current local level of delinquency. These are of course extremely elementary and obvious points, and one would hesitate to make them were it not for the fact that they are constantly being overlooked. It does not follow that the official statistics relating to reporters and hearings bear no relationship at all to community levels of delinquency – only that because of all the intervening complexities, the nature of the relationship should never be taken for granted.

With these reservations in mind, we may begin to examine the scale of operation of the hearings system. Table I shows, for each of the three years 1972–1974, the number of reports received by reporters, and the number of children to whom these reports relate.

Reporters are now receiving more than 30,000 reports each year, and these concern more than 20,000 children. Boys outnumber girls in the ratio of nearly 5 to 1. The figures suggest a fairly steep rise in reports between 1972 and 1973, and a much smaller increase in the following year. Although changes in the frequency with which delinquent acts were committed may account for this trend, we must also consider other possible explanations and in particular consider how far a greater degree of confidence in the hearings system on the part of police officers may have been responsible.

The police are the principal source of reports. In 1973 some 82% of all cases came from police sources. The only other sources of referral of any major significance were procurators fiscal (8% of the total) and education authorities (5%). Between 1 and 2% of all reports came from social work departments, extremely few (0·6%) from the Royal Scottish Society for the Prevention of Cruelty to Children, and almost none (one in 500, to be exact) from relatives. 'Other' sources accounted for just under one referral in 40. As many as 88% of all referrals were on offence grounds. Truancy cases amounted to between 6 and 7% of the total, and children alleged to be 'beyond control' to perhaps 2 or 3%. The small balance – say one in 50 of all grounds of referral – is attributable to cases of neglect, suffering or moral danger; it is perhaps surprising that the hearings system is not more widely resorted to in problems such as these.

About one half of all the offences alleged are crimes against property. In 1973, the most recent year for which detailed figures are available at the time of writing, nearly 15,000 such offences were referred to reporters, approximately equally divided between theft and housebreaking. By comparison, crimes against the person (863) were relatively uncommon. Offences not ranking as crimes amounted to more than 10,000, including some 6,000 cases of breach of the peace and more than 2,000 instances of malicious mischief.

TABLE I

REPORTS TO REPORTER, BY SEX OF CHILD, 1972–74

		Boys	Girls	Total
Reports to reporter:	1972	21,086	3,133	24,219
	1973	25,381	4,003	29,384
	1974	26,998	4,526	31,524
Children reported:	1972	15,185	2,765	17,950
	1973	17,518	3,421	20,939
	1974	17,952	3,796	21,784

Although boys very considerably outnumber girls among the children referred to reporters, the disparity is even greater when only referrals on offence grounds are considered. Table II shows, for the year 1973, the numbers of children referred because of offences. Each year of age from 8 to 15 is shown separately, and the numbers of boys and girls respectively are related to the numbers of children of that age-group in the population; this makes it possible to estimate the frequency of referral per thousand children of that age and sex. The ratio of boys to girls varies between 8:1 and 12:1; even at age 15, the peak year for referrals, not more than 2% of girls are referred to reporters, while among boys of the same age as many as one in seven is brought to the notice of the hearings system. The frequency with which offenders are reported is the same for boys of 9 as for girls of 14 and 15. It will be obvious that in both sexes there is a steady rise in referrals with increasing age, with the likelihood of referral going up by about 50% from each year to the next. It would be of great interest to know what is the statistical probability of a given child becoming the subject of a report at one age or another, but it is not yet possible to compute this from the available data.

The data so far presented relate to the whole of Scotland, with returns from local reporters being aggregated to provide national totals. It would be very surprising if the frequency of reported cases were to be identical in every part of the country, and there is some interest in examining the extent of variation from area to area. The populations of some of the pre-reorganisation local authorities were too small to justify calculations by single years of age, and in any event in inter-censal years the Registrar-General provides only estimates of the size of age-groups in individual districts. We have therefore taken the age-range 10–15 inclusive, and have expressed the number of children of those ages who were reported for offences in 1973 in terms of the frequency per 1,000 of the population group concerned. This calculation has been carried out separately for boys and girls in each of the cities, counties and large burghs which at that time maintained a separate children's panel and reporter. The results are shown in Table III, which also gives totals corresponding to the regions which since May 1975 have replaced the former local authorities for social work purposes (including children's hearings); Orkney and Shetland remain unaffected.

TABLE II

REFERRALS FOR OFFENCES, BY AGE AND SEX OF CHILD, 1973

Age	Boys referred	Rate per 1,000 population	Girls referred	Rate per 1,000 population
8	356	7·4	24	0·5
9	768	16·0	57	1·2
10	1,166	24·5	89	2·0
11	1,739	36·8	126	2·9
12	2,598	56·0	260	5·9
13	3,964	81·3	447	10·4
14	5,793	127·0	688	16·0
15	6,583	145·3	692	16·3

It will be clear from the cautionary comments with which this chapter opened that a statistical table such as this should be interpreted in a very tentative

TABLE III

REFERRALS FOR OFFENCES, AGE-GROUPS 10–15, BY SEX AND DISTRICT, 1973

	Boys referred	Rate per 1,000 population	Girls referred	Rate per 1,000 population
Inverness Burgh	128	71·1	19	11·2
Caithness	95	56·6	9	5·7
Inverness County	151	50·3	18	6·6
Ross & Cromarty	102	34·0	21	7·3
Sutherland	42	70·0	1	1·6
Highland Region	518	51·4	68	7·1
Aberdeen City	711	85·9	101	13·0
Aberdeen County	203	28·2	21	3·1
Banff	50	22·0	15	7·0
Moray & Nairn	111	35·6	11	3·8
Grampian Region	1,075	51·5	148	7·6
Dundee	956	98·4	169	18·3
Arbroath	91	84·3	14	13·0
Perth Burgh	75	36·8	14	7·0
Angus	166	47·4	11	3·3
Perth & Kinross County	123	22·8	12	2·6
Tayside Region	1,411	65·0	220	10·8
Dunfermline	151	59·9	22	9·2
Kirkcaldy	246	97·6	26	10·3
Fife	1,102	90·3	148	12·7
Fife Region	1,499	86·2	196	11·7
Edinburgh	1,950	92·3	189	9·4
Midlothian, East Lothian & Peebles*	639	54·4	42	3·8
West Lothian	425	69·4	30	5·1
Lothian Region	3,014	77·3	261	7·0
Berwick	53	44·8	3	2·6
Roxburgh	146	71·5	42	21·8
Selkirk	48	50·0	4	4·8
Borders Region*	247	59·4	49	12·5

*On local government reorganisation Peebles was incorporated in the Borders Region, but figures for 1973 cannot be disaggregated.

fashion only. To identify differences is one thing; to explain them is quite another. Indeed, a substantial part of the controversial literature of both psychology and sociology relates to issues of interpretation such as this. Whatever our individual stance in relation to such theoretical controversies, we must surely agree to resist the temptation to convert tables of this kind into simple 'league

TABLE III (*continued*)

	Boys referred	*Rate per 1,000 population*	*Girls referred*	*Rate per 1,000 population*
Falkirk	146	81·1	13	7·7
Stirling Burgh	167	99·4	10	6·4
Clackmannan	219	86·8	7	2·9
Stirling County	593	77·6	51	6·9
Central Region	1,125	82·5	81	6·3
Glasgow	6,093	129·6	595	13·2
Airdrie	208	91·2	26	11·4
Ayr Burgh	205	89·9	27	11·2
Clydebank	196	68·0	15	5·4
Coatbridge	292	90·1	15	4·8
Dumbarton	121	77·6	3	2·1
East Kilbride	216	49·1	46	11·3
Greenock	648	159·3	82	21·3
Hamilton	292	110·6	39	16·2
Kilmarnock	344	130·3	31	12·3
Motherwell	113	27·7	34	8·6
Paisley	439	87·1	64	13·0
Rutherglen	86	65·1	10	7·6
Argyll	117	42·4	24	9·1
Ayr County	1,187	82·4	70	5·2
Bute	21	35·0	4	6·7
Dunbarton	421	45·4	33	3·7
Lanark	1,123	57·8	73	4·0
Renfrew	439	43·5	31	3·2
Strathclyde Region	12,561	89·7	1,222	9·1
Dumfries Burgh	203	123·7	27	18·2
Dumfries County	169	54·2	27	9·4
Kirkcudbright	29	20·0	5	3·5
Wigtown	56	35·9	4	2·8
Dumfries & Galloway Region	457	57·1	63	8·7
Orkney	13	15·5	—	—
Shetland	11	13·1	1	1·2
SCOTLAND	21,931	79·5	2,309	8·8

tables', so that the rate of referral to reporters becomes an index of juvenile wickedness, and geographical areas are neatly ranked in terms of their propensity to crime. This is not to assert that the figures presented in Table III bear *no* relationship to the frequency with which offences are committed, but only that that relationship is not necessarily a straightforward one, incorporating as it does many different aspects of public attitudes, police vigilance and police practice which intervene, as it were, between the 'raw material' of delinquent acts and the end-product, a pile of papers on the reporter's desk.

Very roughly, we may say that in the majority of predominantly rural counties, abour 50 per thousand boys aged 10 to 15, or rather less, were referred on offence grounds in 1973. These were some exceptions – Sutherland's figures, for example, were essentially those of an urban area – but we must remember that in some districts we are dealing with quite small numbers and small populations, where very limited fluctuations from year to year may result in fair-sized shifts in the rates per thousand children. The medium-sized industrial towns and the industrialised counties characteristically yielded rates of between 60 and 100 per thousand boys; Motherwell and Wishaw is an extraordinary exception here, with figures such as would normally be met only in a remote rural area. The three cities of Edinburgh, Dundee and Aberdeen all have very similar referral rates, in the region of 90 per thousand. Rates in excess of 100 per thousand occur only in the Strathclyde Region, where four districts, including Glasgow, fall into this category, and in Dumfries; in these areas perhaps one in seven or one in eight of all the boys in that age-group was referred to the reporters. It is worth considering what this means in terms of individual years of age. The available data do not permit precise calculations at this level, but it is safe to say that in the year in question one quarter of all 15-year-old boys in Glasgow and Greenock were drawn into the hearings system.

Referral rates for girls in the 10–15 age-group were everywhere very much lower than for the corresponding group of boys, though the small numbers involved produce some odd fluctuations. Dundee, Dumfries, Roxburgh and Greenock report the highest rates for girls, but nowhere does the figure really rise above 2%. However, virtually all the referral rates for girls fall below the lowest rates recorded anywhere for boys.

This is not the place to embark upon even a speculative 'explanation' of the wide range of differences in the recorded statistics. Tabulations such as these, based upon routine statistical returns, provide the basis of an intelligence system, by means of which trends and patterns may be observed. Fully to understand the significance of these, however, it may often be necessary to move beyond routine statistics and to set up specific, carefully designed research enquiries. The material presented in the table under discussion certainly offers scope for such focussed projects. If we accept as 'normal' or 'to be expected' a steady rise in referral rates as we move from the least to the most heavily urbanised areas (and that assumption leaves many complex issues unexamined), there are some striking deviations from the general pattern which might justify careful local study. Any such study though would have to take account of the way in which the various agencies concerned actually operate, before launching into a search for the presumed causes of atypical delinquency rates.

A further and very important discretionary power is exercised by reporters. As is well known, about one half of all the children reported to them are referred to hearings. The proportions so referred are very much higher for 'non-offence' grounds, but of course these account for only a small proportion of all reports and therefore do not greatly influence the overall percentage. Local variations in the rate of referral to hearings are considerable. Table IV shows these in a summarised form.

It must be emphasised that the percentages attributed to 'regions' relate in fact to the averages of several independent districts (in 1973) which were subsequently incorporated in the new local government regions. Whether these new regions will vary so widely in their practice it is still at the time of writing far too early to judge. In the meantime, the figures presented should be taken to refer to geographical areas and not to administrative units. Lothian, Strathclyde, Borders and Highland areas conformed closely to the national average, but whereas in Dumfries and Galloway and in the Grampian areas little more than one third of all cases reported were referred to hearings, the percentage for Tayside rose to nearly two thirds and for Central to three quarters. Although there were undoubtedly considerable differences between reporters in the use made of informal supervision arrangements and of police warning schemes, it seems unlikely that the availability of alternative arrangements can account for all or even most of these variations in the use made of children's hearings. There is certainly room for further examination of the criteria consciously employed by reporters when deciding on the disposal of cases, as well as of those features of reports which may influence their decisions at a less deliberate level. The exercise of discretion is an admirable part of the hearings system, and it can only be of advantage to understand better the nature of the discretionary process. Here again however it would be necessary to go beyond routine statistics into quite subtle research.

TABLE IV

REPORTS REFERRED TO HEARINGS, BY 'REGION', 1973

'Region'	Reports referred to hearings %
Highland	53
Grampian	39
Tayside	63
Fife	41
Lothian	54
Borders	50
Central	76
Strathclyde	52
Dumfries & Galloway	34
SCOTLAND	52

Finally, what of the disposals made by the children's hearings themselves? Broadly, we find that in 1973, no supervision requirement at all was made in about two cases in five, a non-residential supervision requirement in just under half the cases, and a residential requirement in just over one in ten – 11·6%, to be precise. In this respect too there were striking differences between areas. Table V summarises the position, using the same 'regional' groups as in the previous table.

Once again, apparently simple deductions should be treated with great caution. It would be very dangerous to conclude that some panels are genuinely more prone than others to place children in List D schools. We have no right, for that matter, to say that this cannot be the case, merely that this is by no means the only possible explanation. Can we be certain that in all areas the offences coming before the hearings are comparable in the degree of 'seriousness' however defined? Bearing in mind the complex filtering that goes on beforehand, this would be a very hazardous assumption. On the face of it, the available data would seem to hint at an alternative explanation. A comparison of Tables IV and V appears to suggest that where reporters refer a high proportion of their cases to hearings, the hearings tend to use residential supervision orders less frequently, and *vice versa*. It might be hypothesised that panel members have in mind a particular set of (presumably adverse) circumstances in which a residential supervision order is appropriate. Where reporters pass on a high percentage of all cases to the hearings, many of these are considered fairly minor, and residential orders form only a small proportion of all disposals. Where on the other hand reporters pass on fewer cases, these will include a relatively large proportion of 'difficult' cases, and a residential order appears appropriate comparatively frequently. This, it must be stressed, is the merest hypothesis, broadly consistent with the data but certainly not the only possible explanation. Here again, careful research is required to elucidate this important set of data. It is not the task of routine statistics to solve all our complex prob-

TABLE V

RESIDENTIAL SUPERVISION REQUIREMENTS, 1973

'Region'	Residential SR's as proportion of all disposals %
Highland	7·3
Grampian	12·7
Tayside	18·6
Fife	23·7
Lothian	11·4
Borders	4·2
Central	5·7
Strathclyde	10·1
Dumfries & Galloway	37·0
SCOTLAND	11·6

lems, but only to monitor progress over time and variations between areas, and to suggest lines for intensive study. Unquestionably the statistics of children's hearings perform this latter function admirably.

There is one critically important aspect of the children's hearings system for which even routine statistics are not yet available. We have very little systematic knowledge of the consequences of decisions and disposals. It would be a significant contribution to the improvement of practice if we had information on the subsequent histories of children of different backgrounds who had been under social work supervision or who had spent a period in residential care. In the long run, the credibility of a system which emphasises treatment must rest upon a demonstration of the effectiveness of that treatment. The research required for any such demonstration is likely to be both difficult and time-consuming, and it is to be hoped that the necessary plans can be formulated in the near future.

Section II

THE PRINCIPAL COMPONENTS

OF THE FOUR agencies identified as the principal components of the hearings system, two were created explicitly to serve that purpose; the others had longer histories and different origins, and their involvement in the hearings system raises problems of orientation and priority.

The new system of juvenile justice is crucially dependent on the co-operation of police forces. The police have over the years developed a broad philosophy of crime and punishment which on the face of it does not lie comfortably with the commitment of the hearings system to treatment and to primacy of consideration for the needs of the child. Yet although it would be naïve to dismiss the possibility of conflicts of attitude, the incompatibilities are perhaps less extreme than might have been feared. In recent years the Scottish police have increasingly diversified their classical 'law-enforcement' rôle, moving into a range of activities aimed at deflecting first offenders from delinquent careers and even into positive involvement in community development. It is not necessary that all differences in outlook should be eliminated, only that those that remain should be contained within a framework of mutual tolerance and respect.

The reporter is the administrator of the hearings system, its adviser on matters of law and procedure, and also a decision-maker with considerable discretionary powers. He holds a critical position in relation to the complex process of filtering or selection that goes on. Only a proportion of all the children known to the police find their way to the reporter, the remainder being dealt with by the police themselves. The reporter in his turn has to consider both the quality of the evidence available and the background of the child. He may reach the conclusion that consideration by a hearing is unnecessary and that adequate arrangements can be made on a voluntary basis. The reporter's effectiveness outside the hearing situation depends both on his skill in assessing social and other evidence, and on his links with other statutory and voluntary agencies. If his legal abilities are tested during hearings, his social work skills play a critical part in the exercise of discretion prior to the hearing.

The children's panel exists only to provide the members of children's hearings. It is a striking example of voluntary activity which currently involves some sixteen hundred people. While it is literally true that panel members are drawn from every stratum of Scottish society, it would be idle to pretend that they represent a microcosm of the nation; indeed, it may be quite unrealistic to expect that this can ever be perfectly achieved. A particularly significant feature of the panel system is the importance attached to training. The observer cannot fail to be impressed by the extent to which a sophisticated training programme and regular participation in hearings combine to produce a professionalism of outlook and approach without panel members ever losing, so to speak, their amateur status.

The social work department was created by the same Act of Parliament as the hearings system, but was not created *de novo*. Both the history of social work prior to 1969 and the subsequent unanticipated pressures on the new departments have created problems in maximising the contribution of social work services to the children's hearings. Such shortcomings as have been experienced are not seen as irreparable, although opinions are divided as to whether the key problem is one of resources in general, or whether it is at least in part one of specialisation and deployment. There are, too, subtle issues involved when professionals and informed voluntary workers interact in the process of making and implementing decisions; these issues also are capable of resolution, but only if they are first recognised and examined.

4

THE POLICE

RICHARD W. BETT

THE CHANGING CLIMATE of thought in relation to children who break the law anticipated some modification of practices and attitudes on the part of the police. Traditionally the police have been concerned with law enforcement and protection of the public although they have tended to exercise this with a friendly discretion in the case of delinquent children. The Kilbrandon Committee described the police as 'one of the primary sources of the identification of children in need of special educational measures as well as being part of the sifting or assessment agency'. Clearly this shifted the emphasis from the offence to the offender and his needs; and gave primary importance to the situation, the personality and the family background of the child.

A significant feature of police work with juveniles in recent years has been the strong drive in favour of the development of the policy of community involvement. This translated into urban conditions the traditional rôle of the country policeman whose primary approach to crime prevention depended on securing the respect and trust of the public and particularly of the local community. Prior to the formation of the modern police force, control was conducted on a local basis and carried out by Parish Constables. The Glasgow Police Act of 1800 brought into being a force of two sergeants, six officers and sixty-eight watchmen. Their duties included lighting and cleansing for which they received ten shillings per week.

In the early nineteenth century, the growth of cities led to a rapid increase in crime and some members of Parliament began to press for a national police system. Fears were expressed concerning the possible formation of a police state and the idea was abandoned. By the 1820's however, crime had reached such alarming proportions that the Metropolitan Police was formed in 1829 by the Home Secretary of the day, Sir Robert Peel.

The new force proved successful, and by the middle of the nineteenth century the system was extended to cover the whole of the country, with control being shared between central and local government. As recently as 1947 there were 49 police forces in Scotland: amalgamations brought the number to 20, and although this has again been reduced by regionalisation to the present eight regional forces in Scotland, the basic position remains unchanged. The Chief Constable of a force is chosen by the local authority and approved by the Secretary of State. Thereafter, the Chief Constable is responsible for the appointment, training and organisation of the constables within the police area. Their duty is to guard, patrol and watch; prevent crime, preserve peace, protect life and property and detect offenders. A measure of control and efficiency has been ensured by the introduction of the ranks of assistant chief constable, superintendent, inspector and sergeant.

In an open society such as Britain enjoys, the police have always proved ready to meet the wishes of society in regard to changes that were considered necessary. Such changes will continue in a democracy, but it must be emphasised that, while it is important to be responsive to societal trends, it is of the greatest importance to preserve law and order from possible erosion. The continued growth of crime and the increasing complexities of society make the task of the crime-fighter onerous and difficult. Organised crime with all its attendant dangers requires the unremitting work of a well-led and vigilant police, while such matters as interference with witnesses could confound and hamper their best efforts. Fortunately, both our police officers and our courts have proved equal to such challenges, but watchfulness and the readiness of police and public to meet an ever-changing scene is essential.

Perhaps some of the most interesting changes that have occurred in policing have taken place in Scotland over recent years. This has, in part, been in keeping with the changes made in legislation relating to juvenile offenders, and in particular those brought about by the Social Work (Scotland) Act 1968. Police opinion is no doubt divided as to the advantages and limitations of these changes, but it can be said that the police have made every effort to ensure that nothing has been done which would frustrate the intention of the Act. Indeed, the extent of interchange with social workers, educationists and reporters to the children's panels has grown steadily over the years, and close co-operation between training colleges and the police has resulted in a number of social science students being attached to the police for field training on one or two days every week. This attachment allows the social worker the opportunity to gain a close insight into practical police activities and is a measure of the extent of co-operation offered by the police in order to gain a mutual understanding of problems common to local authority agencies.

The contribution of the police to the new arrangements includes the investigation, the preparation and submission of reports and the classification of cases with a view to allocating to this or that procedure. Prior to 1971 the allocator could either retain a case for police warning – or police juvenile liaison where such a scheme existed – or refer the case to the procurator fiscal. In the new system there are three channels of allocation, each with its own conditions of entry: these are, retention for the police warnings type of procedure; referral to the procurator fiscal; and referral to the reporter.

Police warnings

There has been a long-standing and widely recognised practice of the exercise of discretion by the police in not reporting the available evidence to the appropriate prosecutor for consideration of proceedings but, as an alternative, to administer formal or informal warnings against repetition of anti-social conduct. Such discretion is exercised in minor crimes or offences of every kind, particularly where the conduct of the offender does not appear to indicate a real slide into delinquency. The warnings are applicable to both adults and children, but are generally reserved for first offenders. It is equally true that the police attach great significance to the possible value of a formal police warning for a child whose outlook and disposition would be responsive to such advice and guidance, as opposed to his alienation by further action of the law.

As has been said there are two methods by which discretion may be exercised, namely informal and formal warning. An *informal warning* may be exercised at the time of the detection by the constable on the beat. There is little doubt that the officer is in an excellent position to assess all the circumstances of both the offence and the offender, and everyone recognises that, where the matter is relatively trivial, an informal warning administered immediately is both necessary and appropriate. In this regard the only record may be in the officer's notebook but in recent years forces have been employing a system of juvenile 'contact cards' which is intended to produce a follow-up procedure to any verbal caution administered by a constable, particularly in regard to the following circumstances:

(a) *a child found in unusual or undesirable places or one found frequenting or loitering in such places in the company of undesirable persons, especially at night;*

(b) *a child found playing truant from school and likely to become involved in criminal activities.*

The ideal situation is that all such reports will be followed by a visit to the home and some contact made with the parent or school, but the sheer volume of these reports necessarily precludes action in all but the most needful. Nevertheless, the action taken by the police is considered of tremendous value in the preventive process available to them in dealing with child offenders or potential child offenders, particularly when it is remembered that almost *10,000* such contact cards were issued in one police area in *1973*. Although there are no figures available for the number of informal warnings administered by the police in Scotland, it is interesting to consider that an average of ten informal warnings given each year by every police officer would number over *125,000* warnings.

Administration of a *formal police warning* is the second way in which discretion may be exercised by a senior police officer. This form of cautioning is undertaken in accordance with the recommendations of the 1945 Report by the Scottish Advisory Council on the Treatment and Rehabilitation of Offenders. Conducted in the presence and with the consent of the parents by an officer in the rank of Inspector or above, the warning is not an attempt to settle the appropriate course of treatment for an offender or to invoke punishment. It is a genuine course of preventive action, taken in regard to the child, so that the consequences of anti-social behaviour can be pointed out to him. This formal warning is only given when there is adequate evidence of guilt and an open admission of that guilt has been made by the child. The warning will not be given if the parents have not signified their readiness to co-operate with the police in the matter. As has been said, the warnings are a preventive measure aimed at first offenders, but second warnings have been given for a subsequent offence in exceptional cases where decline in conduct could be arrested. It should be remembered that the *formal police warning* is recorded by the police and results from the process of reporting offenders in a formal way. In other words, the detecting officer has written a formal charge, a summary of evidence and a list of witnesses for his superior officers who then exercise their discretion on whether to warn the individual or pass the information to the reporter. Community Involvement Branches assess the information submitted on children, and it is after consideration has been given to their recommendations that the Divisional Police Commander will make a decision on warning or otherwise.

Although it would be misleading to express the value of this particular form of crime prevention in purely statistical terms, it is worth recording that the system of formal police warnings has resulted in some 60.. of offenders not subsequently being reported for any repetition of offences or crimes. Many would argue that perhaps this number would not offend again in any case, but this view would, nonetheless, fail to recognise the additional savings that have been made to the time of panel members, social workers and others concerned with the treatment of children. It ignores also the considerzble moral support that must accrue to many of the children who become peripherally involved in criminal activities or anti-social behaviour.

Juvenile liaison

In addition to the warnings, a system known as 'juvenile liaison' is sometimes operated as a form of 'follow-up' procedure. This is operated on the 'friendly bobby' lines and consists essentially of a selected police officer maintaining contact with the offender and his parents and providing counsel and advice or whatever guidance appears necessary, often with the co-operation of a social workers.

Since the early days of the introduction of juvenile liaison to Scotland in 1956, there has been an expansion of the community involvement policies initially tested in Gibbshill, Greenock and the Rzploch area of Stirling. These policies involved the local community in its own affairs and sought to produce improvement in the neighbourhood by their efforts. In Scotland at the present time there are about twenty socially deprived areas called 'special project areas' where chosen police officers have been allocated to undertake such support work. A small number of uniformed beat officers undertake their normal police duties in addition to setting up community associations, youth clubs and play groups, as well as aiding other local authority departments to provide a more efficient service to the area concerned. These projects have been encouragingly successful in many problem areas of high crime incidence and it is worth noting that a greater stability has resulted from the efforts of the officers with a consequent reduction in crime figures. Of almost equal importance to the communities concerned there has been a reduction in the numbers of tenants who desire to move to other towns or housing areas.

Today the beat officer remains the most important individual in the whole of the police function. It is through the beat officer that the police continually seek to improve their service to the public. Further, the supporting services of the police exist solely to render the services of the beat officer more effective. As the social problems of the vast housing areas called for a particular social approach, so the problems of change in thought, values and life styles called for the formation of specialist units or departments specially equipped and trained to meet particular crimes or needs. Amongst these are such units as Drugs, Fraud and Crime Squads, as well as specialist firearm and laboratory services. A highly developed training department will also be a constant requirement of an effective police establishment. Nevertheless, society is likely to benefit most from sustained involvement in its own affairs. Co-operation between police and public has proved to be the soundest means by which crime can be countered, and it is not surprising that increasing accent has been placed on service by and involvement with the community by the beat officer. This has brought the following tribute by Professor Michael Banton in his 'James Smart lecture' in June 1974, on 'Policing a Divided Society'. He said, 'In Scotland you have gone further than the police of any other country known to me to develop a positive conception of the police rôle instead of seeing the police simply as agents of the state.' Nevertheless, it must not be thought that the considerable work undertaken by the police in community associations, youth clubs, 'discos' and juvenile liaison is a 'soft option'. The police are postured and trained to counter the worst elements of society and the steady and unremitting tasks of controlling these elements are never ignored. It is with the widest humanity that the Scottish Police Service remains 'Ever Vigilant'.

5

THE REPORTER

ALAN F. FINLAYSON

THE CENTRAL FIGURE in the hearings system is without doubt the reporter, and the varying patterns and emphases which characterise the operation of the system in different places are to a large extent the outcome of the way in which he interprets his rôle. The post carries powers and responsibilities relating to the intake of cases as well as broad administrative duties but principally the reporter has extensive opportunities for creating a system of juvenile justice which suits the character and needs of the local community. This presentation takes the form of a commentary on the professional responsibilities of the reporter followed by a personal account of one reporter's interpretation of his task.

The reporter to the children's panel is appointed by the regional authority from a short leet drawn up by the Secretary of State. In order to preserve his independence, particularly in relation to his quasi-judicial discretion, the reporter cannot be removed from office without the consent of the Secretary of State. The reporter heads a department of the regional authority which is administratively separate from the department of social work.

In terms of the 1968 Social Work (Scotland) Act, the reporter may receive from any person reports relating to a child in need of care. In practice the vast majority of these reports come from the police in respect of children who are alleged to have committed offences. The remainder fall into two general categories of truancy and care and protection. The care and protection cases vary from those of young children who have received injuries at the hands of their parents and others, to the 15-year-old promiscuous girl, with a wide range of care categories in between including lack of parental care and children who are beyond parental control. In each instance, before a reporter can make a decision to refer a child to a hearing, he must be in a position to establish the grounds of referral in court. The various grounds of referral are contained in section 32 (a) to (g) of the Act.

Where a child is alleged to have committed an offence, the standard of proof to be observed is that of 'beyond reasonable doubt' which applies in all Scottish criminal cases and is a very high standard indeed. In care and protection cases, the standard of proof is that of the 'balance of probabilities', i.e. that it is more likely than not that the grounds of referral can be made out. This is theoretically the position but, in fact, in cases of assault on children, some sheriffs continue to demand a higher standard of proof than the 'balance of probabilities', on the grounds that the averments in a case of this kind virtually constitute an allegation of assault by the parents; they therefore tend to require a standard of proof approximating that of 'beyond reasonable doubt'.

From whatever sources the reporter receives a report and whatever the alleged grounds, he will require to decide, on the basis of information which he has been sent or may obtain, whether that child is in need of care other than that provided by the parents themselves. After completing his investigation, the reporter has the choice of three courses of action. If he is satisfied that the parents are capable of exercising the appropriate measures of supervision and care over their own child, he will take no action. If he decides that the matter can be resolved by voluntary supervision, he will refer the child to the regional authority social work department for appropriate advice, guidance and assistance. If it appears to the reporter that the child is in need of compulsory measures of care, he will refer the case to a children's hearing which will then have the responsibility for taking the decision. The most important authority granted the reporter is the making of decisions about children who are referred to him. This is solely his responsibility and one for which he is accountable only to the Secretary of State.

The reporter has various other responsibilities in connection with the 1968 Act. He is the principal officer with responsibility for the organisation of the children's hearings department. When a hearing is arranged the reporter sends out citations to children and parents, together with the grounds of referral, and he is responsible for ensuring the attendance of these persons at the hearing. He is responsible, too, for ensuring that all appropriate information is made available for the hearing and that reports from the social work department and school together with grounds of referral and any other relevant information are forwarded to panel members some four days prior to the hearing taking place. He is responsible for maintenance of the detailed record system and statistical returns. Further, he is responsible for communication of information to agencies who have referred cases or submitted reports.

Arrangements for hearings vary according to the type of situation. In addition to cases of the first instance, there are 'emergency' hearings for children who have been detained in a place of safety. In cases where the court has required the advice of a children's hearing, there must be sufficient time to allow the appropriate report to be submitted to the court. Review hearings must take place within one year.

The reporter must be present at each session of the children's hearing. The actual rôle of the reporter within the hearing has been the subject of considerable discussion among the members of the Reporters' Association. It can, however, best be summarised by saying that the reporter acts in some quasi-legal advisory rôle to the hearing members and also in a clerical rôle to record the minutes of proceedings of the actual hearing.

The reporter also has to make appearances in court. If a child or parent denies the grounds of referral or if the child is incapable of understanding the grounds of referral, the hearing have two options open to them. They may either discharge the referral themselves or, if they wish to proceed further, they must instruct the reporter to report the matter to the sheriff court for a finding as to whether or not the grounds of referral are established. In these cases the reporter will be responsible for preparing the case for court, citing the witnesses to attend the court and conducting the proof before the court.

If a child or parent appeals against a decision of a children's hearing, that appeal will be to the sheriff court and the reporter is responsible for ensuring that all papers which were available for the hearing members are available for the court; he may also be directed by the sheriff to be present when the appeal is heard in order to provide information. He may also decide to take a stated case to the Court of Session on a point of law should he feel that he is aggrieved by a decision taken by the sheriff. If on the other hand a parent or child takes a case to the Court of Session on a point of law, it would be the responsibility of the reporter to answer as the respondent in the case.

After this brief outline of the statutory reponsibilities carried by the reporter, it may be helpful to review the way in which these responsibilities are interpreted in practice in one region.* In relation to offence cases, the first question to be considered is how decisions are taken as to whether or not a child is to be referred to a hearing. It is not the practice of the Lothian Region to use the gravity of the offence as the sole criterion for deciding whether or not a child is in need of compulsory measures of care, nor is the apparently trivial nature of the offence used as a reason for taking no action. The total needs of the child must be considered. Nevertheless, the nature of the offence is obviously of considerable interest to the reporter in making his decision and in addition to that he will be interested to know from the police report the time of the offence, who the child's companions are, whether he is a leader, whether he appears to be led and all these matters which can come out from the evidence. He must of course be satisfied on evidence that he can prove the case in court.

In addition to the actual evidence, however, additional information which can be provided by the police in regard to the child or family is very much appreciated. In many cases they will perhaps have given the child an informal warning in the past and they will be in a postion, if they know the area well, to report on the company that the child is keeping and whether he has been a source of trouble in the area. In other cases they will know whether other members of the family have previously been in trouble with the police and in all cases they will caution and charge the child with the offence in the presence of his parents, normally in his own home.

Initially information is requested from the social work department. While it would be ideal if a home visit could be carried out in every case, this is not always possible because of the exigencies of the department. In these cases therefore the department will simply advise the reporter what they know of

*It must be emphasised that practices vary from region to region and no doubt even within regions. It should not be assumed that the region referred to here is in any way representative – or for that matter that it is unique.

the child and family. In many instances the child and family may be already known because another member of the family has been in trouble and a probation report supplied for the court's consideration. In other cases children may have been taken into care or the parents may have consulted the department about a variety of matters such as electricity disconnection, eviction notices or matrimonial difficulties. In areas which are better supplied with social workers it is possible to obtain information by means of a home visit; and if in any area a specific request for a home visit is made in any particular case this will be carried out and a report presented.

It is accordingly on the basis of these three sources of information: the police, the social work department and the school, that the reporter's decision might be made. On other occasions the reporter will have the benefit of other information from the Department of Psychological Medicine and the Division of Special Educational Services, if there is reason to believe that the child is already known to one of these departments.

Care and protection cases emanate from a wide variety of sources. The normal sources would be the social work department, the police, schools, hospitals, family doctors, voluntary agencies and, in particular, the RSSPCC, neighbours and parents themselves. Clearly when one considers this large number of bodies or individuals who may present reports, it is difficult to be specific about the nature of information which is obtained. Basically however the reporter is in a position, having received an original report, to look to a variety of agencies or individuals for information to assist him in deciding whether the grounds of referral exist and if they do, whether the child may be held to be in need of measures of care over that provided by the parents.

Another ground on which many children are referred to a hearing is that of truancy or in its more appropriate form, failing to attend school without proper cause. Whereas in the past these reports were received from a sub-committee of the Education Committee with responsibility for school attendance, history has shown that truancies so reported were normally so deep seated that by the time they were referred to the hearings system, panel members and the reporter found it impossible to deal efficiently with any but a small percentage of cases. It has now been arranged that reports will be sent direct from the school to the reporter and he will then decide which children are in need of compulsory measures of care.

The system of decision-making in the Region takes the form of a joint exercise between the reporter, his depute and assistants. This sharing of responsibility among colleagues discourages any excessive concentration of power and stimulates thoughtful discussion of the implications of decision-making. It is generally known that there are conflicting views as to the qualifications required for the reporter to the children's panel. Whereas there is a strong lobby of opinion to the effect that such persons should be qualified in law, if one accepts that the major responsibility which the reporter has is that of deciding how and when to intervene in the lives of children, there are solid arguments for asserting that the most appropriate qualification for the reporter would be that of a social worker. However, there are clearly legal requirements in assessing evidence and presenting matters in court. Perhaps the best way of meeting the requirements for a reporter is for the department to have a balance of previous experiences. In the Lothian Region therefore the system which has been adopted is to recruit to the department reporters with previous experience of different disciplines.

If the reporter believes that the child is in need of special measures of care he may either refer the child to a hearing or ask the social work department to undertake voluntary measures of care. In any other case where he believes that the parents can cope with the situation themselves or that other situations demand it, he will take in the words of the statute 'no action'. The use of these words in the Act has caused a great deal of harm to the system. It seems to imply that the reporter ignores much of what is referred to him, and it is easy to understand the feelings of police officers and indeed school teachers and others who report matters, if they are simply advised that no action has been taken, with the implication that nothing has been done. In fact, something and in many instances a great deal is done in every case, even though the final classification is 'no action'. At the very least a letter will be sent to the parents pointing out the decision which has been taken, or is required by statute. The letters that are sent point out to the parents that the reason for the decision is that the reporter is satisfied that the parents can exercise the appropriate measures of care and discipline over their own child. They go on to point out that if this belief is mistaken, and is shown to be mistaken by the fact of a subsequent referral to the reporter, it would obviously be difficult to take a similar decision in the future; it would be much more likely for the child to be referred to a children's hearing for compulsory measures of supervision. This is perhaps not a great deal but it is in its own way a warning, and the percentage of cases which are re-referred to the reporter on matters of any gravity suggests that it has a salutary impact.

In other cases – and it is appreciated that this is not general practice – the reporter will frequently meet a child and parents sometimes with the same objective as the letter to parents but at other times with different purposes. In particular, the opportunity is often taken to defer a decision, in order to give the child and his parents a chance to show what he can do in the next three months, particularly in relation to performance and attitudes at school. This can operate as a bolster to the parents' authority and many parents and children have found this helpful.

There is of course a category of cases in which the case is marked 'no action' because the reporter is not satisfied that there is sufficient evidence on which it would be possible to proceed in a court of law to prove the case beyond reasonable doubt. Whereas the police claim they would never submit a report without sufficient evidence, it will be borne in mind that the witnesses in many of these cases are children and for various reasons they have good cause not to give the same account in court as the account which they gave to the police officer some weeks or months before. In other cases where meetings are held with parents and children encouragement is given to make good any damage that has been done. 'Deals' with parents and children in which they are told that if they do not, say, remove spray painting they will be sent to a hearing are not acceptable. The matter may be discussed with the child and parents and the 'no action' decision taken but if the parents have been assessed rightly they will be the kind of parent who would be anxious that the child be involved in such an exercise. It is not possible in the course of this chapter to give details of the various people with whom the reporter's department has been involved in these matters and it is not claimed that this is done in all cases; but much emphasis is laid on encouraging children to put right what they have done wrong in relation to vandalism and in relation to thefts. In certain cases the recovery of stolen money is arranged. The City Engineer's Department and the Corporation Transport have allowed youngsters to put right what they have done wrong. Arrangements have been made for children to be involved with the Fire Service and with Youth and Community workers. These are all finally classified as 'no action' and while the police may be aggrieved at the terminology they are coming increasingly to appreciate that 'no action' does in fact mean that compulsory measures of care are not necessary but that nevertheless in many cases a great deal of positive work is achieved. In similar meetings with children and parents it is often possible through the reporter's knowledge of youth organisations to refer the boy to some useful activity with the co-operation of his parents. Many would claim that this is no part of the reporter's function and it is undeniable that when the social work departments are sufficiently well staffed and organised to be able to cope with all the responsibility and deal constructively with cases referred for voluntary measures of care, these matters could be appropriately handled without the intervention of the reporter.

Other 'no action' disposals relate to children who are in List D schools. Children frequently abscond from these establishments and when they are in abscondance they will invariably commit offences. Other children commit offences when they are on leave from establishments. In these cases the probable decision will be 'no action' but in all these cases contact is first made with the headmaster to find out what steps will be taken by the school. Normally the headmaster will be arranging forfeiture of privileges and particularly of home leave. The reporter, having heard from the school, writes to the child advising him of his decision and pointing out that the length of time which the child will spend in the establishment will depend very much on the reports received from the school and other people, that the present offence has been noted, that it will be brought to the notice of the hearing members when he ultimately returns for review. He is further told that the reporter looks forward to receiving better reports in the future from the school and the social worker. Copies of that letter are sent to the boy's social worker and to the parents. In these cases when the ultimate decision which is open to the hearing members has already been taken, it is arguable that it would be pointless to bring the child before a children's hearing simply for a statement of this kind to be made. Should the school feel that it would be useful for a hearing to take place for that purpose or to involve the parents more in the matter, this will obviously be arranged. Similar considerations frequently apply to 'no action' decisions which are taken when children are the subject of supervision requirements while they are living at home.

The 'no action' decision has been discussed at some length because of the adverse publicity which it receives and because it may be helpful for panel members to be aware of the various categories of 'no action' which obtain. In all cases too, a record is kept of the situation so that if the child is referred again at any time, the previous information and correspondence will be available.

There are seven categories of offences contained in a letter by the Lord Advocate to procurators fiscal in August 1970 relating to offences which will be jointly reported to the procurator fiscal and to the reporter.

1. High Court offences. These are offences which can only be dealt with in the High Court. The obvious ones are murder and rape. The others are in fact incest, treason and deforcement of messengers.

2. Offences of such a nature that they would normally be dealt with in the High Court such as attempted murder, assault with intent to ravish, assault with a firearm, assault to the danger of life.

3. Offences which could involve disqualification. Since the hearing is not a court and has no power of disqualification, contravention of the Prevention of Crime Act, such as possession of a knife which could involve forfeiture, must be reported jointly to the procurator fiscal and the reporter.

4. Offences committed by a child between 14 and 16 which may involve disqualification from holding a driving licence. Again, since a hearing is not a court and cannot impose penalties, and since the procurator might believe that disqualification might be appropriate, the matter is reported jointly to the procurator fiscal and to the reporter.

5. Offences committed by a child while acting along with an adult. In these cases, where there may be prejudice to the prosecution if the cases were split the rule is that the cases are in the first instance reported jointly to the two persons mentioned.

6. Offences committed by a child who is a child by definition of the Act in that he is someone between 16 or 18 who is the subject of a supervision requirement. Again in cases of these kinds they are jointly reported.

7. Offences of such a character that the prosecutor believes that they should be prosecuted in the public interest. An example of this could be a charge of malicious damage in children placing a sleeper across a railway line which could disrail a train but in fact, because of other intervention in removing the sleeper, causes no damage.

Criticism has been levelled in Parliament at the high number of children who are prosecuted in court. In Edinburgh last year only 113 fell into all these seven categories. The reason for this may be the good communication which exists between the procurator fiscal and the reporter. Custody cases are discussed every morning, so that decisions can be reached on the appropriate ways of dealing with them. In cited cases the police co-operate in ensuring that the reporter receives a set of papers of all cases every Monday and the procurator fiscal receives an identical set. A weekly meeting is held to discuss again whether the child should be prosecuted in court or whether the children's hearing should take the responsibility. The procurator fiscal and his deputes have proved to be extremely co-operative in this regard and to be operating the spirit of the 1968 Act and the Lord Advocate's letter of instructions of August 1970. Category 1 cases must be prosecuted in court. Category 2 cases tend to be prosecuted in court if the child is 15 or over. Category 3 cases are dealt with by the reporter, and it is usually possible to obtain the weapon. In category 4 cases the procurator fiscal does not believe that disqualification now with the raising of the age for driving would be appropriate and they are normally handed to the reporter. Category 5 cases are discussed on the basis of the difficulty of prosecution if the cases are split and in particular if the child is going to deny the grounds of referral and the adult is going to deny the charge. It is undesirable for witnesses to be inconvenienced by coming to court on two occasions to speak to the identical facts. Children should however be prosecuted in court in cases falling into category 6. It is inequitable if two 16-year-olds are charged with com-mitting an offence, that one who has a history of delinquency and is the subject of a supervision requirement should simply be dealt with by a children's hearing whereas his co-accused, a first offender, is liable to the penalties of the court. If a child is already subject to a supervision requirement it is of course necessary for the court to remit the case to a children's hearing for advice before the sheriff can finally dispose of the case; this opens a wider variety of options to the hearing than are normally available to them. In practice again it has been interesting to note the very high percentage of cases in which the sheriff accepts the advice of the children's hearing. Category 7 cases are reported from time to time to the procurator fiscal and the reporter and in these cases they are normally passed to the latter.

As mentioned earlier, it is the responsibility of the reporter to arrange for children to attend a hearing. Panel members and reporters agree that it is at the very least highly desirable that there should be continuity of panel members for continued or reviewed cases. While the making up of the panel roster has all along been the responsibility of the chairman of the panel, he normally provides the reporter with that roster some three months in advance. It is possible therefore to arrange with cited continued cases for at least one member of the original hearing to be present at the adjourned or reviewed hearing. There is no doubt that this is of considerable benefit to the hearing members, and to the children and their families.

This outline of the basic responsiblities of the reporter has omitted certain ancillary functions which are not strictly written into the Act but which seem necessary for the children's hearings to operate efficiently. In particular, the reporter is in the front-line as a communications person between the various agencies with which the department is involved and must be closely connected with the panel members, the social work department, the education department, the police, the procurator fiscal, hospitals, voluntary agencies (including the RSSPCC) and other bodies. He is responsible for maintaining good links with these bodies, and for ensuring that they understand fully the work of children's hearings.

6

THE CHILDREN'S PANEL

KATHLEEN MURRAY

THE CHILDREN'S PANEL shares with the office of reporter the distinction of having been created solely as an instrument of the new system. Independent of both the courts and the local or regional authority, it is the public agency which provides volunteers to staff the hearings. Its independence is clearly reflected in the machinery of appointment: recruitment, selection and training involve a unique partnership of central and regional government which ensures an essential minimum of standardisation while at the same time encouraging innovation and a flexible response to local circumstances.

It was feared that members of the public would not come forward in sufficient number to staff the panels but contrary to expectation the first recruitment in some areas attracted three or four times the number required. Initially 850 members were appointed to 52 children's panels serving the social work areas of the local authorities. This figure rose to more than 1,500 members before May 1975 when the reorganisation of local government transferred responsibility for social work to the nine regional and three all-purpose island authorities. Members in office and those eligible for reappointment were invited to serve on the regional authority panel and vacancies were filled by the appointment of new members. Unfortunately some panels became so large that the maintenance of effective leadership and fluent lines of communication between members has been a considerable problem.

The Secretary of State's functions under the Social Work (Scotland) Act are exercised through the Social Work Services Group, a body formed in 1967 by bringing together relevant divisions of the Scottish Home and Health Department and the Scottish Education Department. The Group was responsible for the early planning and continues to keep a watching brief over the system's operation. The special quality of the Group lies in the collaboration of administrative civil servants with professional social workers. Although the Secretary of State is responsible for the appointment of panel members as well as their regional chairmen and deputies, the task of finding suitable candidates for each panel is entrusted to the Children's Panel Advisory Committee of each regional and island authority. As indicated in chapter 1, the CPAC may perform a number of tasks but it is concerned principally with the recruitment and nomination of panel members. Each committee consists of five members of whom three including the chairman are appointed by the Secretary of State and two by the regional authority. The one exception is in Strathclyde where the CPAC has ten members of whom six including the chairman are appointed by the Secretary of State and four by the regional authority. Because of the CPAC's influence in determining the character of the panel, its membership has aroused considerable interest. The regional authority nominees are very often elected members who not only represent the community but through personal contacts may also stimulate recruitment and community support for the system. The Secretary of State's nominees include persons who are knowledgeable about family and social problems, and former panel members who contribute valuable advice from their experience of hearings.

The CPACs are sometimes criticised by panel members for a lack of continuing interest in the work of the panel. The situation has been improved recently by the appointment of former panel members to regional committees and by the increasing readiness to consult with regional panel chairmen. Further trust will develop as the CPACs learn to communicate with the panel and to use their potentially favourable position for conveying and interpreting the needs of the system directly to the decision-making bodies of central and regional government.

As panels occupy a central place in the operation of children's hearings, the character of the system and the interpretation of its objectives are likely to be influenced greatly by the kind of people who are attracted and subsequently appointed to panel membership. It is not surprising that so much importance has been attached to obtaining 'the right kind' of people and that the composition of panels has been the focus of continuous discussion.

Selection proposals

The first reference to the characteristics desirable for panel membership is found in the Kilbrandon Report. This stated that panel members should be specially qualified by knowledge or experience to deal with children's problems. Although they might include members of the legal profession, teachers, doctors and local authority members, they should be chosen more for their personal qualities than for their specialised training or official position.

The White Paper of 1966 dramatically changed the emphasis to 'community involvement' and indicated that the panel should be composed of people 'drawn from a wide variety of occupation, neighbourhood, age group and income group', and that decisions should be taken by members with personal knowledge of the neighbourhood to which the child belongs. It was hoped that 'the new system will attract suitable people whose occupations or circumstances have hitherto prevented them from taking a formal part in helping and advising young people or who might not previously have thought of themselves as candidates for public service'. The aim here was to build up a sense of local responsibility for the less fortunate members of the community. Although the concept of 'community involvement' is considered central to the panel process, its definition is far from clear. Smith and May[1] have commented on the far reaching consequences which could result from a literal interpretation of the White Paper's proposals: 'If taken at their face value they would seem to imply a redefinition of delinquency and law-enforcement, and a system of juvenile justice reflecting the standards of each local community.'

The 1968 Act offered no guidance on the requirements for panel membership but subsequent official circulars, taking a less radical view than the White Paper, have tended to discourage the introduction to the panel of a cross-section of attitudes and diversity of response to delinquency problems. One circular stated, 'Persons appointed as panel members should have shown themselves capable of taking reasonable unbiased attitudes towards children in trouble. While panel members may be expected on occasion to take differing views on the appropriate measures in individual cases, in general it is desirable that persons with a clear pre-disposition towards taking a "hard" or a "soft" line with all, or even particular types of case, or children, or with other apparent prejudices should be excluded from panel membership as far as possible.'*

Initial government circulars emphasised the personal qualities desirable in every panel member. These include intelligence and good judgement, the capacity to be objective, concern for people and their problems, an absence of bias and prejudice, knowledge and understanding of children and their families and a belief in the individual's potential to change. The concept of 'community' persists and CPACs are constantly reminded of the importance of ensuring that the composition of the panels is representative of the community in respect of age, sex, occupation and geographical location. Only people who might be professionally concerned in advising hearings or in helping to implement their decisions are excluded.

Smith and May[2] have commented on the conflicting principles embodied in the selection proposals. One is concerned with the principle of 'diversity' and seeks to create a panel reflecting a varied cross-section of the community. The other is concerned with finding panel members possessing the relevant personal qualities. The task of the CPACs has been largely one of striking the appropriate balance between these two different sets of advice.

Selection procedure and results

Each CPAC is free to decide on the selection method most suitable for its area but in practice its recruitment and selection procedure tend to conform to the pattern suggested by the Social Work Services Group. The publicity and advertising, the design of the application form, the method of assessment, the definition of selection criteria have all been provided by the Group after wide informal consultations. There is no limit to the breadth of recruitment but imagination and skill are needed to develop this fully. Research indicates that

*Social Work Services Group Circular No. SW7/1969, appendix A, para. 1; Paper 5 of a series of papers presented to a Consultation for Children's Panel Advisory Committees, and issued by the S.W.S.G.

personal contact has been one of the most effective methods of reaching interested persons, and CPACs and panel members have tried to make contact
with local groups. The community councils could have an important rôle in
making available to the residents all relevant information and encouragement.

The standard selection procedure employs three stages – an initial written
application, an individual interview and a group discussion interview. Commonly the CPAC calls on professional 'selectors' who advise on the assessment
of personal qualities while CPAC members concentrate on the social characteristics.

National and local studies of the results of selection have drawn attention to
significant gaps in panel membership. While there is no evidence of a major
departure from the original selection procedure, efforts have been made recently
to broaden the intake and further research is now required in order to assess any
change in composition.

Table VI illustrates the way in which the idea of panel service tends to
attract to a disproportionate extent people from certain social groups and how
this is reinforced by selection.

The significant feature of these figures is the extent to which it is demonstrated that panel members, particularly in relation to social class are self selected.

TABLE VI

THE EFFECTS OF SOCIAL CHARACTERISTICS ON THE SELECTION PROCESS

	Total number of applicants	% successful	% unsuccessful
Social class			
1 and 2	1,970	39	61
3, 4 and 5	842	31	69
Married	2,755	34	66
Single	327	33	67
Age of leaving school			
under 17 years	1,608	32	68
over 17 years	1,196	43	57
1–2 teachers in household	657	45	55
No teachers in household	2,270	34	66
Male age group			
20–35	327	37	63
35–50	719	36	61
Female age group			
20–35	356	40	60
35–50	797	36	64

These figures are taken from Andrew Rowe's analysis of the initial
selection for children's panels in Scotland.[3]

Whereas 70%–80% of the general population occupy social classes 3, 4 and 5, only 30% of those volunteering for panel membership come into this category. Further it is shown that the system attracted a large proportion of middle-aged married people who stayed on at school beyond their seventeenth birthday, and a high percentage of teachers.

In general the effect of the selection process was to reinforce these tendencies toward self selection with the interesting exception of young women; they are far less likely to apply for membership than are older women but once having volunteered are more likely to be selected. The differences in terms of the proportions selected and rejected are relatively small and consistently less important than the process of self selection.

The reasons most commonly put forward for wanting a broader social mix on the panel is that middle-class members will not understand the problems of children from underprivileged backgrounds and that they will have greater difficulty in communication with these families. However the recruitment and selection methods could to some extent be held responsible for the imbalance in the applicants and final membership. In a discussion of the Social Work (Scotland) Act, Smith and May have argued:

> . . . such a process of selection will not only deter a great many people from coming forward in the first place . . . but will also in any event effectively discriminate against major social groups. . . . Panel membership will in effect, if not by design, be drawn from a limited and fairly homogeneous group – literate, articulate, familiar with thought at an abstract level, familiar too with the notion of 'public service', distant from the majority of families with whom they will be dealing, and with very little direct experience of poverty and hardship. Even with predominantly working class areas, where inevitably these characteristics will be somewhat modified, those who survive the rigorous selection procedure are hardly likely to be typical of the population they are to represent.[4]

In her thorough study of the selection of the County of Fife children's panel, Elizabeth Mapstone has commented on the skill needed by the panel member in the setting of the hearing.

> Their task would seem to require not only the social confidence and intellectual discipline which may result from further education or long participation in public affairs but also the controlled involvement, a combination of concern and detachment, commitment and independence, characteristically developed in training for the professions.[5]

It is not surprising, therefore, that when choices had to be made between the two objectives, the CPACs placed the objective of a panel composed of individuals suitable for the quasi-professional task to be performed above the objective of a panel carrying out the function of community representation. Moreover a group of students in the Department of Social Administration of Edinburgh University investigating the professional selectors' backgrounds and attitudes concluded that the selectors produced a panel chosen on criteria based on qualities very similar to those found in themselves.

There is no evidence however, that absence of a cultural bond with the families inhibits communication in the hearing. Understanding people's problems does not require the sharing of an environment and the qualities of sympathy and understanding required of panel members are just as commonly found in middle-class as in working-class cultures. Indeed some writers have gone so far as saying that middle-class values might be more relevant to the hearings. Elizabeth Mapstone refers to comparative studies of child rearing which have shown that the very process of discussing reasons for and results of behaviour is typical of white-collar families, unfamiliar in the homes of manual workers. Louise Higgins[6] draws on evidence from various psychological studies which might suggest that a predominantly middle-class panel might not be out of sympathy with the ideology of the Social Work Act. American studies indicate that the better educated and those in occupations enjoying higher levels of prestige tend to be less authoritarian than other social groups. Tolerance in general has been found to be greater among those in professional and related occupations as has the propensity to take part in voluntary associations.

If panel members do not always share the problems of their clients they are nevertheless not entirely unaware of their significance. Many members are in close contact with the communities from which the children come, sometimes through working there in a professional or voluntary capacity. There is also evidence that many panel members have their roots in working-class areas. Louise Higgins examined the social mobility within the Glasgow children's panel and found that 50% had moved upwards by at least one social class. She found that the average panel member was in social class 2 but had come from a social class 3 background and as a result may be very well aware of the problems of young people in the poorer areas.

Although the studies of the results of initial selection have not been followed up, there are signs of a gradual shift in the balance of panel membership. Certainly there have been constant reminders from the Social Work Services Group that a better cross-section is needed and there have been sincere efforts by CPACs to attract a wider spread of society. One urban area advertised specifically for 'manual workers' and directed the recruitment at particular areas which were under-represented. There are now more young people and a recent circular estimated that manual workers occupy 20% of the membership.

There is great need for more extensive research into the validity of the selection procedures. For instance there has been no evaluation of the 'suitability' criteria. It is important to establish whether the personal qualities identified at the selection stage are predictive of good practice in hearings. There are however, massive problems in designing 'effectiveness' scales and indeed this kind of measurement could be seen as conflicting with the principle of obtaining a lay panel representing society.

At the end of their term of office members have an opportunity to apply for reappointment and a recent circular from Social Work Services Group advised CPACs that three terms amounting to a total of nine years might be considered

the upper limit. Although it is desirable to obtain maximum public participation through a regular intake of new members, it has been recognised that a
very rapid changeover would deprive the system of valuable experience and
knowledge. So far there has been little more than the change resulting from
natural wastage in which geographical mobility is a major factor. In Glasgow
City panel the average loss to annual intake has been 15% in one year, 32% in
two years and 49% in three years.

Former members of the Glasgow City panel were invited by the writer to
report on their reasons for resignation. Information was received from only 50%
of the sample and many of those who did not reply were known to have left
the district. In addition, of those who did reply about half were known to have
left the district. Only a small number mentioned frustration and disillusionment
with the system as a major factor in their decision to resign. Only one or two
resigned on account of the heavy work load. Although there are wide variations
in the time given by panel members, the average commitment is considerable.
It involves not only attendance at hearings but a lot of time in preparation as
well as time given to area meetings and regional training. Members can claim
for travel, subsistence and loss of earnings but there are no financial rewards.
In 1975 the Social Work Services Group conducted a survey of the time spent
by panel members outside hearings on related business and although this
ranged very widely, there was no evidence of dissatisfaction with the high level
of demand.

According to the legal statute panels have responsibilities only within the
operational situation of a children's hearing. In some areas, however, the
members have initiated and taken part in the extension of their rôle. They have
tried to spread ideas and stimulate interest within the community at large; they
have formed links with other elements in the system; they have contributed
suggestions for extending resources; and they have offered advice on the
management of local problems. For example the 'resources group' of the
Aberdeen City panel with the support of the director of social work established
a scheme for the use of volunteers in social work supervision. From the start
this scheme was the responsibility of a small group of panel members and its
development is evidence of the validity of this kind of initiative. The City of
Glasgow and City of Edinburgh panels each organised working parties which
have examined and reported on some relevant issues such as truancy and creating
links with professional services. The Greenock and Port Glasgow panel initiated
a research project concerned with the working of the system in the area. The
Dunbarton County members obtained a grant from the Quality of Life Experiment for the purpose of setting up an 'intermediate treatment' scheme and they
continue to supervise and support the project.

The panels have been moving slowly towards the formation of a National
Association which could provide the machinery for expressing their views and
for setting their experience in the broadest context. While the Associations of
Regional Panels are gathering support for a national body, they continue to
promote the aims of the hearings system and draw attention to some of its
needs. Possibly it is an advantage that these endeavours have moved slowly and

have been looking closely at the purpose and function of any representative body.

The initiative for these external activities most frequently comes from the panel chairman. His official duties are restricted largely to choosing members for children's hearings but the energetic men and women holding this office have contributed very significantly to the corporate activities of their local panel as well as giving moral support to individual members. Following regionalisation the chairmen were advised that subdivision into areas would be appropriate and they were left to work out the method of appointment of area chairmen. A variety of practice resulted: in Strathclyde the area chairmen were elected democratically; in Lothian Region nominations were given to the regional chairman who then consulted with the CPAC; in Grampian Region the chairman himself appointed a team of deputies.

Training

Outwith the hearings, one of the most time-consuming activities is members' attendance at initial and further training which is a condition of the appointment. The organisation of training reflects again the subtle relationship between central and local government. Regional training is the responsibility of university-based tutors who are supported financially by the Social Work Services Group while the regional authorities meet the training costs. At the local level, panels are also expected to be involved in training and these arrangements are made by the regional chairmen in association with area chairmen, reporters, social work department, CPAC and other interested persons. Since 1974 the regional tutors have collaborated in the organisation of a national summer school. Potentially this three-tier structure is a most creative and effective arrangement and enables opportunities for discussion of local problems, consideration of issues across area boundaries and examination of the purpose and progress of the system against the backcloth of the broadest range of experience and practice.

There is no standard training syllabus but some guidance on content is offered from the centre. The Social Work Services Group convenes a group which represents all the interests and maintains an overall review of the programmes in order to ensure that core elements are included. In practice there is great variation between regions in the amount and to some extent the content of the training of different panels and of different members within each panel. For example, new members appointed to an urban area may have to attend prior to commencing service, an all-day introductory meeting and a series of fourteen tutorial sessions held weekly. These introduce the members to appropriate officials; the legal framework including powers and procedures of hearings; the skills of interviewing and communication; the assessment and treatment agencies; theories of human growth and development. Members also attend hearings as observers and visit a comprehensive range of assessment units, residential schools, homes and hostels, clinics and other agencies. In a small rural panel the preparatory training is far less elaborate and may include two week-ends of regional training with other panels, some talks locally with appropriate officials, a few visits to residential establishments and to hearings.

In-service training encourages members to look in depth at specific issues, to examine their practice in hearings critically, to increase their sensitivity and awareness of society's problems, to stimulate interest in the development of new resources and to communicate their experience and understanding to a wider public.

One difficulty which has led to some inconsistency in the amount of training offered in different areas is that local responsibility has not been allocated to any specific part of the system. It could be predicted that panel members themselves will eventually take over their own training with some administrative help from the regional authority and professional backing from the universities. This trend is beginning to appear in the current programmes where panel members feature significantly as the principal contributors to the courses. Perhaps this has been one of the main changes in approach to training over the five years of operation. Initially the teaching was carried out entirely by academics and professional workers but over the years panel members themselves have gathered experience and developed a sophisticated understanding of the hearing situation. Their contribution will be enlarged as literature on the system, such as texts and research reports, becomes available. Working as a tutor opens up a whole area of new understanding and perception for the experienced panel member. Information is updated, familiar questions are re-examined and enthusiastic, often critical trainees are encouraged to share their fears and doubts about the validity of the operation. This experience seems to have the effect of reinforcing confidence and restoring to the serving panel member strong belief in the creative potential of the system.

While the provision of training may appear inconsistent with the idea of a lay panel, it is very rare to hear its importance seriously questioned. Because training is always subsequent to selection the extent to which it can interfere with the character of the system is limited. Indeed at the preparatory stage the demand is usually for more training. Panel members appreciate very quickly the complex responsiblities of their work and welcome relevant training experience. About 12% of any intake withdraw from membership during the preparatory period but this has been due so far to removal from the area or to recognition of the scale of the commitment.

As panel membership extends to a broader cross-section of the community, the provision of training meets a greater challenge. Ways have to be found for bringing members from contrasting cultural and educational backgrounds into a shared understanding of their common purpose within the hearings system. It represents a significant process of community education. Nowhere is there such a unique opportunity for confronting the general public with the whole range of social and individual problems, for encouraging the development of understanding not only of anti-social behaviour but also of the institutions and of the society against which that behaviour is a reaction. The community is encouraged to find within itself greater humanity and the strength to offer relevant support to those with less fortunate life experiences.

The machinery of appointment provides the means for shaping the hearings system into a progressive, imaginative and sensitive human endeavour. The effective recruitment, selection and training of panel members can build up in the community a body of concerned and knowledgeable people who are in a position to convey to society at large their understanding of the problems presented in hearings. How successfully they are able to influence society's subsequent response will depend largely on the stature of the hearings system in the eyes of the public; and this in its turn will reflect the effectiveness of the processes described in this chapter.

REFERENCES

1. May, D. and Smith, G. (1969), Policy Interpretation and the Children's Panels: a case study in Social Administration. *Applied Social Studies*, 2.
2. Smith, G. and May, D. (1971), The Appointment of the Aberdeen City Children's Panel: a comment on the Social Work (Scotland) Act, 1968. *British Journal of Social Work*, 1, 1.
3. Rowe, A. J. B. (1972), *Initial Selection for Children's Panels in Scotland*. London, Bookstall Publications.
4. Supra, reference 1.
5. Mapstone, E. (1972), The Selection of the Children's Panel for the County of Fife. *British Journal of Social Work*, 2, 4.
6. Higgins, L. T. (1972), A Psychological Study of the First Glasgow Children's Panel. Unpublished thesis.

7

THE SOCIAL WORK DEPARTMENT

F. M. MARTIN

MODERN SOCIAL WORK had its beginnings in late Victorian charitable endeavour. The salaried staff who towards the end of the nineteenth century were increasingly employed by charitable organisations to take over much of the work among the poor that had traditionally been carried out by volunteers may be considered the first professional social workers. But gradually other small groups of workers were brought into being to provide a personal service for those in distress, in sickness or in moral danger. Each new group of social workers however had limited and specialised responsibilities, having been created to meet a specific social need or legislative requirement. Thus, the creation of the probation system required the establishment of a body of probation officers to 'advise, assist and befriend' offenders. Similarly, some forty years later, the Children Act of 1948 imposed on local authorities the duty of setting up a comprehensive service for children deprived of a normal home life, staffed by specialist officers. In medicine, the introduction of social work came almost unintentionally. The first almoners, as they were called, were appointed at the turn of the century to assess patients' means and ensure that free treatment was not received by those deemed to be capable of paying for it; but they showed more concern with their patients' needs and problems than with their ability to pay hospital fees, and rapidly became organisers and providers of personal services.

Towards generic social work

These groups, it may be said, were not so much specialised as segregated, with different clienteles, different professional training and different professional organisations. By no means all practitioners were in fact professionally trained while the welfare services provided by local authorities after the demise of the Poor Law were staffed almost wholly by untrained workers. A major influence on the evolution of a unified profession came, paradoxically, from the highly specialised psychiatric social workers. Whereas most practitioners had hitherto operated on fairly empirical lines, the new psychiatric social workers, originally trained in the United States, brought back a body of theory heavily influenced by the psychodynamic orientation of American psychiatry. This incorporated distinctive views of human development, relationships and psychopathology, defined the nature and objectives of social work intervention, and provided in some degree a professional ideology. In respect of both professional training and general education psychiatric social workers formed something of an élite within social work, and an obvious source from which ideas might be diffused. In a modified form casework theory and practice came gradually to be seen as the appropriate standard equipment for all trained social workers. Two further lines of thought, related but by no means identical, flowed from this: one, that there should be a basic pattern of generic training for all social workers, irrespective of the settings in which they were going to work, the other, that a generically-trained social worker should forthwith be competent to engage in any type of social work practice. Changes in the system of training were initiated quite rapidly in the sixties, with specialist courses being terminated and new generic programmes being introduced. For the notion of the general purposes social worker to be fully realised, however, major administrative changes were needed. In fact, legislation preceded the administrative innovations, because questions of the future of the social work profession became caught up in a wider consideration of the pattern of social service provision.

The first step forward was in Scotland. As earlier chapters have shown, the report of the Kilbrandon Committee pointed to the need for a family-oriented social service and led in due course to the considerably more extensive proposals eventually embodied in the Social Work (Scotland) Act 1968. This required *inter alia* the establishment of a comprehensive social work department by each major local authority, taking over responsibility for the personal social services formerly provided under the auspices of the health, welfare and children's committees, and for the work of the probation service. When part III of the Act was implemented in April 1971, one of the major commitments of the new social work departments would be to work in close conjunction with the children's hearings, providing background reports on children and undertaking the supervision of those who were judged by the hearings to be in need of this 'compulsory measure of care'. In many respects the effects of the Act on the pattern of social service have been far-reaching and largely unpredicted, and as a consequence the actual rôle of the social work departments in relation to children's hearings cannot be adequately understood other than within the wider context of social service provision and its development since 1969.

A unified service: problems and progress

Looking back over the few years that have passed since the Social Work (Scotland) Act became law, it is difficult not to feel a sense of amazement at the degree of optimism which permitted a major new public service to be launched on such a slender basis. Fifty-two departments of social work were to be created, at a time when there were fewer than 300 professionally qualified social workers in the whole of Scotland. The complex skills of social work management can scarcely be said to have been available in profusion. As to the range of problems which would confront the new service, there had not been even the most superficial research. No attempt had been made, however tentatively, to estimate the likely levels or types of demand. There was a general assumption that the new departments would carry out, more effectively, the duties formerly discharged by the small, separate departments which they replaced, in spite of the fact that the Act defined their responsibilities in terms so broad as to defy almost any drawing of boundaries. Prison welfare services at first remained independent, but were brought within the scope of the local authority departments in November 1973; social work support for the health services was added at the time of the reorganisation of local government in May 1975.

In the five and a half years preceding local government reorganisation, the achievements of the new departments were varied but for the most part disappointing. Certainly in the industrial areas of Scotland, few if any would claim that the social work services provided were at any time adequate, either quantitatively or in terms of the level of professional expertise. The promulgation of a new service had a powerful impact on levels of demand and expectations of service. Earlier thinking had failed to take account of the full extent of social deprivation, especially in the Clydeside connurbation, or of the way in which that deprivation would, appropriately or otherwise, generate a demand for personal social services on an unanticipated scale.

The new departments were ill-equipped to respond to this challenge. Organisationally, they had not long succeeded in welding together into operational teams personnel drawn from separate and often mutually suspicious departments when the shadow of a major new reorganisation began to loom ahead. Staffing levels remained almost uniformly unsatisfactory. The small pool of trained and experienced field workers was depleted as new opportunities arose in management, in central government and in social work education, while the build-up of a new corps of generically trained social workers proved to be a good deal slower than had been hoped. Perhaps most important, the social work services had – and have – no means of balancing demand and supply. The open-ended commitment of the 1968 Act accorded well with the social work profession's ethos of unstinting responsiveness, and the task of defining an explicit system of social work priorities has never been attempted. In the full sense, such a task implies a systematic understanding of the structure of personal and social needs, and the capacity to identify priorities for intervention, involving judgements both of the intensity of need and of the appropriateness and likely effectiveness of social work measures. Too little has been done to separate out either problems which can be resolved only through major environmental changes or social and economic reforms, and in relation to which intervention at the personal level is impotent, or problems which are generated by the policies and practices of other public service agencies. Deliberate stock-taking of available skills as well as of presenting problems, and deployment of resources according to rational plans, have not generally been characteristic of local authority social services.

It might well be concluded from the foregoing analysis that the most urgent task confronting social work departments is to increase their establishment of trained workers. That almost all authorities are severely understaffed is undeniable, and the importance of maintaining training programmes can scarcely be exaggerated. But the present-day tendency to assume that the admitted shortcomings of social work services will be made good when 'sufficient' staff are available is questionable. It tends to rest on an essentially static conception of needs as existing in the community in fixed quanta, and ignores the many factors which influence people's expectations of services. Experience has already shown dramatically how the creation of a new service raises the level of demand, and although no one would claim that the demand is infinitely elastic, it seems quite probable that a very substantial injection of resources may be necessary before a levelling-off occurs. If this is indeed the case, the expansion of the number of trained staff is likely to redefine rather than to eliminate the management problem of setting boundaries.

Conflicting demands on the time of social workers have led to tensions in relationships with other agencies and frustration and disappointment among social workers themselves, when attempts to meet one demand produce a storm of criticism from those hurt by lack of attention or inadequate performance. This criticism often takes the form of advocating a return to past forms of organisation – for example, a restored probation service – without any attempt to assess the implications of such a change. It is of course a particular version of a debate which has gone on over a number of years, on the 'generic' versus the 'specialist' approaches to social work education and social work practice. Unfortunately, the alternatives in the debate have usually been inaccurately defined.

The social work task: diversity and specialisation

It may be helpful to begin by reviewing, even cursorily, the types of task which confront field workers. The range of knowledge and skills required is formidable and work is carried out under pressures that call for quick decisions. Making arrangements for the admission of children, the elderly and the mentally handicapped into residential care often follows a long period of systematic work with the same people in their own homes, as well as with their families. Supervision of youngsters who have appeared before the hearings or the courts; investigation of applications from prospective adoptive parents and handling the sensitive relationship that exists when a natural mother is plagued by doubts whether it is right to part with her child; a continuous search for more foster-parents and ongoing contact with them and the children placed in their care; investigation of allegation or suspicion of the ill-treatment of children; concern for the social work needs of the physically handicapped; the after-care of patients discharged from hospital; examination of applications for financial help to meet rent arrears, unpaid gas and electricity bills and negotiations with housing authorities and the public utilities to stave off eviction or the withdrawal of fuel supplies. This is by no means a comprehensive list; the work involves home visits, reports on the circumstances and recommendations as to appropriate courses of action. Though detailed legal knowledge is not required, it is necessary to know where legal advice can be obtained if the client is to be fully protected. Increasingly social workers are conscious of welfare rights and advise clients how to obtain benefits to which they are entitled. This can include helping with appeals to tribunals and, if necessary, appearing with the client to ensure that the appeal rests on knowledge of all the relevant facts.

Clearly, no single social worker can have complete knowledge of every social problem that may arise or deal with them effectively. There are nevertheless powerful arguments against any suggestion that we revert to earlier styles of professional education or of deployment, in which, as outlined earlier in this chapter, social workers were trained to work with a delimited range of problems and used their skills within a specific setting. There *is* a communality of methods, working principles and underlying philosophy, but more importantly there is the need to ensure that social work problems are not undetected because the relevant professionals are not trained to view social work as a whole. However much they may be conscious of their limited skill in dealing with particular problems, very few generically trained social workers wish that they had received only the type of specialist training which would have equipped them to deal competently with a narrow range of tasks. Must we then accept breadth and shallowness as the only alternative to depth and narrowness? There is surely another possibility, even though it is one towards which we could hope to move only by degrees. This is to see generic training as the essential foundation for all social work practice, but one upon which many practitioners will subsequently wish to undertake specialist training in a particular area of social work, depending on their own blend of skills, interests and temperament. Specialisation thus becomes a matter of post-qualifying study rather than of separate training from the beginning. There is an instructive analogy to be drawn with the history of medical practice in Britain. Until the Medical Act of 1858, physicians, surgeons and apothecaries were quite distinct professions, differing in training, in functions and in social standing. The 1858 Act fused them into a single profession, with a common mode of basic training. Subsequently, specialisation re-emerged and developed profusely, but always at a postgraduate level. This may well be the appropriate path for social work education to follow, though on a more deliberately planned time-scale.

Social workers of course do not – and emphatically should not – work in isolation. Individual workers function as members of teams and should have access to advice and support from senior social workers. In principle, the field worker should be able to draw upon the collective knowledge and experience of a whole department; and the resources of a department should include the services of specialist advisers or consultants with highly developed skills in particular areas of social work. In this way, it is sometimes suggested, the limitations of generic training can be made good; as long as the basic grade worker can recognise problems which are too complex for him to cope with unaided, and as long as he has a range of specialists on call, we can have the best of both worlds. The argument has considerable force, but it does not constitute a case against specialist training. One should not underestimate the extent to which social work departments are dependent for their specialist advice on members of staff who received training and experience in pre-generic days. It is not easy to see from what sources their successors will in due course be drawn, unless new cadres of specialists can be trained in the meantime through post-qualifying studies.

The effects of regionalisation

The wide range of specialised personnel and facilities on which a large department can draw was put forward as a major argument in favour of the regionalisation of social work functions, when the future organisation of local government was being debated. A regional social work department, it was claimed, would also be better able to deploy resources where they were most needed than a department responsible for a geographically limited and socially more homogeneous area. Many social workers however opposed the idea, fearing the creation of large impersonal bureaucracies and arguing that the effective provision of services demanded sensitivity to local needs. In the event, social work became in May 1975 the responsibility of the nine regional and three island authorities. The largest of these was to be responsible for one half the population of Scotland. It is impossible as yet to pass any judgement on the success or otherwise of the regionalisation of social work. The resources with which the new developments began were simply those inherited from the local authorities whose functions they assumed. Regionalisation could not in itself produce more trained staff, more buildings or more ideas and imagination – the latter perhaps the most precious resource of all. Indeed in some respects regionalisation was responsible for delays in progress, as the capital building programmes in particular of the predecessor local authorities were not neces-sarily compatible with the broader policies of the new regions. It was also necessary for the larger regions to devise and put into effect complex new management structures, raising difficult issues of balance between central control and local autonomy. Inevitably, time is needed before smooth working relationships and acceptable systems of decision-making can be achieved, and it is perhaps not altogether surprising if in the early stages of reoragnisation communications are confused and field staff feel remote from what seem to them to be the centres of power. Even though this stage may be transitory it does nothing, while it lasts, to promote the interests of clients. Neither, for that matter, does the prolonged period of uncertainty and anxiety that precedes reorganisation, and both of these must be taken into account among the prices to be paid for whatever benefits the new form of organisation may yield. Unfortunately, it will take longer to reap such benefits than might have been expected. The birth of the new regional authorities was accompanied by a national economic crisis of extreme severity, postponing indefinitely any hope of substantial expansion in social services.

One possible gain may come not from the new scale of local government organisation but from the general acceptance, at least in theory, of the principles of corporate planning and management. The possibility of forging compre-hensive rather than departmental policies could have important implications for social work. In particular, it opens up for the first time some scope for a serious attempt at preventive work. Social work by itself can do little to control the environmental factors which help to shape people's lives and attitudes and which contribute in varying degrees to the failures and tragedies which social workers and panel members encounter in their practice. Corporate management allows for the infusion of social work ideas and principles into education policy and town-planning policy. Ideally, housing policy too should be co-ordinated with social work thinking, but the division of responsibilities between region and district means that separate machinery is necessary. All of this is easier to recommend than to accomplish. Departmental prerogatives are less readily abandoned than management theorists like to admit; and social workers often lack skill in moving beyond morally impeccable generalisations to the statement of precise objectives for social policy. None the less, it is a goal which deserves high priority if we are seriously concerned to improve the quality of life in our urban communities.

Relationship between social workers and panel members

The provision of services for children's hearings is a major responsibility of all social work departments, and in most areas it accounts for a very substantial fraction of all social work activity. Two major tasks are involved: the preparation of reports on children and their circumstances, for the benefit of reporters and panel members, and the carrying out of supervision requirements when hearings decide on these as appropriate measures. Each of the tasks is discussed in considerable detail elsewhere in this book (Chapters 10 and 13) and there is no case for reviewing the issues again in this chapter. It may instead be more useful to consider briefly some general matters affecting the relationships between panel members and social workers; to deny that tensions and mutual criticism have been quite common would be neither honest nor constructive.

The criticisms levelled by panel members at social work departments concern the quality of social background reports and the failure to deliver them promptly, though complaints on these grounds have become very much less common, and, more persistently, the inadequacy of supervision given to youngsters put under the social work department's care. The shortcomings of much social work supervision cannot be denied, but at the same time the resentment often felt by social workers when exposed to such criticism is itself understandable. While the panel member sees that his decision in a particular case, arrived at after very careful consideration of the child's needs, is brought to nothing by skimped supervision, the social worker on the other hand is aware that time spent on supervision means less time available for other clients whose needs may seem to him no less pressing or less worthy of attention. The problem then is largely one of competition for social work attention, arising from the imbalance, discussed above, between the pressure of demand and the scarce supply of professional resources. But it would be an over-simplification to argue that this is the whole problem, for the primary difficulty is compounded by at least two other considerations.

There is first the conflict that often arises from the management of a generic caseload. The same social worker will have clients of different age groups and a very wide range of personal problems. Possibly he can cope with all of them with equal skill and equal interest, but it would be astonishing if social workers did not in fact vary quite widely in their preference for working with the young as compared with the old, say, or the physically handicapped as compared with the mentally ill, or the delinquents as compared with the homeless. Supervision cases constitute a statutory obligation and cannot be ignored; but those social workers who find this type of work less well suited to their talents and temperaments may easily be tempted to give the clients in question a relatively low level of attention, and feel themselves justified in this by the manifest seriousness of the problems experienced by those other clients with whom they prefer to work. Not all social workers can relate equally well to children and young people; and although, as Chapter 13 makes clear, many social workers are extremely skilled at working with clients who have become clients by compulsion, others, it must be admitted, find it very difficult to come to terms with the notion of a client who did not choose to enter into that relationship and who is not free to leave it. The long-term answer then may be not merely an increase in the number of social workers, but also a formal recognition that social work with young delinquents requires specialists.

There is another and less tangible aspect of the relations between social workers and panel members. The dependence of the hearings system on close and quite subtle working relationships between a number of groups, makes it inevitably subject to strains and tensions, and these are likely to be intensified if one of the groups is made up of voluntary workers. Volunteers who are involved in the provision of services tend to be perceived by the relevant professionals as competitors and are therefore a source of anxiety. There is little or no problem when the voluntary workers have a clearly segregated rôle. For example, hospital nurses are delighted to have volunteers come in to man tea trolleys; but volunteers who take on the job of establishing personal links with patients in the psychiatric wards may be seen by nurses as invading their territory. Again, acceptance of the voluntary workers is likely to be greater, the more self-assured the professional in his own status. Thus, in the hospital example, doctors are much less likely than nurses to be troubled by the presence of volunteers. As far as children's hearings are concerned, it should be remembered that social work, as indicated early in this chapter, is still a youthful profession; its standing in the eyes of the public is still very uncertain. In the children's hearings system the voluntary workers (panel members) rightly have the central rôle. They are guided by reporters and advised by social workers, but they alone make the decisions. Opportunities for mutual misunderstanding abound. Social workers may feel aggrieved if their professional recommendations are not accepted, and may question the judgement of panel members. The latter for their part are likely to resent any suggestion that they routinely endorse social workers' recommendations. The difficulties which some social workers experience in undertaking compulsory measures may be intensified if they see the decisions as having come from a lay rather than a professional body; and so on.

The question is not whether one is 'right' and the other is 'wrong'. All participants in the system need to understand its inescapable sources of tension, and to acquire a deeper awareness of their own feelings and attitudes. In particular, we need to recognise that whenever we are troubled by inner doubts about the rightness or the value of our own actions, we have a natural tendency to seek someone else who can bear our guilt. The hearings system makes decisions of far-reaching importance for the lives of young people and necessarily imposes considerable emotional strain upon all who take part in it. There is no simple organisational rule for ensuring that in these demanding circumstances professional and voluntary workers relate to one another with tolerance, understanding and mutual respect. The only hope lies in greater self-awareness, in a growing ability to accept and absorb criticism, and in an increase in the sense of inner security which comes from an acceptance of both the value and the limitations of one's own rôle. We always hope to see growth and development in those who come to us as social work clients or as children in need of special measures of care; but on another level it is the goal to which all of us must move if we are to contribute as fully as we are capable, in our rôles as social workers or as panel members.

Section III

THE HEARING PROCESS

THE FOCAL POINT of the entire system is the hearing itself, where panel members and professionals come together with the child and his parents. There is an obligation, in the conduct of the hearing, to balance two very different sets of requirements; these are the aims of free and unfettered communication and of conformity to legally proper procedures. It may well be that there is a degree of conflict between these aims such that a complete reconciliation can never be achieved, and that they must always be held in a certain tension.

The reports provided by social workers on children and their backgrounds are a vital source of information for panel members anxious to understand the child's circumstances and background and to reach a relevant decision. Like all professional reports, they may vary greatly in the comprehensiveness of their coverage and in the skill and sensitivity with which they are compiled. The preparation of a good social background report requires common sense – and a great deal more: it needs a professionally informed judgement in eliciting information, in tracing connections and relationships, and in accepting where necessary apparent contradictions. In addition, it demands the special skill of creating a record which can inform and guide panel members and is not merely a demonstration of the writer's esoteric knowledge.

Advised but not overwhelmed by reports, panel members taking part in hearings must also use the evidence of their own eyes and ears in building up the best account of the child and the circumstances of his life. If the facts incorporated in professional reports were all that mattered, justice could be dispensed by quite simple computers. The meeting of persons, and the deeper understanding to be derived from it, is all-important. In the hearing, observing and listening are not merely mechanical processes. In the first place, there is a need for a high degree of skill in understanding the meanings of both verbal and non-verbal communications. Secondly, if a free flow of communication is to be achieved the members of the hearing must be much more than observers, and be able to put questions capable of opening up important issues and eliciting significant information.

Combining many different items of information about a young person and his environment, and making use of the resulting pattern to interpret the behaviour that has brought him to the hearing, is in a real sense a creative act. The facts rarely speak for themselves; their message depends on the ideas and beliefs that we bring to bear, consciously or otherwise, on their interpretation. All practical men are theorists; judgements and decisions in all human affairs imply certain more general underlying assumptions about behaviour and motivation which we would be justified in calling theories if we could make them explicit. Many writers have made explicit their ideas on the subject of delinquency, and in varying degrees have related these theories to the findings of systematic research or of clinical observation. Many theories, useful within limits, fail because overweening ambition leads to untenable monopolistic claims; perhaps the wisest attitude to the multiplicity of theories is one which involves a reluctance to rely unduly on any one type of explanation, an acceptance of pluralism and a search for ways of integrating ostensibly diverse approaches.

A children's hearing is a fascinating psychological process, but it is meant to lead to decisions; and these decisions can have far-reaching and perhaps very painful consequences for the child and his family. Civil rights must therefore be safeguarded and the entire proceeding carried out within a framework of rules designed to prevent injustice. Inevitably, the demand for formality and standardisation of procedure and the demand for easy, open, wide-ranging communication pull in opposite directions. The challenge of the children's hearing is to demonstrate how far an honest and uninhibited discussion of intensely personal issues can be carried on without disregard for the essential principles of the administration of justice.

8

THEORIES OF DELINQUENCY

A. RUSSELL FORREST

IT IS POSSIBLE to classify theories of delinquency into two broad types. The first would include all those theories which attribute delinquency to some inherited characteristic or some innate deficiency in the child (biological inferiority, glandular malfunction, mental retardation, and so on) while the second type of theory tends to place the primary focus on environmental factors, either in the action and interaction of social forces on the individual, or in the dynamic of forces within individuals and between individuals which arises whenever human beings exist together in relationship.

Biological theories and theories of inherited characteristics

Throughout history an enduring assumption that people have made about delinquency is that it is committed by individuals who are born that way. One of the best known theories of this type was developed a century ago by Cesare Lombroso.[1] He postulated that the criminal was a kind of throwback to a more primitive form of man and that such people could be recognised by their physical characteristics. The study of criminals around this time indeed was known as the science of criminal anthropology and was conducted largely, if not exclusively, by medical officers in prisons.

An early root of this scientific enterprise may well have its place in the popular generalisations (even proverbs) which were embodied in the works of Greek and Roman writers and physiognomists. When Homer described Thersites as ugly and deformed with harsh or scanty hair and a pointed head 'like a pot that had collapsed in the baking', he spoke to the existence of a criminal type of man. And Aristotle and Galen and Seneca all would speak to the view that those individuals with criminal physiognomies and certain shaped heads should be destroyed 'not in revenge, but for the same reason scorpions and vipers are destroyed'.

Later on, a mediaeval law even declared that if two people were suspected of a crime, the uglier or more deformed was to be regarded as the more probably guilty. Developments from this position into the 1800's however also included ideas about 'degeneration' (defined as 'a morbid deviation from the normal type of humanity') caused by 'intoxications, famines, social environment, industries, unhealthy occupations, poverty, heredity, pathological transformations, moral causes'. And so to a first recognition of the importance of social factors in criminal behaviour, but still within the view of the criminal as specially and abnormally prone to these influences as well as to hereditary transmissions of 'bad nature'.

Leaving aside the study of the criminal's physical nature, Despine[2] in 1868 sought to make an exhaustive study of his mental nature, proving to his own satisfaction and to that of other authorities that the instinctive criminal was a 'mental monstrosity'. The criminal was not, in his view, necessarily insane or diseased but 'morally mad'.

In 1872, Maudsley[3] writes, 'It is a matter of observation that this [instinctive] criminal class constitutes a degenerate or morbid variety of mankind, marked by peculiarly low physical and mental characteristics', and like Despine he concluded that since the criminal was 'a moral imbecile', it would not matter much whether he was sentenced in anger and consigned to prison or sentenced in sorrow and consigned to the asylum.

In 1890 Havelock Ellis[4] reviewed fifteen years of such studies into 'the criminal type' and 'the criminal mind'. He clearly recognised that many of these reports and reporters lacked adequate methodology; that they were often overly dogmatic and opinionated in their convictions; that they failed consistently to take account of sampling and other statistical biases, and that in being preoccupied with the elements of innate disposition, they largely ignored the social factor. He concluded thus: 'There are first the cosmic causes of crime (temperature, climate, diet) . . . then there is the biological factor (anatomical, physiological, psychological) which may be atavistic, atypic or morbid . . . lastly, there is the social factor (the price of alcohol, the price of wheat)' and quoting Lacassagne, 'every society has the criminals it deserves'.

Ellis thought that it was impossible to overestimate the importance of the social factor in crime and delinquency, and in particular he identified alcoholism (although he mistakenly thought that alcoholism, even temporary intoxication, at the time of conception 'modifies profoundly the brain and nervous system of both parent and offspring') as a social evil, a poison which would 'loosen morbid impulses'. The erroneous view that social characteristics could be acquired genetically in this way, of course, was very much around at the time. This view also carried a lot of authority from archaic sources in the Bible where the hereditary character of crime was fully recognised in the Hebrew God who visited the sins of the parents upon the children unto the third and fourth generation.

And so, in 1877, when R. L. Dugdale[5] produced a study of the 'Jukes' family, which produced, from the 709 traced descendants of five illegitimate daughters of an American backwoodsman, a vast number of criminals, prostitutes, vagabonds and paupers, it could be simply concluded 'there is no more instructive study in criminal heredity than that of the Jukes family'.

Against the theoretical background of inherited characteristics and biological inferiority, it could be safely concluded therefore that criminals were physically and morally insensible, intellectually stupid (comparisons were constantly made with idiots), ape-like in appearance, vain, emotionally unstable, workshy, sexually perverted, ugly and deformed.

Despite advances in our knowledge of the way inheritance works and our greater sophistication in the application of research methods to social problems, it is interesting that in some ways the idea of the 'born criminal' still haunts us. It is as though from our own unconscious we are unable to resist childlike ideas of 'good' and 'evil', and unwilling to come to terms with the confusions, anxieties, conflicts, uncertainties and mixtures of good and bad which are *all* part of the adult in the adult world. The theoretical view which takes account of the idea that the 'monsters' are not 'out there' but part of ourselves, locked away in our sometimes unconscious internal environment, will be discussed in a later section.

Delinquency as the result of mental deficiency

This theory is worth looking at on its own within the group of biological theories since it reached its zenith in the 1920's when standardised intelligence tests were being developed, and also worth noting since it exemplifies the 'nature versus nurture' issue which Havelock Ellis pre-empted in his review of anthropological studies. Prisoners were tested on the 'new' intelligence tests and were found to be 'feeble minded'. This finding was regarded as evidence for the theory that mental deficiency was *the* cause of delinquency.

The influence of low intelligence as a factor in delinquency persisted well beyond the time when increased sensitivity to the verbal, educational and cultural components in these tests argued against the simple acceptance of their results as evidence for a direct relationship between test scores and intellectual endowment. And the issues of the availability of provision, differential selection and the effects of labelling (to be looked at later in some detail) were also left out of account.

However, even as late as the 1960's the average IQ of delinquents was accepted as generally falling below the average figure of somewhere about 100 for the general population. But an interesting Scottish study in 1964[6] showed that if an intelligence test constructed specially for use with deaf children was given to delinquent boys in an approved school (now List D school) their scores were not significantly different from non-delinquent children on that test. This was argued to be a result of the lack of emphasis on verbal material in the test (which could be administered by mime).

And in 1969 a major study of 'social class and delinquency'[7] which also looked at intellectual and educational factors, concluded that the variable most strongly associated with delinquency was social class and that the second strongest association was with type of school. The author finally concludes, 'It is not intelligence or any academic aspect of education that is so important [as factors in delinquency] but the social consequences of being defined a failure.'

Theories of environmental factors as causes of delinquency

Theories within this class might be divided into two broad groups. One group might be called sociological, and the other group psychological. The first group looks to the way social and political forces shape the behaviour of individuals and the second group tries to identify delinquency within that area of human functioning which has to do with individual personality. Within the group of sociological theories, four differing emphases in approach might in particular be identified.

1. *Strain theory* where conformity to social behaviour norms (non-offending) is taken for granted and deviance from these norms is explained in terms of discontent, frustration and 'anomie'.

2. *Cultural deviance theory* where deviance is defined as conformity to a sub-cultural set of values which are 'conventional' for the people upholding them.

3. *Control theory* where social and psychological factors interact to produce an inability to accept community norms and controls.

4. *Labelling theory* which takes seriously the remark somebody made that delinquency is caused by society's attempt to deal with it. This approach looks especially at the *process* by which offenders are categorised and disposed of by various agencies, thereby, it is argued, enhancing the likelihood that they will be regarded and treated as 'deviant' (object) rather than as 'person in difficulty' (subject) or 'person in distress' or 'person reacting normally to an intolerable situation'.

(i) In *strain theory* terms, delinquency is seen as a kind of 'innovative adaptation' to the stresses and conflicts which arise when people are 'blocked' in some way from achieving approved goals.[8] Variations on this theme speak to ideas of 'differential-access-to-legitimate-means', of 'normlessness', of 'alienation'[9] – the disintegration of part of society so that there is no body of common values or morals which effectively govern conduct; and where, there is a feeling of being totally controlled by forces outside oneself, ends of action becoming contradictory, inaccessible or insignificant. So, according to this theory, approved goals or ends are shared by all of society but only one part of society has the approved means of achieving them. In essence, strain theory tells the story of delinquency in terms of the haves and the have-nots, the environment of the have-nots being characterised by value confusion, family disorganisation and feelings of powerlessness. One consequence of growing up within this kind of environment is that problems will certainly arise in the area of 'rôle identification', especially in that part of identification which has to do with taking on a stable sexual identity and the theory therefore predicts quite well the often reported observation that delinquents have a special need for masculine identity, overvaluing a tough-aggressive posture as one aspect in a pattern of pseudo-masculinity.

There is certainly much evidence which relates to these ideas about the divided nature of society and the differential distribution of authority within society, and perhaps even we have our own experience of feeling frustrated, angry and impotent in the face of anonymous and unyielding bureaucracy.

Children in List D schools often see things in terms of 'them' and 'us'; often feel they cannot influence their own destiny; are often out of touch with those legitimate means of complaint and protestation which, say, the child of middle-class parents learns how to use to his advantage.

Why is it, we might ask on their behalf, that planners can produce (even win awards for producing) vast, destructively anonymous housing estates or high-rise flats with impunity, while at the first suggestion of a lowering of amenity in select residential areas the articulate and influential lobby of local house owners can be so oft heeded?

Studies of so-called high delinquency areas have certainly found that they fall into certain types, namely run down residential areas in which businesses are being established, industrial areas and areas with a highly unstable population. And they have also shown that in such areas there is also increased incidences of other social problems such as poverty, suicide, adult crime, unemployment, educational underachievement, alcoholism, mental illness, inadequate recreational facilities, overcrowding and congestion.[10]

The connection between area of residence and personal-social attitudes/behaviour has been looked at by architects and planners, although it is more complicated than simply looking at the effects particular building structures have on their occupants. One recent study[11] however did compare different areas of Dundee in terms of detected delinquency rates and found that people living in those areas with the highest delinquency rates also scored highly on measures of anxiety and 'deterritoriality' – that is a feeling of anonymity. Interestingly these areas are often called in social background reports 'high delinquency areas', rather than areas of personal/social deprivation (sometimes more accurately slums). And further, an address in some of these areas will be enough to deny access to employment, credit and other forms of security, if not actually to promote a view of the incumbent as malingerer, thief, failure.

Strain theory also predicts quite well the experience of the child from this impoverished background at school. As the child finds himself ill-equipped in linguistic and conceptual terms to cope with the demands of school he is likely to become frustrated and ill at ease. For some of these children have lacked the necessary experience of creative play; have lived with adults without hope; have been catapulted prematurely into disillusionment; have reduced awareness of their own personal worth. And so as this child becomes frustrated and disruptive, truancy will arise in his experience as an 'innovative adaptation', reflecting a way of achieving a goal (of both teacher and pupil at this point), namely his being removed from classroom and school.

But contra strain theory notions of disorganisation and valuelessness, some studies have shown that while not organised in middle-class terms about institutions like church and school, these areas of the community have just as strong organisational values about street, cafe and police.[12] One study, in fact, has shown differences in self-concepts between lower-class and middle-class delinquent boys. Lower-class boys conceived themselves as being tough, fearless and dangerous, while middle-class delinquent boys viewed themselves as clever, bad and loyal.[13]

(ii) Indeed it is the presence of these strong values which has given another sociological theory its foundation since it recognises the existence of a 'sub-culture' of delinquency which is organised about 'focal concerns' and lower social class membership.[14] These focal concerns have been defined as trouble, toughness, smartness, excitement and autonomy, and are seen as being transmitted from generation of children to generation of children through imitation, gang drafting and initiation, and through other forms of cultural transmission.[15] Because of the frequently adverse family circumstances which characterise the backgrounds of these children, the consequent pattern of precocious personal and emotional independence will include an over-dependence on the acceptance of the street group and therefore a special vulnerability to its attitude and value system.

In *cultural deviance theory* terms it is also easy to predict that school is anathema to the delinquent child, and to explain why school is poorly adapted to his needs. For success even in Primary 1 will depend on abilities like good manners, respect for authority, well developed habits of work, neatness, punctuality and tidiness. The school then is seen by this theory as the arena of conflict between the lower social class child and expectation by teachers of middle-class standards of behaviour.

How is this to be reconciled with what is known of child rearing practices in 'hazardous environments'?[16] For the Wilson-Herbert study[16] has shown that there is considerable uniformity in child rearing attitudes in these areas – attitudes which in some senses mirror environmental conditions. For example, the invariable answer by mothers to questions about intervention in children's quarrels was 'let the kids fight it out'. In conditions of cramped personal space, in conditions of overcrowding (which anyway encourage aggressiveness as self-defence), attitudes which put peace with adult neighbours first have high survival value. Harmony with neighbours thus takes priority over the administration of justice and denies adults the possibility of helping children learn how to negotiate with others in situations of conflict. As the authors have noted, while this aggressive independence is essential in the unsupervised street playgroup (where 'territoriality' is an artefact of groups rather than a feature of property) it is not a good preparation for school.

Perhaps this theory should really be called cultural deprivation theory since deviance implies a deviation from 'normal' – and the fact is that such children may be well adapted to the tough world which is their home environment; children only rendered incompetent (and alienated) by 'the interaction of the class system and the technological revolution'.[17]

(iii) Some sociologists have tried to take into account individual personality variables as well as social factors and have argued delinquency to result from a failure of *personal and social controls*.[18] Conformity is explained by the special bonds which develop normally in relationships out of social commitment and involvement. When these primitive ties have been broken or where they have failed to become attached, the individual is in a condition of 'drift'[19] (not unlike the idea in strain theory when the individual lacks a clear sense of rôle-identity) and is therefore highly dependent on external sources of control for the 'direction' of his behaviour.

One development of the theory has been towards the notion that a favourable self-concept acts as a kind of insulator against falling into delinquent behaviour patterns when these are endemic in the social environment of the child's home.[20] Since a favourable self-concept comes from experience of affectionate, interested and consistent patterns of family experience, this theory would account well for the fact that children from one street to another, or one close to another, vary greatly in their expressions of delinquent behaviour.

The emphasis here on the interaction of personality and social setting and the identification of different types of delinquency, to some of which the theory does not apply (for example so called 'socialised delinquency' or 'career delinquency') has given some indication of the great complexity of facts and factors any single theory of delinquency would have to subsume, a complexity indeed which has so far rendered most theoretical approaches quite incomplete and underpowered.

(iv) The fourth type of theory within the sociological perspective, known as *labelling theory*,[21] deserves closer attention than it can be given here. The basic assumption is that certain terms – 'delinquent' for example or 'neurotic' or 'schizophrenic' – carry unattractive or undesirable connotations, and that when they are applied to someone by a supposedly authoritative figure there is a risk that the individual's future behaviour may be interpreted as a confirmation of the label. The theory usually goes on to argue, more controversially, that the person labelled comes himself to believe that he must really be 'bad' or 'abnormal'. Not only do we give a dog a bad name, but he agrees with us that he is a bad dog. Many of the movements concerned with human rights have stemmed from the recognition that 'labelling' can be a powerful and destructive process, producing conditions of stigma[22] from which people cannot recover their own personal or social identity and from which individuals may not be able ever to regain a normal relationship with systems of authority and control.

Consider the earlier example of the child going to school at five lacking the necessary prerequisites of language and conceptual ability, of experience of toys and creative play, and of compliance to authority, good manners and so on. He becomes frustrated and disruptive, his teacher may label him defective, or dull, or delinquent, or disturbed, and if he survives to Secondary stage, he will arrive there with a set of expectations about him which will determine to a great extent how he will be treated. Even the fact of his having seen an educational psychologist or a psychiatrist can become part of the process of identifying him as 'odd' or in some way deviant, thereby enhancing the likelihood that he will be odd or deviant. Information may be differentially selected from his history to confirm his 'delinquent' character, indeed children have been known to do this themselves after a time and to 'take on' the rôle they have been given so that at least they can make a success of failure (using this stigma for so-called 'secondary gain').

A study in America[23] claimed to show such an effect (the Pygmalion effect) when it divided some children at random into three groups. The groups were called A, B and C, and although the way they were divided ensured that each group was the same in terms of the range of ability, their teachers were told that they had been divided according to their ability so that group A was brightest and group C least bright. At the end of a year the three groups were tested for their educational attainments and results showed group A highest, followed by group B, with group C lowest. That is, the groups had performed according to the expectations of their teachers and not according to their natural abilities. This is certainly a striking finding, but it might be a mistake to build too many conclusions on it in the absence of further experimental confirmation.

Labelling theorists would therefore attach much importance to the *process* by which children in trouble are identified and disposed of in the system set up to deal with them and they would tend to underplay the significance of explanations of behaviour coined simply in terms of individual pathology.

Labelling theory of course has a much wider relevance to understanding the nature of social interaction. The normal and the stigmatised are seen not as different types of person, but as differing perspectives within a common process of human encounter: a process which includes the management of personal and social identity, the use of anticipation in classifying strangers into categories (or stereotypes), and the imputation of a wide range of attributes on the basis of one observed (for example, mentally ill people assumed to be dangerous, or blind people attributed with unique judgement on the assumption that they draw on special channels of communication). The way the individual responds defensively to being categorised may be wrongly interpreted as a direct expression of the observed 'defect', and both the defect and the response may even be used as a justification for the way we treat him.

Even where it is possible for the stigmatised person to attempt to correct his 'failing', through, for example, plastic surgery, remedial education or psychotherapy, what often results is not the acquisition of 'normal' status but a transformation of self from 'someone-with-a-particular-blemish' to 'someone-with-a-record-of-having-corrected-a-particular-blemish'. (For a wide ranging discussion of these issues the reader is referred to the most readable account of *Stigma: Notes on the Management of Spoiled Identity* by Erving Goffman.)

Much of the argument and observation which underpin this theoretical perspective is directly relevant to the replacement of juvenile courts by the system of children's hearings. The Kilbrandon Report in debating the underlying principles of the two models (court-based and hearing-based), for example, notes, 'Because of the high degree of personal responsibility which [the court-based model] attaches to the criminal, a stigma is attached in the public eye to conviction of a crime, which bears no necessary relationship to the harm done by the action itself or the actual responsibility of the person who did it'.

Labelling theory of course would have questioned the idea that 'stigma' had very much to do with the legal setting, and would instead have argued, as we have seen, that it resides with us all as a profound aspect of the way human beings deal with each other in everyday social intercourse. In support of this view it might be argued that despite the introduction of a social welfare system for children which does not segregate children in trouble from children at risk or those in need of care and protection, the same stigmatising forces operate to render 'delinquent' just as status-degrading and identity-reducing as before. It will be of considerable interest to see whether or not in a longer space of time, with greater understanding of the nature of conditions from which delinquent behaviour springs, with greater awareness of its forms, incidences, and outcomes, and consequently with less mystery (and fear) about its properties and effects, 'delinquency' as a label with strongly pejorative connotations will slide more neutrally into a respected body of knowledge and thereby become more acceptable.

Psychological theories of delinquency

Most psychological theories of delinquency have focussed on the psychodynamics of the individual. That is, they have sought to abstract from individual case studies patterns of internal organisation, including unconscious processes, which help to extend and develop an understanding of the nature of human personality and its response to conflict, crises and developmental distortion.

Identity crisis theory

One type of theory, for example, has focussed especially on the problems confronting the adolescent in his growth to maturity and has speculated that the critical conflict in early adolescence is between 'ego–identity' and 'rôle diffusion'.[24]

This theory argues that there are three processes of experience, that is (i) as an organism or body, (ii) as ego or person, and (iii) as member of society, and it is suggested that the meaningfulness of an experience which is located in any one of these three is co-determined by its meaning in the other two. It follows, therefore, that particularly in early adolescence when faced with a rapidly changing body and ambiguous or confusing cultural expectations, there will be a great struggle for the person to find some definition of himself, some certain feeling of his own value and self-worth, some awareness of having a personal identity. In the course of this 'identity crisis' he may experiment with various rôles and behaviours to see how they 'fit', and some of these may well be delinquent.

The emphasis here on the nature and processes of personal growth clearly requires a formulation of related ideas in the whole area of family relationships, what is normal or within normal limits, and what is not. Criticism of this type of theory is indeed often made because the case study approach defines (*a priori*) the condition under scrutiny as 'abnormal' and then seeks to explain the condition perhaps selectively recognising in the life history those factors which tend to support the view of it already taken . . . in the manner 'post hoc ergo propter hoc'. Stronger criticism of the whole field of psychoanalytic and psychodynamic theorising (see following section) would have it that they are not theories in the strict sense at all since they do not readily submit to traditional ways of testing by measurement, observation, prediction and statistical evaluation.

The identity crisis theory, however, is more than a case study approach since it attempts to bring together social, personal and anthropological data in a way which simplifies and enlightens in the manner of valid theorising.

Psychoanalytic theory

As earlier mentioned, psychoanalytic views of delinquency are very much concerned with the internal environment of the personality and the way this is protected from hurt or damage (the main predator is anxiety) by mechanisms of defence. Where other approaches to delinquency have concerned themselves with social and personal factors of a rational kind, psychoanalytic theory is primarily interested in the developing nature of the human personality in contact with meaningful others.

In order to make this a little clearer it is necessary to say something about the psychoanalytic view of normal development, keeping in mind that the original (classical) position as outlined by Freud is now very much modified.[25] It is worth mentioning, however, since his name is so well known and so closely identified in everyone's mind with the 'discovery' of the unconscious mind.

The classical Freudian model of psychoanalysis was concerned with the *structure* of personality – the 'ego' as the part of personality which had to do with organising the adaptation of the person to the outside world, regulating the means by which he sought satisfaction for his drives (known collectively as 'id'), and reconciling those with a more primitive control system (the 'superego') which operated unconsciously within the ego.

Freud's view of personality, however, has come to be recognised as an oversimplification and developments towards 'ego-psychology' took psychoanalytic theory away from its more restricted form (mainly concerned with the nature of conflict, symptom-formation, and clinical manifestations of unconscious processes) into a more general psychological perspective where the ego is seen to be structured, not only by the experiences of the infant and young child in the satisfaction and frustration of its drives, but also by the maturation of 'autonomous ego capacities' (motility, perception and so on).

Post-Freudian theorists, then, have concentrated their attention not so much on Freud's (now overpopularised) clinical concepts concerning symptom formation, symbolic function, infantile sexuality and so on, but on the in-depth study of the developmental process and of those personality structures which are consequent upon the nature of transaction between child and parent as each is engaged in their own growth towards personal identity, independence and responsibility.

The development of psychoanalytic theory in Britain has been particularly identified with what is called *Object-Relations Theory*. Its interest is in developing a view of personality from the very start in terms of the relationship between the infant and its environment, and it describes how, from the time he leaves his mother's body, the emotional experiences of the infant lead to their segregation into 'good' and 'bad' feelings. The earliest good experiences make an idealised good-object-image inside the child – a kind of (symbiotic) emotional fusion with the real good-satisfying-mother. Correspondingly painful frustrations and the aggressive feelings associated with attempts to get rid of these 'pains' begin to build an inner 'bad' object which threatens the developing self with disintegration and destruction. Between these two poles of idealised blissful fusion with the good-satisfying-mother and the dread of loss-of-self associated with an 'attacking' mother-image, there grows the 'central self' in which the more reality-based differentiation between the self and the mother takes place. A similar development takes place, according to the theory, leading to the creation of an inner world of structures which mediate relationships with the good-powerful-father – the prototype of independent achievement. And so an idealised father, along with a more threatening one, are also differentiated in the inner world of personality, part of the ego structure.

The individual personality is then patterned by its growth into a number of dynamic object-relations systems which seek to effect certain kinds of interaction with others (that is, they are personal need-systems). And each of these systems represents a part of the self related to an inner object which defines in varying degrees the 'other' in the sought-after relationship.

Some of these need systems of course are unconscious so that sometimes in relationship with others we can be totally unaware of how we have 'selected' them to fit our internal object 'mould' (and perhaps settle through them old scores). These so-called 'repressed' relationships are, as we have seen, 'split-off' from the central part of the self, and often contain angry and destructive components ready to emerge into action when a close on-going relationship (say with a therapist or with a spouse) will allow it. Sometimes these 'bad objects' are represented in the mechanism of 'projective identification' – that is, when the 'other' in a relationship is used not only as the 'target' of a repressed need but also where the other is manipulated into playing the part of the self which wants the 'forbidden' relationship.

Many children in List D schools have their inner worlds overfilled by bad objects in this sense. That is, their patterns of social and personal relationships are dominated by repressed needs related to an experience of parenting which has not been 'good-enough'.[26] This will see put on to others, therefore (through the mechanism of projective identification) the anger, frustration and hate which actually were focussed originally, but unspoken, against parent figures, leaving the self in a (self-destructive) condition of chronic challenge against itself.

Because the theory is based on central social relationships within the family, it throws much light on how the individual distributes his 'needing' relationships in the groups to which he belongs, and therefore it bridges the gap between personality theory and the nature of group processes.[27] (The development of this work is being continued in Edinburgh at the Scottish Institute of Human Relations.)

If all this sounds complicated it may be because human nature is complicated and too often perhaps in our attempts to understand it we oversimplify. Critics of more straightforward accounts of human behaviour, like the theory proposed in the following section where people are regarded simply as accumulations of learned habits or sets of conditioned responses, have argued that such psychologists are alone amongst scientists in reducing the conception of their object of study (human beings) to a less wonderful state than actually exists. Physicists, for example, can see bundles of neutrons and electrons hurtling around in states of dynamic tension and interaction when they look at a table or a chair, while these psychologists can look at human beings and see only puppets.

Psycho-biological theory

A notable example of a psychological theory of delinquency which is based on the idea that human behaviours are learned habits, related to genetic (and therefore inherited) characteristics of personality, is to be found in the work of Professor H. J. Eysenck.[28]

Eysenck argues that there are only two or three fundamental aspects of human personality (plus intelligence). These are primarily inherited and measurement of them can be used to predict who will become delinquent and who will not. He argues that according to the (inherited) 'strength' of these few given factors, will be determined how easily a person is 'conditionable', that is how easily he will acquire a 'conscience' about his behaviour. Eysenck sees conscience as a set of fear/anxiety conditioned responses (induced by parents and other authority figures). Children who fail to develop conscience, that is children who are difficult to condition by the punishment/reward devices through which, such consciences are achieved, are likely to become delinquent. Because Eysenck lays the foundations for his theory in the area of genetically given physiological and neurological structures, he puts strong emphasis on the biological bases of behaviour and he is therefore closer to theories of inherited characteristics described in the earlier part of this paper than to those sociological and psychological theories which speak to environmental causes as primarily important.

Eysenck has developed special questionnaires which purport to measure the inherited characteristics he speaks of in his theory and so there is a great deal of research evidence available (usually on institutionalised delinquents and riminals) which can be studied and evaluated. Reviews of these studies generally produce equivocal results.[29] On the one hand, some reviewers (and some critics of Eysenck's basic position) have pronounced the theory 'dead', while on the other hand others argue that the theory has never been adequately tested due to either a misunderstanding of the critical hypotheses to be tested or to faulty selection of control groups (of non-delinquents) against which to compare delinquents' scores.

A recent Scottish study,[30] which tried to take account of all these important selection and test variables examined the scores of nearly 1,000 West of Scotland children in the age range 13–16 on one of the Eysenck questionnaires and found the theory wanting in several crucial respects. This study showed that whereas Eysenck's theory was developed from the idea that genetically determined personality 'traits' or characteristics would distinguish delinquents from non-delinquents, a more accurate view would be that delinquency is associated with 'a set of attitudes related to unfulfilled needs incorporating ideas of parental rejection and punitive or inconsistent methods of child rearing'. This would be close to a human growth model (with elements of security, stimulation and identity), earlier mentioned and to be discussed again later, where parent and child behaviours 'reciprocally augment' each other in a rather complicated way. The results of this Scottish study (perhaps the most comprehensive yet made of Eysenck's theory) were also consistent with the views of other writers in this area who have concluded that 'juvenile delinquency is a manifestation of a wide range of personalities from the normal to the pathological',[31] and that 'while a given personality characteristic may occur more frequently or in greater magnitude in a delinquent group, it cannot be argued that this characteristic is pathognomic of delinquency.[32]

Paradoxically a related approach to Eysenck's conditioned-response one, is contained in a theoretical view which *discounts* the importance of enduring personality traits and which emphasises instead the extent to which human behaviour is determined by specific environmental conditions. This is called *social learning theory* and argues that behaviour of a certain kind will only recur when a new set of environmental circumstances closely enough approximate the original ones (in which the behaviour was elicited). It is thus argued that delinquent behaviour will be highly resistant to change so long as there is the possibility of a replication of the circumstances in which it was first produced (and probably rewarded). The original behaviour, it is argued, arises from chance motivational states rather than from enduring personality-trait pre-dispositions, and where these (tension) states 'match' environmental opportunities for their resolution, a behavioural response will be established and will become a permanent part of the individual's 'behavioural repertoire' so that whether or not he makes that response again will depend upon (i) whether he finds himself subsequently in a similar situation and (ii) the extent to which the original behaviour was reinforced (rewarded).

Proponents of this theory[33] have therefore argued that three kinds of 'mechanism' should be employed to reduce delinquent behaviour. These are (a) reducing opportunities to commit delinquent acts, for example fitting steering locks to all cars; (b) using behaviour modification techniques, for example punishing behaviour which is undesirable and rewarding behaviour which is appropriate in a specially regularised and systematic way; and (c) teaching the individuals concerned responses which compete directly with the anti-social ones in their repertoires, for example giving practical advice on how to deal with everyday problems such as getting on with the police, finding a job and so on.

As the authors readily admit, apart from the practical difficulty of exercising these 'manipulations' over the individual in his own family environment (as every parent knows), there is the 'fundamental ethical problem of trying to reconcile demands for personal autonomy with the need for social control'.

The typological approach

One of the problems which faces the researcher using special statistical techniques of analysing 'personality' data is that he cannot be sure if his results are to be interpreted as factors *within* individual personalities, that is as different aspects of one person; or if they represent groups of people responding similarly to the items on his questionnaire, that is he cannot be certain whether he is speaking of 'traits' or of 'types'.

Increasingly too it has been recognised that delinquency is a blanket term for a wide range of actions . . . 'a miscellaneous aggregate of quite different kinds of actions presented by a markedly heterogeneous population of agents' (see reference 31). It has therefore become important in theorising about delinquency to try to define different *types* of offenders. And there have been different theoretical approaches to this problem. For example, there have been:

A. *Psychiatric* typologies[34] which speak of three distinct groups,

    (i) an overinhibited type with parents who are cold, unsocial and strict;

    (ii) an underinhibited type with parents who are full of 'bottomless hostilities and endless bitterness', and are therefore children who are rejected and actively hostile; and

    (iii) a pseudo-social type who are defiant and deceptive (as in type (ii)) but who are loyal in a group or gang. Parents of this third type are described as indifferent and inadequate.

B. *Behavioural classifications*[35] which produce three or four different types such as,

    (i) a socialised group whose delinquency is due almost entirely to social and ecological causes (these are sometimes called 'career delinquents');

    (ii) an unsocialised-aggressive group likely to be highly impulsive and difficult to get to know;

    (iii) a neurotic-disturbed group likely to be solitary and inhibited; and

    (iv) an inadequate group likely to be intellectually dull and socially inept and perhaps part of the next generation of chronic sick, alcoholic and depersonalised.

C. *Psychological typologies* such as the one which speaks of 'levels of maturity'.[36] Seven stages of maturity are defined within this approach and they are described in terms of the way an individual's needs are related to his construction of the world, especially his inter-personal world. Various measures of these stages were developed and delinquents were to be more commonly found at the lower levels of maturity:

    (i) an asocial, self-centred group with no understanding of inter-personal dynamics. These children are described as 'not interested in things outside themselves except as sources of material supply' – children preoccupied by the need simply to survive.

(ii) a slightly more mature group 'seeking external structures for controls, manipulating within a dimension of giving-receiving' – that is, children aware of rules and experimenting with relationships in the way of the adventurous three- or four-year-old; and

(iii) at the next level of maturity, a group 'aware of expectations, concerned about status and respect, influenced by people he admires'. Here are children caught between imitation and identification, between a process of acting-out 'false selves' and developing the feel of 'real' authority which comes from having a personal identity.

D. *Factor-analytic typologies*[37] – analysing information from questionnaires mainly, it has been possible to identify some four major groupings:

(i) an unsocialised-aggressive, sometimes called psychopathic, group;

(ii) a neurotic-disturbed group characterised by so called acting-out behaviour and likely to feature large as a group in referrals to child guidance clinics;

(iii) a subcultural-socialised group of delinquent behaviour very much a feature of family and social experiences (see cultural deviance theory); and

(iv) a type of delinquent who is immature and inadequate and out of his depth in coping with complex situations.

The difficulty with typologies, of course, is that not many people actually fit clearly into one category or another. Usually it is found that 25% of cases cannot be allocated to a 'type' because either they fit equally well into two or more categories or they do not fit into any at all (and so new sub-types are created and so on, and so on . . .).

A related problem also is evident in this approach when institutionalised offenders are used as the basis of study.

For example, in 1965 a study[38] was made of the population of 100 boys in a senior List D school near Glasgow. Children were interviewed and assessed as to their possible allocation to other forms of provision, based on defined categories of mental handicap or emotional maladjustment, were these other forms of local authority provision sufficiently available. Some 10% of this List D population could have been ascertained mentally handicapped and placed in residential special schools; 15% was deemed severely maladjusted and would have been well placed in schools for maladjusted children; and a further 10% was identified as needing in-patient psychiatric care. Regarding these 35 children then as falling primarily within the official category 'delinquent' (that is, as types of delinquent) obscures the fact that their presence in the List D schools says perhaps more about the poverty of appropriate educational and hospital provision and the nature of decision taking within overburdened field services than about the population of delinquents represented by them.

Typologies, therefore, tend to oversimplify the situation. This is put very well by one researcher[39] who concluded out of his study of 'assaultiveness':

'It is apparent that even within the relatively simple category of aggressive behaviour, there are vast differences in personality patterns among the people who engage in such behaviour. If we expand the horizon to include the whole panorama of illegal behaviour subsumed under the heading of crime, ranging from dope peddling to income tax evasion, from safe-cracking to homo-sexuality, from sit-ins to murders, the futility of finding a single cause or a simple cure can be seen.'

Delinquency as a multifactorial phenomenon

On the other hand, approaches to theorising about delinquency as a multi-factorial phenomenon have been criticised because, like single case study approaches, they are regarded as unscientific. Each case from a multifactorial perspective is argued to be determined by a unique set of factors combining to produce so called delinquent behaviour and therefore few general explanatory principles apparently can be set forth. These approaches are said to answer a question like, 'Why is the room cold?' by statements like 'Because the tempera-ture is low', that is, they offer elaborated descriptions rather than true causal explanations.

However, in trying to take account of the complexity of the interaction of biological, social and interpersonal forces (as well as the unconscious processes and defence mechanisms which are part of personality) students should not be deterred by cries of 'unscientific' just because established scientific methodology cannot yet take account of the full available range of observations and experience.

For example, an interesting attempt to take account of this complexity of forces in terms of scientific method has been made,[40] using a computer to handle the large number of measurement interactions involved. The idea in this study was to make sense of behaviour by seeing it as based on the impulse to respond out of biological, psychological, and social needs or drives as these are carried by physiological mechanisms in the body. A formula was proposed to define what the authors called the 'ergic tension equation', that is, an equation which describes a set of relationships amongst the various components of behaviour so that from the vast range of information possible about a human being's condition at any one point in time, measurement of perhaps five or six variables would be enough to predict states of 'ergic tension' or 'excitement to act'. The variables proposed in this study were to include (i) a measure of the incentive value of stimulus (S) – that is, some estimate of the attractiveness of the object or goal the behaviour would achieve if undertaken; (ii) some measure of the constitutional (biological) strength of the body system (C); (iii) an esti-mate of the kind of habits previously learned by the person (H); (iv) a measure of those temporary physiological conditions which affect drives or instincts (P) – for example, blood-sugar level, alcohol level, blood pressure, oestregen level, and so on; and (v) measurement of the degree of 'current goal satisfaction' (G) – that is, the degree to which the organism or person is satisfied with what it has got already or how it feels already.

Apart from the difficulty of measuring some of these variables, already it will be recognised how tenuous the relationship might be between measures of these factors and a prediction about actual behaviour based on the simple formula $E = (S+k)(C+H(P-G))$, where k is a constant, and E is 'excitement to act'.

The authors of the study, however, did manage to take measures from people on these variables and fed the data into a computer. They produced a number of 'ergic factors' which the authors interpreted as 'pugnacity', 'gregariousness', 'fear', 'assertion', 'narcissism' and 'curiosity'. So far so good, but when these factors were then included with 'family sentiment factors', that is, measures of relationship between the people studied and their families (mother, father, brothers and sisters and so on) as they would have to be to take full account of the social and psychological environment of the subjects, the results were so complicated that they could not be readily interpreted!

The study remains nevertheless a rare example of an 'objective' attempt to get beyond the simplified (some would say sterile) view of human beings which often underpin unifactorial theories.

And it is necessary to be able to demonstrate a 'frame of reference' or a view of the way human beings grow up and a value system against which observations and experience can be checked, examined and shared with others.

A model of human growth and development*

One interesting and useful frame of reference as such is contained in the proposal of a set of basic human needs[41] as they develop from primary dependency relationships. In the beginning there are physiological needs, the need for food, the need for sleep. Then there is the need for freedom from fear/pain, the need for safety. There is also the need to belong, the need for a place in the group. And the need to give and receive affection, the need for esteem and self-respect, the need for identity and responsibility. This relates to a view of personality as based on an underlying integrative/adaptational system which seeks to sustain survival of the individual beyond the level of a primitive biological consciousness ('provisional existence') and towards a hopeful, growth-motivated attitude to living which will include ideas of self-fulfilment, self-actualisation, and personhood through relationship with meaningful others.

Delinquent behaviour within this organic model of human growth and development would arise in consequence of unmet needs. Delinquency then would have something to do with failure in the basic human and social contract (which a child's birth expresses), a developmental distortion in the establishment of a 'dialogue' between infant and parent and those who care for him throughout his waking life, which is a matter of critical and fundamental importance.[42, 43]

This approach would find significant support in the levels of maturity model earlier mentioned. The finding that levels two, three and four within that

*Janet Hassan has been particularly identified with the extension and development of this model into child care practice in Scotland.

scheme were well represented amongst delinquent groups would suggest children deprived at different levels of growth and therefore (defensively) showing behaviour and personalities organised about 'gaps' in experience (that is, organised about need motivation rather than about growth motivation). This growth model is clearly also linked conceptually with object-relations theory where the inner world of the person is structured around personal-need-systems related to 'good' and 'bad' objects. 'Gaps' in experience, as used here, may therefore not really be gaps at all but feelings of 'emptiness'. There would also be much favourable evidence for this model from the vast number of studies which have found a strong connection between what broadly might be called the 'quality' of family relationships and delinquency in its widest sense.[44, 45]

Attention here would also be drawn to the extreme degree of social deprivation which characterises the areas from which the families of institutionalised delinquent children are drawn,[46] and which produce whole 'subcultures of despair' (see reference 17). Here, therefore, is a conceptual system which links together biological, psychological and sociological approaches by postulating a 'drive for growth', an inbuilt urge towards survival which requires the organism to organise its defences according to the way in which its basic needs are met. If this has been 'good enough', the child will have trust and hope and will not be afraid of his own anger and hate. If it has not been good enough, the child will be anxious and insecure and will only be able to manage his anger and hate by putting it on to others, as his parents had managed theirs by putting it on to him, thereby denying him satisfactory dependency relationships. And so, just as the child's behaviour will mirror his experience of adults in the family (and be 'reciprocally augmented'), the experience of the family in society will be determined by the opportunities afforded it to live and to grow, to achieve its own identity and so come to realise its full potential as a trusted, responsible and independent unit within the family of man.

Summary

Theories and some research findings have been reviewed in this chapter showing that a number of theories have been proposed which attribute delinquency to some innate characteristic of the individual. These have included ideas that the delinquent was some throwback to primitive man, that he was biologically inferior, that he had innate defective intelligence or suffered other kinds of abnormal stigmata.

Theories and findings relating delinquency to environmental factors were additionally described with reference made particularly to the influence of family structure, school and neighbourhood organisation, social class membership, value systems and personality. The rôle of social forces was examined in terms of labelling theory and other socio-legal processes which serve to highlight the relationship between the nature of existing provision and deductions from the measurement of population characteristics.

Samples of delinquency typologies were also described and finally some attempt was made to argue the case for a multifactorial view of delinquency within an integrated framework of a theory of human growth and development.

Perhaps the final summary, however, should be left to Havelock Ellis who wrote at the end of the nineteenth century: 'Criminality like insanity waits upon civilisation. . . . In an epoch of stress, and of much change and readjustment in the social surroundings and relations of individuals, ill balanced natures become more frequent, and the anti-social and unlawful instincts are more often called out than in a stagnant society. . . . It is a problem that on closer view is found to merge itself very largely into all those problems of our social life that are now pressing for solution and in settling them we shall to a great extent settle it . . . it is not an argument for pessimism or despair. It is merely an additional spur to that great task of social organisation to which during the coming century we are called.'

REFERENCES

1. Lombroso, C. (1876), L'Uomo Delinquente. (See 4 below.)
2. Despine, A. (1868), Psychologie Naturelle. (See 4 below.)
3. Maudsley (1872), Responsibility in Mental Disease. (See 4 below.)
4. Ellis, H. (1890), *The Criminal*. London, Walter Scott.
5. Dugdale, R. L. (1877), *The Jukes: A Study in Crime, Pauperism, Disease and Heredity*. New York, Putnams.
6. Forrest, A. R. and Moffatt, G. B. (1964), Using a Dutch Intelligence Test for Deaf Children with Approved School Boys. Unpublished M.A. theses, University of Edinburgh.
7. McDonald, L. (1969), *Social Class and Delinquency*. Faber and Faber.
8. Cloward, R. A. and Ohlin, L. E. (1960), *Delinquency and Opportunity: A Theory of Delinquent Gangs*. Glencoe, Illinois, Free Press.
9. Merton, R. K. (1957), *Social Theory and Social Structure*. Glencoe, Illinois, Free Press.
10. Short, J. F. Jnr. (1966), *in:* Hoffman, L. W. and Hoffman, M. L. (eds.), review of *Child Development Research*, vol. 2. New York, Russell Sage Foundation.
11. Briody, W. (1975), town planning thesis. Duncan of Jordanstone College of Art, Dundee.
12. Whyte, W. F. (1955), *Street Corner Society*. Chicago, University of Chicago Press.
13. Fannin, L. and Clinard, M. (1965), *in: Journal of Social Problems*, 13, 2.
14. Miller, W. B. (1958), *in: Journal of Social Issues*, 14, 3.
15. Salisbury, H. E. (1959), *The Shook-up Generation*. New York, Harper and Row.
16. Wilson, H. and Herbert, G. (1972), Hazards of Environment. *New Society*, June.
17. Connolly, K. and Bruner, J. S. (eds.) (1974), *The Growth of Competence*. Academic Press.
18. Reiss, A. J. Jnr. (1951), *in: American Sociological Review*, 16.
19. Matza, D. (1964), *Delinquency and Drift*. New York, Wiley.
20. Reckless, W. C. (1961), *The Crime Problem* (3rd ed.). New York, Appleton-Century.
21. Becker, H. S. (1963), *Outsiders: Studies in the Sociology of Deviance*. New York, Free Press.
22. Goffman, E. (1968), *Stigma: Notes on the Management of Spoiled Identity*. Pelican.
23. See report in Deutsch, M., Katz, I. and Jensen, A. R. (eds.) (1968), *Social Class, Race and Psychological Development*. New York, Holt.
24. Erickson, E. H. (1950), *Childhood and Society*. New York, W. W. Norton.
25. Sutherland, J. D. (1963), Object-Relations Theory and the Conceptual Model of Psychoanalysis. British Journal of Medical Psychology, 36, 109–121.

26. Winnicott, D. W. (1965), *The Maturational Processes and the Facilitating Environment*. London, Hogarth Press.
27. Sutherland, J. D. (1964), paper given to VIth International Congress of Psychotherapy, London.
28. Eysenck, H. J. (1970), *Crime and Personality* (2nd edn.). London, Granada Press.
29. Passingham, R. E. (1972), *in:* Nebylitsyn, V. D. and Gray, J. A., *Biological Bases of Individual Behaviour*. New York, Academic Press.
30. Forrest, A. R. (1974), Personality Organisation and Delinquency. Unpublished Ph.D. thesis, University of Strathclyde.
31. Wootton, B. (1959), *Social Science and Social Pathology*. Allen & Unwin.
32. Quay, H. C. (ed.) (1965), *Juvenile Delinquency: Theory and Research*. Princeton, Van Nostrand.
33. Cornish, D. B. and Clarke, R. V. G. (1975), *Residential Treatment and its Effects on Delinquency*. Home Office Research Studies No. 32.
34. Hewitt, L. E. and Jenkins, R. L. (1946), *Fundamental Patterns of Maladjustment*. Chicago, Institute for Juvenile Research.
35. Supra, reference 29.
36. Sullivan, C., Grant, M. Q. and Grant, J. D. (1957), *in: Psychiatry*, 20.
37. Peterson, D. R., Quay, H. C. and Tiffany, T. L. (1961), *in: Child Development*, 32.
38. Vallance, R. C. (1965), mimeographed report.
39. Mergargee, E. I. (1969), *in: Deliquency in Three Cultures*. Austin, University of Texas Press.
40. Delhees, K. H., Cattell, R. B. and Sweney, A. B. (1971), *in: Journal of Genetic Psychology*, 118.
41. Maslow, A. H. (1961), *Towards a Psychology of Being*. Princeton, Van Nostrand.
42. Newson, J. (1974), *in: Bulletin of the British Psychological Society*, 27, June.
43. Paterson, M. H. (1971), Growth and Responsibility. Mimeographed paper.
44. Bowlby, J. (1969/1973), vol. I – *Attachment*; vol. II – *Separation: Anxiety and Anger*. London, Hogarth.
45. Peterson, D. R. and Becker, W. C. (1965), *in:* Quay, H. C., supra, reference 32.
46. Wedge, P. and Prosser, H. (1973), *Born to Fail*. Arrow Books.

9

ASSESSMENT OF CHILDREN

JANET HASSAN

IMPLICIT in the terms of reference of panel members, as they attempt to put into practice the philosophy of the Social Work (Scotland) Act, is a concern to ensure that intervention in the life of the child coming before them should be relevant to that child's needs. If panel members are to make informed judgements – and hence valid decisions – they must understand the behaviour or symptoms which have brought the child to the hearing. The understanding to be aimed for is one which permits the presenting symptoms to be understood in the context of the growth and life pattern of the individual child, and it needs to be shared also by the various professional groups involved in intervention and possible remedial action.

This move towards understanding requires both a body of knowledge and a faith. From research findings, theories and studies of human development is derived knowledge. This knowledge is not a static body of doctrine but is under constant scrutiny in its practical applications and in the various therapies and treatment procedures which are based upon it. But without due regard also to our value systems – or faiths – assessment reports can become compendia of facts. If we do not make our values explicit, we may find that the facts have been weighed by unseen scales which incorporate unexamined values, and distorted by this weighing process. This need to be aware of values becomes highlighted in the hearings system. Panel members will wish to intervene helpfully with children but they are also accountable to local communities and to the community at large where many disparate value systems confront one another with no apparent logic. In this dilemma panel members may seek a quick solution by turning to those aspects of the behavioural sciences which are ostensibly 'value free'. On closer examination we realise that none of the human sciences provides us as yet with 'pure' data, uncontaminated with value judgements; most of us think they never will. In drawing attention to faiths and value systems, it is not suggested that professionals are not affected in the same way as other people, sometimes consciously, often unconsciously. The professionals' span of attention, the areas which are highlighted for relevancy, the vocabulary used – all are affected by their values. Training, whether as professionals or as panel members, should make us more aware of these issues, more in control of their influence on our judgements, more open to challenge and discussion on our point of view, more ready to accept cross validation of opinions and judgements. No pure science of assessment exists; no perfect instruments for testing any human characteristic have, to date, been found. All available techniques can be employed with varying degrees of skill and sensitivity; all methods of assessment are open to improvement, and none is infalliable.

What are some of the faiths and value systems which affect the weighing and relative weighting of the social and personal histories given in assessment reports? The genetic thesis still influences our thinking; many of us hold some remnant of this, often side by side with other views of the state of being human. We can spell out and even seem to measure inadequacy, dullness, poor resources, as genetically determined factors which predetermine possible outcomes. Concepts of genetic inferiority or superiority tend often to be equated with class, race, religion, occupational status of father, success as implied in the Education Acts and in the school system. A high level of literacy on the one hand and cultural deprivation on the other may both be seen as deviations from the cultural norms reflected in the mass media. To state these possibilities is but to be a participant member of the maelstrom of our time and place, with no easy answers to the problem of growing, developing and being.

Again, however humanistic the principles underlying the system in which we work, few in the Scottish culture are totally free from the influence of religious faiths. What is unfortunate is that the value systems which have grown from these roots are no longer respectable matters of discussion or even of interest, but tend to be held as hidden agenda. One example which comes to mind was provided by an educationist who said 'I believe in Original Sin' – and was met by silence – the silence of assent on one side and the silence of contempt and disbelief on the other. The discussion of purely educational data then continued as if the statement were totally irrelevant and had not been made. Yet at best, it had aroused feelings which would affect the hearers' participation in the remainder of the debate. Our public discussions are conducted as if there were no value systems on the basis of which we make judgements on social behaviour – as if people could live at any level without value systems, however varied, however primitive, however self-contradictory. To draw attention to this is not to suggest that we should not draw boundaries to our social contracts, or to deny that certain behaviours are uncivilised in our social groupings and that behaviour which damages or hurts other people should be defined, condemned and prevented. To look coolly and effectively at the diversity and conflict of values requires awareness and self-awareness in the setting of the hearing; this awareness, and all that it implies in terms of sensitivity, self-direction and tolerance of criticism, can be strikingly developed by training.

Recognising the importance of the interpretative skills that must be brought to bear on the information presented in children's hearings, can we identify the principal areas of the child's life and environment with which the assessment process should be concerned?

The child or young person is a member of a family or family group. Social workers, in giving an account of the child's circumstances, should aim to provide a definitive map of that field of forces which is a family while recognising the difficulty of capturing the essence of something so complex and dynamic. Pressed for time, they may narrow the scope of their assessment and restrict it to bare facts without exploring the implications of the facts. Death, illness, unemployment, family size, to take but a few examples, may be recorded simply as 'facts', but they are facts which are likely to have wide emotional repercussions. A thorough assessment will try to take account of what we may think of as the ripple effects flowing from these events – their influence on the life style of the family, on levels of responsibility, on feelings of depression. But however much time is available, selection from the mass of possible material is unavoidable. Criteria of relevance are therefore of the greatest importance. To take a single example: if the reason for intervention in family affairs is a referral to a hearing, the detailed personal history of the father may or may not be relevant. What is unquestionably relevant is the way in which that personal history has influenced the development of the family member who is the present focus of concern. Each person carries, in a unique pattern, the imprint of family pressures and family strengths, and it is to these individual constellations that individual assessment must address itself.

Beyond the family setting, each child is open to, and in varying degrees influenced by the culture of his neighbourhood, while through the school, television, pop music and other media he is exposed to the messages of the wider society. Some of the messages he picks up are contradictory; we can sense the contradictions as well as the young people. 'Do as I say, not as I do,' runs one message; 'Don't be found out' says another. How can the assessment process take account of all this? Ideally, it should aim to examine the impact on the individual child of both the formal education of the school and the unofficial education of the streets; to find out what use he has made of his cultural world, what aspects of it he has incorporated in his own attitudes and values; to ascertain to what extent and in what ways he is still his own person, capable of making choices in spite of pressures both internal and external. Above all, it should be the aim of the assessment process to throw light on the means by which the young person can grow beyond the constricting limits of his present situation and achieve greater autonomy.

A good social history presents the members of the hearing with a view of a unique individual, and it is in terms of his uniqueness that they will see him as answerable to the community, in greater or less degree, for the grounds of referral. The further exploration of the individual's unique pattern of growth and development is the responsibility of the various specialist professionals. Psychiatry, psychology and social work have different standpoints, but share a common framework of interest in personal growth within which this unique child can be seen and better understood. Since assessment is a complex, multi-dimensional affair, it is quite legitimate for different professional groups to concentrate their respective skills on different aspects of the developmental process. The use of a number of skills in the assessment process may lead to differences of view but should not produce total inconsistency; any suggestion of the latter calls for further explanation and exploration. It follows that professional reports do not merit criticism if they seem to duplicate one another in certain respects.

In exploring assessment reports further, some systematisation of data which might enliven our shared understanding could be helpful. There was a long period during which the human being was conventionally seen as divided into Body, Mind and Spirit (including feelings or emotions), and it was assumed that different professional groups had an exclusive concern with one or other division. Few practitioners however found it satisfactory to confine their skills within these narrow boundaries. With our growing knowledge of inter-relationships it has become much more common, indeed standard practice among professionals, to assert that the influence of parts must be considered holistically; all relevant therapies are now based on this view. But such is the complexity of the very many factors which add up to an assessment of a person, that some subdivision is frequently necessary. There remains the problem of making sense of the whole when presented with separate assessments of 'parts'. This is best achieved when parts are examined and brought back into the context of the whole person. Again a commonplace example from the hearings system: 'I see you hate PT – why?' To discover the ramifications of this 'why' is part of assessment – for the answer may be fear; it may have to do with dress; it may be related to feelings of physical inadequacy (real or imagined); it may lie in the personality of the teacher; it may be a fantasy of possible physical damage – and the possible reasons can be extended *ad infinitum*. Normally there is a publicly acceptable and ostensibly rational 'why' and a host of unspoken, unrecognised 'whys' which lie below the surface and which the sufferer himself may not fully understand, experiencing them only as unease and anxiety in the situation.

But this suggests an interminable process. We should recognise that we can only have 'good enough' assessment which must be as expert as our time and skill can make it. But there is another systematisation which may do more justice to uniqueness and individuality. We can try to arrive at both the Sum (the separate aspects of the individual as they affect one another) and the Centre (the uniqueness and separateness of his individual identity as a person) if we try to keep both in view in personal interaction. A useful mnemonic can be found by borrowing from the traditional use of dimensional terms to express aspects of the person: we may speak of the length, breadth and depth of personality. Most people assess one another in terms of these dimensions; our social skills are based principally on our capacity to make these assessments quickly, skilfully and intuitively.

> (i) *Length:* Every person has a dimension in time, depending on his age and experiences of growing in a family, in a community. Such details form an essential part of his social history; their implications will impinge on every person who sees or speaks to the child and who takes account of his age, height, weight and health; his speech, his confidence and awareness; his capacity to relate, to interact and to take responsibility appropriately. These areas of the person may

be, and are, interpreted and assessed by all of us, using our social skills in our daily intercourse with other people. Professional skills in this area are normal social skills sharpened against known theories and research findings. The professional's viewpoint is a necessary check for our areas of partial knowledge and hence of prejudice, when for example we assume that all children coming from a particular area are bound to be socially deprived, or undersized, or delinquent – or to have whatever characteristics we attribute to the area to which they happen to belong.

(ii) *Breadth*: Assessment in terms of this dimension requires a more focussed skill for various aspects of development may contradict or be out of alignment with each other. This is most clearly seen where the young person may act out of character; or where a relatively well-adjusted child may start to fail or opt out; or the obedient conventional child may have a sudden aggressive outburst. More subtly, the adolescent who presents himself as a big tough may revert very quickly under pressure to infantile levels of dependency and we are presented with the problem of deciding which aspect of his personality is more 'real'. How can both make sense? These and numerous other instances are everyday questions of assessment and offer a real challenge to the professionals. Objective tests may help – but only if used with subtlety and an interpretative vocabulary which throws light on the problem, and where test findings can be related to other modes of judgement and assessment. Of particular value in this respect are straightforward reports from day schools and from residential situations where different behaviours, often contradictory behaviour patterns, may be noted. Adaptability to the expectations of adults or groups may be recognised either as weakness or as strength. Our exasperation at not having pure uncontaminated samples of behaviour should not blind us to this very normal phenomenon. But who is this person, this individual who carries with him his history, his experience – how do we know him, how do we glimpse his uniqueness? It is perhaps worth reiterating here that part of the art and skill of the hearing process is the assessment of 'hearing behaviour' as yet another example of adaptation to a new situation and a new set of expectations.

(iii) *Depth*: The uniqueness, identity, awareness and inner strengths, the fears, anxieties, uncertainties of an individual all have inner meanings without which any judgements of Length and Breadth are but isolated phenomena – aggregations of evidence which we may interpret more or less correctly but may not 'know' other than in exceptional situations. Trust in the process may make it easier for these personal dimensions to be opened up and shared, but provide no absolute guarantee. The child's unease may be a powerful inhibitor, and its signs should be seen or heard. Interviewing skill is vitally necessary and that skill involves more than just 'being a good listener'. The professional has to help and interact in a way that will be productive and not damaging. He must maintain a firm awareness of the purpose of the hearing while at the same time exercising the skills necessary to create an atmosphere of trust and acceptance and to encourage free comment. Many people may feel that such advice is exaggerated and that 'getting at the truth' (whatever that is!) should be our main aim. Understanding in this dimension of depth has its own validity in which objective truth may be only a small and perhaps unimportant part. Contradictions between 'truths' are commonplace in this dimension – for example, the social history may indicate that the father is a good provider and a stable support; the child may convey the reality of his feelings of hate and violence towards his father – feelings which may be merely transitory, or perhaps long-standing, perhaps even irreparable. The truth of states of feeling is not co-terminous with the truth of social data. This dimension of depth has its own rationality and irrationality, and this is an essential aspect of all we know and feel to be our private internal selves.

Through the examination of the many facets of the individual in a 'dimensional' frame of reference, there should emerge the individuality of the child, his strengths and weaknesses, his relationships with his family, especially his relationships with his parents both as a pair and as individuals with whom he is involved. His loves and hates, his aggressions both positive and negative, his capacity to learn both in the educational system and as a social being, his confrontations and his retreats into group rather than individual identity – all of these are relevant to our understanding of the individual. Our discoveries need not take volumes to express but should arise from the economical use of skills focussed on the task. For this task to be accomplished, panel members must make their own assessment of the reports placed before them and check them against the actual behaviour of the family in the hearing. Panel members will be alerted for example by reports which highlight weaknesses and omit strengths, and those which seem to give all their attention to 'badness' and omit any mention of 'goodness' and normal functioning.

The professional report may sometimes appear too narrow and specialised, but the information in question has probably been obtained in a very subtle interaction of two people. The attitudes of those involved on each side of the exercise require comment and interpretation; a sense of nearness, feelings of trust, co-operation or suspicion will almost certainly have influenced results and provide a significant field for interpretative comment.

From the assessment data before them the members of hearings are asked to make judgements and arrive at decisions. They have a responsibility to ask professionals who may use specialised terms or mere jargon to explain what they mean, and they should not shrink from this responsibility. Such private languages must be translated into shared concepts if we are ever to bring about appropriate responsive action in the community. We tend too readily to obscure the real issues by using such terms as 'inadequate', 'dull', 'poor resources' as though they left nothing more to be said or done. Such omnibus assessments foreclose options and thus reduce the range of relevant interventions, thereby contravening the very spirit of the Act.

When emphasising the responsibility of the professionals to panel members we should not forget that a reciprocal responsibility is owed to the skills and insights of the paid professional person. A whole class, and not merely one child must engage the concern of the class teacher; judgemental statements which ignore the span of the teacher's responsibility may indeed make matters worse in the long term. To cut across or to ignore personal commitments to amelioration and treatment is to disregard the lengthy experience of those who believe in fundamental amelioration rather than in symptomatic treatment; such people may for example view growth crises as phenomena to be lived with, and lived through rather than cut short by removal or disposal which ignores the underlying issues. To substantiate these faiths of minimal hope and crawling, snail-like progress in certain cases demands a commitment shared between professionals and panel members alike; to accept responsibility and to face possible community opprobrium must be a shared decision which is not easily reached and which must involve a painful experience.

Assessment is time-consuming, challenging and demanding. It must be multi-dimensional if it is to do justice to the many dimensions of human behaviour and the individual uniqueness of human beings at every stage of life. All the professions involved in assessment must possess skills in interviewing within an intellectually coherent frame of reference; they must also work to evolve a vocabulary that conveys areas of understanding and makes it possible to underline areas of special concern; and this vocabulary must be capable of translation into measures of treatment and intervention.

For members of hearings assessment is a necessary foundation for the processes of discussion, confrontation and decision-making. On the basis of the findings of the professionals, they are entitled to command the services necessary if recommendations are to be put into practice. The resources required may never be as rich or as full as panel members would wish, but the availability of resources should not circumscribe their thinking about desirable courses of action; such coherent demand is a necessary pre-condition for the provision of relevant resources on any appropriate scale.

IO

REPORTS FOR CHILDREN'S HEARINGS

VERA HIDDLESTON

THE EMPHASIS laid on treatment means that reports from professionals concerned with children play a central part in the hearings system. Since the written word has a power of its own in relation to its influence on decision-making, it is essential to examine carefully the preparation and use of reports. Statutory authority is to be found in the Social Work (Scotland) Act 1968, as follows:

> Where the reporter has arranged a children's hearing . . . he shall request from the local authority a report on the child and his social background and it shall be the duty of the authority to supply the report which may contain information from any such person as the reporter or the local authority may think fit (S.39(4)).

> Where a reporter receives information from any source of a case which may require a children's hearing to be arranged he shall, after making such initial investigation as he may think necessary, proceed with the case in accordance with the provisions of the next following section.
> Paragraph (b) of Section 17(1) of the Police (Scotland) Act 1967 shall, in relation to a child to whom this part of this Act applies, have effect as if that paragraph imposed a requirement on constables of a police force to make the reports thereby to the appropriate reporter in addition to the appropriate prosecutor (S.38).

And in the Children's Hearings (Scotland) Rules 1971, Part II, 6:

> (1) Where the reporter arranges any children's hearing . . . as soon as possible, but not later than three clear days before the date of the hearing, he shall give to each of them [i.e. panel members] any of the following documents if it is relevant to the case of a child to be considered at the hearing:
> (a) a copy of a report of a local authority on the child and his social background;

> (b) a copy of the statement of the grounds for the referral of the
> case to the children's hearing given to the child under rule 14
> below;
> (c) a copy of any judicial remit or reference or of any reference by a
> local authority;
> (d) where the child is subject to a supervision requirement, a copy of
> that requirement.
> (2) If the reporter has obtained any information or any document, other
> than a document mentioned in paragraph (1) above, which is material
> to the consideration of the case of a child at any children's hearing,
> he shall make that information or, as the case may be, that document
> or copies thereof available to the chairman and members of the
> children's hearing before the hearing.
> (3) Subject to paragraph (4) below, the chairman and members of a
> children's hearing shall keep securely in their custody any documents
> made available to them under this rule and, except as otherwise
> provided in rules 17(3) and 19(4) below, they shall not cause or
> permit any information contained in the said documents or otherwise
> disclosed during the hearing to be made known to any person.
> (4) Immediately after the conclusion of a children's hearing the chairman
> and members shall return to the reporter any documents which have
> been made available to them under this rule.

Rules 17(3) and 19(4) state that the chairman shall inform the child and his
parents of the substance of any reports, documents and information if it appears
to him that this is material to the manner in which the case of the child should
be disposed of and that its disclosure would not be detrimental to the interest of
the child.

The statutory duty of the local authority social work department to provide
a social background report is clear, but except in the case of the police in relation
to the reporter's initial investigation, the duty of other agencies and authorities
is less clear. Their obligation rests on the decision of the reporter or local
authority that they have relevant information. This presumes considerable
professional trust and collaboration and can make for practical difficulties. The
implications will be discussed later.

It is interesting to make a comparison with previous legislation on this
subject contained in the Children and Young Persons (Scotland) Act 1937. At
this date children at risk were the concern of the Education and Poor Law
Authorities who were not superseded by the Children's Department until 1948.
The nature of information required was specifically stated.

> An Education Authority who have received a notification under the
> last foregoing sub-section and an education or poor law authority who
> have themselves charged any child or young person with any offence
> or bring any child or young person before a juvenile court as in need
> of care or protection shall, except in cases which appear to them to be of a
> trivial nature, make such investigations and render available to the

court such information as to the home surroundings, school record, health and character of the child or young person and in proper cases, as to available approved schools as appear to them to be likely to assist the court: Provided that an education authority shall be under no obligation to make investigations as to the home surroundings of children or young persons in any probation area in which by direction of the probation committee arrangements have been made for such investigations to be made by a probation officer (1937 Act, S.43(2)).

The most notable difference lies in the arrangements for the decision-makers to have copies of reports at least three days before decisions are made. It underlines the focus on children's needs and the kind of work that is expected of panel members.

SOURCE OF REPORTS

At this stage it might be helpful to identify the range of reports which may be obtained. It is obligatory to have a social background report from the local authority social work department for every child, and, where the child is of school age, a school report is considered essential. The panel members may additionally receive or request a report from a local authority child guidance clinic; a department of child psychiatry; a department of forensic psychiatry; a psychiatric hospital where there is a psychiatrist specialising in work with children or adolescents; an assessment centre; a residential establishment. While these are the reports most commonly received, there is no reason why they should not also be requested from other relevant people, such as doctors, or from workers in voluntary organisations.

Collaboration between agencies is important and in this the social worker has a key rôle. If the hearing is continued for further investigation, and reports are requested by the reporter, the social worker should offer to collaborate with the other agency and invite a copy of the report before the hearing.

At the initial hearing the only report normally available in addition to the social background report is a report from the school. This report could be obtained by the social work department as part of the information they consider appropriate, or it could be obtained by the reporter as part of his initial investigation. Head teachers have sometimes been reluctant to pass reports to another professional whom they may not know, and who may then incorporate the information in his own report. If, however, the reporter obtains the school report, care has to be taken that the social worker receives a copy before the hearing. Ideally the social worker would himself visit the school before writing his report and comment on the situation as he sees it. In some cases a social worker will find during his initial inquiries that a child is attending a child guidance clinic or a psychiatric unit. It is often too late for him to arrange for these bodies to send reports, and the hearing has to be continued so that these may be obtained. The social worker would be expected to obtain the families' permission to alert other agencies.

CONTENT OF REPORTS:
THE PANEL MEMBERS' PERSPECTIVE

In writing reports for an outside body a professional needs to be aware of the purpose of the report and the needs of those who will be using it. An attempt will therefore be made to put this forward in very general terms.

The reports are an aid to decision-making as to which plan of action best fits the needs of the child. It is also an aid to the development of discussion during the hearing. The following are some pointers to the kind of content that is helpful to panel members in the fulfilment of their task.

Social work reports

1. *Initial referral*

   The report should aim to provide a picture of the child in his family and neighbourhood and would mention
   (a) factors in the family or immediate and wider environment which might be contributing to the grounds of referral: relationships, illness or handicap, patterns of coping, difficulties relating to employment, low income, housing, neighbourhood resources and patterns, school;
   (b) personal factors which might be contributing to the grounds of referral: developmental difficulties, health, personality;
   (c) strengths in personal, family, school and neighbourhood life;
   (d) significant referrals to other agencies, such as child guidance service or hospital and how the child and family view these;
   (e) previous social work with the child or the family and the response;
   (f) reaction of the child and family to the immediate situation;
   (g) the social worker's judgement about
      (i) why the situation has arisen,
      (ii) possibilities open to the hearing,
      (iii) possible difficulties in communication at the hearing,
      (iv) areas to be avoided or explored in discussion.

2. *Continued hearing*

   The report should link with the previous report(s) and should add details of
   (a) changes in the situation;
   (b) additional information;
   (c) changes in the social worker's assessment in the light of new knowledge;
   (d) placements available and what they might or might not offer the child.

3. *Assessment centre report*

   This report describes the nature of the experience given by the assessment centre. It should comment on
   (a) the child's reaction on entry and how he has adapted;
   (b) his relationships with other children, with adults and with adults in authority;

(c) the extent and nature of the child's contact with his family;
(d) how the family relate to the assessment centre staff;
(e) additional information in the areas covered by the social background report;
(f) an assessment of the problem and how the child might be helped particularly in terms of his likely response to residential care of differing kinds.

4. *Review of supervision requirement*

This is a report which links with the original report(s) and should refer to
(a) changes in the situation and modification in assessment in the light of additional knowledge;
(b) the goals of supervision and how far the child, the family and the social worker have been able to work towards them;
(c) the extent of achievement and the reasons for achievement or lack of it;
(d) a reasoned recommendation for future action.

5. *Review of residential requirement*

The social worker's report should link with the original report(s) and should recall the reason for a residential requirement. It should provide
(a) a statement of the rôle of the social worker vis-à-vis the child, his family and the residential establishment;
(b) a clarification of goals and a statement of how far these goals have or have not been achieved;
(c) a recommendation for future action with reasons.

The residential establishment should report on the nature and aims of the provision and give details of

(a) the child's reaction and how he adapted during the initial stage of placement;
(b) the initial assessment of the child and his difficulties indicating the goals which were set and what the child might derive from the placement;
(c) development during the placement including relationships with other children, with adults and with adults in authority;
(d) educational attainment;
(e) links with his family;
(f) relationships of residential establishment and family and of child and family;
(g) modification of assessment and/or goals in the light of emerging knowledge;
(h) how far the child and the residential establishment have been able to work toward the goals;
(i) progress or lack of it with reasons;
(j) recommendation for future action with reasons.

School report

The school report should refer to every aspect of the child's experience in school and his response to this. It should give information on

(a) size of school, size of classes, curriculum opportunities, the neighbourhood and its effect on the school;
(b) courses followed by the child, interests and attainments, intellectual assessment, learning problems such as poor reading attainment and poor concentration;
(c) pattern of attendance and reasons for absence;
(d) relationships with teachers and with other children;
(e) response to the classroom situation;
(f) parents' contact with school and any known home problems;
(g) health record and referral to other agencies such as child guidance, social work, medical clinic;
(h) the involvement of the guidance teacher and career advice;
(i) the school's estimate of the child in the school situation;
(j) school facilities available to the child
   (i) guidance,
   (ii) remedial help,
   (iii) leisure activities.

Child guidance report

Where the child is already known to the clinic, the educational psychologist would report on

(a) the reason for referral;
(b) nature of the work done with the child;
(c) the child's response.

The report would comment further on

(d) the parents' and child's reaction to the referral;
(e) intellectual assessment with comments on any impairment and its effects on the child;
(f) family and personal factors contributing to the problem;
(g) developmental needs of the child;
(h) whether attendance at the clinic is likely to be effective with reasons;
(i) a reasoned opinion of the child's likely response to the different methods of care open to the hearing.

Psychiatric report

This should include information on

(a) the response of the child and his family to the referral;
(b) assessment of the child's development and any malfunctioning;

    (c) family relationships;
    (d) indications of psychiatric disorder or psychopathology, its nature and
        possible treatment;
    (e) the psychiatrist's estimate of the features in the child's background or
        behaviour which caused the referral;
    (f) the developmental needs of the child and his likely response to the
        different measures of care open to the hearing.

CONTENT OF REPORTS:
THE PROFESSIONAL PERSPECTIVE

The social worker, and reports for hearings

The social work report is primary, being obligatory in every case, and it forms a statutory part of the duties of the social worker. While reports to hearings are of recent origin, reports to courts, in particular to juvenile courts, have a long history. The literature relating to the probation service has a good deal to say about the purpose, content and the style of reports to courts. In the introduction to a 'commentary on the preparation and presentation of social work reports to courts, hearings and to associated agencies', Social Work Services Group note, 'The replacement of the Juvenile Court system in Scotland by the Children's Hearing system has brought a new dimension to the field of social work reports on children at risk and created opportunities for new and imaginative contributions by social workers in the spirit of Kilbrandon. The changes introduced by Part III of the Social Work (Scotland) Act 1968 are based on the recognition that behaviour in children is an apect of the growth process and an alternative method to the Court – The Children's Hearing – was given a remedial function which essentially requires a careful skilled social history as a basis for consideration of the matters before it.'

It should be stressed that the skills of social assessment, social case recording and report writing are central features in the training of social workers. The relevance of social assessment to the children's hearing can readily be seen when it is defined as – the gathering of all material which throws light on the client and his problem; the reviewing of this material in terms of its relative significance, and the arrival at tentative conclusions, based on the evidence, on causes, the client's ability to work on the problem and the appropriate treatment methods. A diagnosis is made after a thorough study which includes the basis of concern, the wider social environment, housing, the family relationships and functioning, the care and training of children, employment, school, finance, health, social relationships and activities, experience of and attitude to social institutions, individual behaviour and adjustment, and if appropriate, personal development. Social workers are particularly concerned to assess how far the situation is affected by social and environmental factors and how far by emotional or behavioural factors, and their training includes some study of sociology and of human growth and behaviour.

The social worker records his findings and analysis in his agency records and where information is required for an outside body, such as a children's hearing, he draws up a special report. In writing the report he has to bear in mind the aim of the report, the needs of those who use it in relation to their task, the clarity of its style and language, and the effect the report has upon the client.

One of the tasks of the social worker in meeting the child and his family before the hearing, is to prepare them for the nature of the experience and encourage them to enter into discussion. He will as far as he is able at that stage convey to the family the social assessment he has made.

At the hearing the social worker is likely to be the only person known to the child and his family. He is also the author of the report in front of the panel members. This makes it possible for him to play a significant rôle. He is there in the words of the Act as 'a person whose presence is necessary for the proper consideration of the case which is being heard'. The only official guidance is given by Social Work Services Group in their memorandum on Part III of the Social Work (Scotland) Act which states that 'the representative of the social work department present – who may often be the social worker who prepared the social background report – will be of assistance in cases where the members of the children's hearing or others concerned, such as parents, with the agreement of the chairman, wish to ask his views on aspects of the social background report for elucidation of any suggestions it contains concerning appropriate measures of care, and for advice on possible alternative measures'. This suggests a very formal rôle for the social worker and, bearing in mind that unless the case is dismissed he may well have a continuing rôle with the family, the social worker may usefully play a positive part in the interaction and discussion during the hearing. He may suggest discussion of a significant area which has been overlooked. He may in the light of emerging material wish to modify his assessment. Social work training includes some focus on group processes so that it can be expected that trained social workers will play an appropriate rôle, facilitating and clarifying, but not dominating.

The teacher, and reports for hearings

It is not surprising that reports from the school are considered essential for children's hearings since the child over five years spends a high proportion of his life at school. The teacher therefore will have a good deal of knowledge of the child, but his professional education, unlike that of the social worker, did not include learning to write social assessment reports. It is therefore frequently the practice for precise guidelines to be given to the teacher to aid him in compiling his report. It is unfortunate if this sometimes limits the response from teachers who have a great deal to contribute. The importance of precise information, and the need to spell out reasons for subjective judgements, needs to be underlined. In the area of behaviour and personality it is particularly important to describe rather than to use adjectives such as 'lazy' or 'unco-operative'. Panel members are more interested than teachers may be aware in the details of the child's educational performance and interests. A positive school experience can help to sustain a child in the midst of family difficulties, and if a child's school experience is unsatisfactory, they will be concerned to know reasons for this and any possibilities of changing the situation. In considering a residential school placement, the greater the understanding of the child's educational needs, the better. The choice of a residential school which gives priority to helping children educationally, can be of major importance for certain children.

Where the referral to the children's hearing has arisen from the school situation, accurate information about the problem must be forthcoming. In considering truancy, for example, details are needed of the immediate as well as the past record – of weekly absence as well as of attendance over a period of weeks.

In secondary schools the reports are normally made by the guidance staff who have to deal with large numbers of children and may not know the individual child well, so that the teacher will be collating the views of a number of members of staff, and the time he can spend in obtaining the necessary details from staff will be crucial. In the primary school the report may be written by the head teacher, who will not have much individual contact with the child. The class teacher is however in a position to have a rounded view of the child and his ability and it would seem wholly desirable that he should be the one to deal with the report. The teacher does not normally attend the children's hearing, but where he feels that he has something to contribute which cannot be effectively dealt with in a report, there is no reason why he should not ask to be present for at least part of the proceedings. The chairman would consult the child and his family to find out their wishes in the matter.

Other agencies, and reports for hearings

These will normally be made at the request of the hearing and may be recommended by the social worker. In many cases panel members will not be in doubt about referral because the symptoms will be florid or obvious, but borderline cases can present a dilemma as panel members are unwilling to add to the demands on overworked services, but are equally concerned that real difficulties should not be overlooked. The most difficult group are probably those children from unstable families whose development has been adversely affected by their circumstances and who are acting out their conflicts. The difficulty does not arise if the social worker is knowledgeable and experienced with this group, but if not, the question whether the child guidance service or the psychiatric service can offer any help will be asked, and the need for clarification of function among local services becomes very obvious. It may be more appropriate in the long run that the specialist knowledge required for skilled assessment and management of these cases should be developed within the social work departments.

USE OF REPORTS BY PANEL MEMBERS

The Children's Hearings Rules are quite specific about the confidential nature of reports. Panel members, like all professionals, must constantly bear this in mind.

Names should never be used, except in the hearing itself, and, where situations are discussed for learning purposes, they should be heavily disguised.

Before the hearing

The amount of work involved in assimilating material before a hearing should not be underestimated. A number of tasks can be identified and ideally the papers should be studied on at least two separate occasions. The main tasks are

1. *making sense of the papers and checking for omissions;*
2. *digesting the content of the papers;*
3. *assessing the material in the papers, noting problems, raising questions;*
4. *formulating tentative views about the nature of the problems and the kinds of decisions that will have to be made;*
5. *identifying the kinds of questions that may help to open up fruitful discussion with the child and his family;*
6. *refreshing one's mind on basic details as shortly before the hearing as possible.*

The papers that panel members receive on a new case are likely to be relatively straightforward, but where a child has been before several hearings, they may be faced with a mass of information. A helpful aid is a front sheet which lists the dates of all the hearings that the child has attended, giving the reasons for referral and the decisions taken. It is also helpful when the social worker writing the up-to-date report is aware of the additional material which is being sent to panel members and can relate to it accordingly. If these systems are not in operation then panel members must themselves sift the information, write down dates, note decisions and build up a picture of what has been happening to the child over the period of time. If vital information is missing, then the reporter's department should be asked to supply it.

In order to comprehend and get a feel of the child and his family and their situation, the documents relevant to the hearing have to be studied conscientiously. All reports should be scrutinised carefully to see whether the writers have differentiated between facts and opinions; whether they give evidence for views put forward, and whether the reasoning and recommendations match. It is particularly important to pick out any statements about the child's behaviour which must be put to the child and his parents before they are allowed to influence decision-making. An example of this would be a statement that a child has been stealing at school. Panel members will also wish to note gaps in information, points they would have wished to be developed further, or discrepancies between reports.

Tentative views will be formulated about the nature of the problems and the kinds of decisions that will have to be made. It is helpful to be clear about what one thinks at this stage, rather than to be influenced by material which one has read without being aware of it. It becomes more possible to test out hypotheses in a hearing situation if one is aware of them. Hopefully panel members will also try to identify their own prejudices. It is useful to have thought through why one would be more inclined to one decision than another. In this whole process panel members will be bringing to bear, even if not consciously, the knowledge derived from training, from life experience, and from their experience as panel members.

Panel members can at this stage decide the areas they feel it would be helpful to explore with the family and the kind of information they need to know to aid decision-making. If the picture of the family in the social work report is alive, then they can begin to imagine themselves into the family situation and think of the kind of comments or questions that are likely to help the family respond. Encouragement or recognition of difficulties convey interest and concern.

It is very easy, even if papers have been studied most carefully, to confuse cases and get mixed up over detail. One of the most important aspects of the whole hearings system is that individual needs and problems are being considered with care and regard for the person. If a panel member is confused or mistaken in his knowledge about a child, then the message that gets across is not of concern for the individual.

At the hearing

The Rules state that '. . . the children's hearing shall consider the case of the child and during such consideration shall

> (a) consider a report of a local authority on the child and his social background and any judicial remit or other relevant document and any relevant information available to them;
>
> (b) consider any report, submission of which has been requested, by the manager of the residential establishment in which the child is required to reside' (Rule 17(2)(a) and (b)); and:

'The chairman shall inform the child and his parent of the substance of any reports, documents and information . . . if it appears to him that this is material to the manner in which the case of the child should be disposed of, and that its disclosure would not be detrimental to the interests of the child' (Rule 17(3)).

It is very easy when involved in ongoing discussion to forget to refer specifically to reports. Although the family will have been told that reports will be made available to panel members, they may not have grasped the significance and it can be helpful to say early in the hearing that these reports are on the table. Where material from reports is influencing discussion, then this should be made explicit, and the child and his family given an opportunity to put their point of view. Specific recommendations should of course always be stated and discussed.

Apart from this specific use of reports in discussion panel members will also be testing out the facts, the views, the hypotheses put forward in the report as they try to assess what kind of child, what kind of family, what kind of problem, what kind of decision.

Mention has already been made of the rôle of the social worker at the hearing. In their study of the papers panel members may have noted questions to be put to the social worker and others will arise during the course of discussion. It should perhaps be said that openness with the child and his family is at the heart of the system. The content of reports are to be shared unless disclosure is to the detriment of the child. Discussion with the social worker about his report should therefore take place during the hearing, unless panel members are unsure about a point which is material to decision-making and which it might be detrimental to the interests of the child to discuss openly. This is not likely to be a frequent occurrence and is most likely to involve information which parents have not disclosed to the child, or which the child has not disclosed to the parents.

In conveying information contained in the report to the child and his parents it may often be necessary to use different language. Not only may the language require to be simplified, it may require to be softened, so that for 'a low IQ' the phrase 'does not find it easy to learn at school' may be substituted.

This chapter began by underlining the centrality of reports to children's hearings. Where professional presentation on the one hand and careful assessment on the other is lacking, the treatment aspect is correspondingly weakened and the aims of the system are undermined. Panel members should be prepared to spend time, and to develop in their ability to study and use the professional assessments they receive, in order to increase the potential of the hearing and to lessen the risk of the taking of inappropriate decisions. The continuous development of knowledge and skills in this area for social workers and for panel members alike is vital.

II

THE RULES OF PROCEDURE*

CARYL GODWIN

ONE of the objects of the hearings system is to avoid the sometimes awe-inspiring formality of courts of law and to create, as far as possible, a relaxed and sympathetic atmosphere in which parents and children will feel free to express their views. Too rigid a procedure can defeat this object. At a hearing much of what is said and done must depend on atmosphere and on personalities; much that is valuable will develop from the sensitivity and flexibility which members can bring to the task of working in harmony and adapting procedure to each new situation.

Then why have statutory rules? Society has evolved certain concepts of freedom and of justice which it expects to be embodied in the legal system. We are shocked by the idea that adults should be sent to prison without a fair trial, and we must not forget that a decision reached at a hearing may drastically affect the lives of a child and his parents. To send a child to a residential establishment may be a move seen by panel members as a way to a new and better life, and by the family as a despotic deprivation of liberty. Many of the statutory rules are there to give parents and children an opportunity to challenge the right of the hearing to interfere with their lives.

Many potentially conflicting elements are present within the hearings system. The rights of parents and their privilege of privacy may be opposed to the child's right to grow up in a healthy and happy environment; the need for flexible individual judgement should be balanced against the need for objective decisions; the need to respect confidentiality may conflict with the need for openness so that 'justice may not only be done, but manifestly be seen to be done'. The rules attempt to reconcile these elements.*

*The main statutory provisions which regulate procedure at children's hearings are set out in the Social Work (Scotland) Act 1968 and the Children's Hearings (Scotland) Rules 1971.

*During the summer of 1975, visits were made to hearings in Strathclyde and Tayside Regions to find how far normal requirements were observed. Hearings varied greatly in character. In general, the smaller and more close-knit communities tended to have less formal procedure. At such hearings the statutory requirements were least observed. Sometimes ignoring rules did not appear to have a harmful effect but the practice can be dangerous, for each rule has a purpose.

Rules govern the procedure even before the day of the hearing. The reporter must, except in certain kinds of cases, send to members a statement of the grounds of referral, a copy of the social background report and of other relevant documents, at least three clear days before the date of the hearing (Rule 6(1)) – although this requirement is not always met. These documents may contain highly damaging and possibly erroneous statements about families, so all papers must be kept securely (Rule 6(3)) and the information contained in them not discussed except at the hearing (Rule 17(3)) or where advice is made to a court or local authority on appropriate measures of care (Rule 19(4)). At the conclusion of the hearing, these documents must be returned to the reporter (Rule 6(4)).

On the day of the hearing, members frequently discuss among themselves the case which is coming up and the course of action they may wish to follow. Sometimes the social worker talks over the case with the panel members. Pre-discussion with the social worker however can lead to legitimate allegations of breach of natural justice and there should be no opportunity given for the social worker to bias the hearing's decision. Indeed the reaching of provisional decisions is clearly contrary to the spirit and intentions of the Act and any decision so reached would be struck down by the sheriff on appeal. It is wrong to consider the case in this way in the absence of parents and child. However, it is not necessarily objectionable to review the approach to various problems in a preliminary discussion.

Rule 5(1) gives the chairman of the regional panel the power to appoint the chairman and members of particular hearings, and if he is absent this power may be given to the deputy chairman or he may, if he wishes, make standing arrangements. The intention is that the person best able, from experience or by temperament, to control procedure should take the chair.*

Where not otherwise specified, the procedure followed at hearings can be arranged at the chairman's discretion (Rule 9(1)). A statutory right of attendance at a hearing is strictly limited. At the start, the chairman should identify those who are present to ensure that only those with a right to attend are there. The Act and rules do not confer on the reporter or social worker an express right of attendance, though it is implicit. Rule 12 lists those who *may* attend at the chairman's discretion. These are:

(a) *members of the Children's Panel Advisory Committee and the clerk to the local authority;*

(b) *members or possible members of children's panels and their instructors;*

(c) *students or researchers;*

(d) *any other person whose presence is, in the opinion of the chairman, justified by special circumstances;*

(e) *clerks, etc., to help with the work of the hearing.*

*At several hearings observed, the members took it in turn to chair, feeling that this spread the strain for them, and allowed for greater flexibility of approach in dealing with the needs of different families. This rotation is not a breach of the rules so long as the regional chairman has a standing arrangement to allow for it.

The chairman should always object to overcrowding. If he has not been informed beforehand of the number of observers to be present, he should insist that some or all be excluded if the number is excessive. The only persons he cannot exclude (other than the family and, presumably, the reporter and social worker) are members of the Council on Tribunals, or of the Council's Scottish Committee, and bona fide representatives of a newspaper or news agency (S.35(3)).

Both parents have a right to attend at all stages of children's hearing which is considering the case of their child (S.41(1)); where a child is adopted, the word 'parents' means adoptive parents to the exclusion of natural parents. The father of an illegitimate child has no general right to attend. When a parent fails to appear the chairman should confirm with the reporter that he has been notified. The hearing may continue the case in order to give the absent parent an opportunity to attend if it is felt that this is in the best interests of the child. It should be noted that the 1968 Act (S.41(2)) states that . . . 'his parent *shall* attend at all stages of the hearing unless the children's hearing are satisfied that it would be unreasonable to require his attendance or that his attendance would be unnecessary to the consideration of the case'. While attendance cannot be enforced by the hearing, non-compliance with this provision constitutes an offence (S.41(3)) punishable by fine on summary conviction. The hearing does not have to accept excuses for non-attendance which are unreasonable. A child and his parents may each be accompanied by a representative to assist them in the discussion at the hearing. If a representative is disruptive, or if the hearing is satisfied that his behaviour is detrimental to the interests of the child, the chairman may exclude him (Rule 11(1–3)). This move cannot be used against a recalcitrant parent since he has a right to attend at all stages, but the chairman may adjourn the hearing for a while (Rule 9(2)), to allow a parent time to calm down.

When the chairman has clearly identified the child, it is usual to introduce members and others who are present. It is essential to check with the child his age and whether he is subject to a supervision requirement to ensure that the child comes within the jurisdiction of the hearing (S.55). Where this has been done, no decision can later be invalidated on the grounds that the age of the child was stated incorrectly.

The chairman should then explain the purpose of the hearing and inform the parents and child of the grounds stated by the reporter for the referral of the case. This should be done in simple language which parents and child can understand. If the child is not able to understand the explanation, the hearing must, unless they decide to discharge the referral, direct the reporter to apply to the sheriff for a finding as to whether the grounds are established. The child must be present at this stage of a hearing as his acceptance of the grounds is necessary, but it is not necessary that a parent who has failed to attend should accept the grounds (S.42(8)).

Unless the child and his parents accept the grounds (it appears that acceptance by *one* parent is sufficient), the hearing must direct the reporter to apply to the sheriff to establish the grounds (S.42(2)(c)). It is essential that this part of the procedure be done carefully and impartially, and the possibility of an application to the sheriff must not be used as a kind of threat to induce unwilling acceptance. The grounds for jurisdiction are set out in S.32 of the 1968 Act – unless one of these grounds is accepted by the child and his parent, the hearing has *no legal right* to proceed further with the child's case. If the child and his parent accept the grounds in part, the hearing may consider the case on those grounds alone (S.42(2)(b)). It is at this point that difficulties frequently arise – for the hearing must be sure that the essential elements which give jurisdiction have been accepted.

Errors are frequent where the statutory ground for referral is that the child . . . 'has committed an offence' (S.32(2)g)). The elements which constitute an offence *must* be accepted – otherwise the grounds are, in effect, denied, and the case must be discharged or sent to the sheriff.

The kind of mistake that is sometimes made is illustrated by three cases observed:

(1) *Ground – assault. The boy admitted that he had been fighting. He gave an account of how the incident arose, stating that he was attacked and was trying to defend himself. Self-defence, if proved, may be a complete defence. The boy was thus denying that he had committed an assault and was not accepting the grounds of referral.*

(2) *Ground – 'acting in concert' in a case of theft. When the grounds were read to him, the boy stated that he was in a sweet shop with a friend (he was there legitimately, there being no question of breaking and entering.) He saw his friend steal sweets but said that he had not known this was going to happen and did not receive any sweets. Mere innocent presence at the scene of the crime did not constitute 'acting in concert'. The boy was thus denying that he had committed an offence which gave the hearing jurisdiction.*

(3) *Ground – malicious damage. Boy admitted breaking a window but said that it was an accident. Malicious damage requires malice – it is not the same as an accident. The hearing wrongly proceeded with the case.*

In the case of adults, members would probably have understood that these were basically pleas of 'Not Guilty'. The fact that an offender is a child does not alter what is essentially non-acceptance. While excuses of the kind cited above are frequently common, and may be irritating, it is clearly the hearing's duty not to pressurise the child into acceptance of the grounds, and not to continue in such cases. In most cases of this kind, the reporter keeps the hearing right on such points, but not all reporters are legally qualified and the members themselves must accept some responsibility for ensuring that there is jurisdiction or the right to proceed.

What if the child admits that he has committed an offence not stated in the grounds of referral? Rules 14 and 15 state that seven clear days notice of grounds must be given to the child and parents unless in specified circumstances (i.e. where the child is detained in a place of safety and must be brought before the hearing on 'the first lawful day'). It is therefore invalid to alter the grounds at the hearing. The practice is sometimes followed of getting the child and parent to sign a waiver of their right of notice, but as this is a statutory duty and right it is doubtful if this practice is valid.

Once the grounds have been accepted, the hearing then considers the case. The manner in which the hearing has been conducted up to this point may well influence the whole atmosphere of any ensuing discussion. At some hearings parents and child remain standing until the grounds have been accepted; they are then invited to sit. There is no rule against this (which comes within the area of the chairman's discretionary control of procedure) but it does introduce an element of court-like formality which may inhibit frank discussion. It is more common, and better practice, to invite families to be seated as soon as they come into the room.

During consideration of the case, the hearing is required to examine the social background report, any judicial remit, or other document or information that might be available to them, and any report which the manager of the residential establishment in which the child is required to reside may have to submit (Rule 17(2)(a) and (b)). Every attempt must be made to elicit the views of the child and parent, and the chairman should ensure that the child and his parent really are involved in a frank and fair discussion (Rule 17(2)(c) and (d)). At an early stage it is important to find out from the reporter why it appears to him that compulsory measures of care are necessary, and from the social worker why he has recommended a particular course of action. This raises the vexed question of how much of background reports should be revealed at the hearing.

One of the most rigid requirements of law is that a person should know the case he has to meet; this is an essential element of natural justice. The 1971 Rules 17(3) and 19(4) *require* the chairman to inform the child and parents of the substance of any reports etc., if it appears to him that this is material to the manner of disposal, unless the disclosure is detrimental to the interests of the child. Members must be sure that the child's interests *justify* non-disclosure of a fact. Potential annoyance to social workers or teachers is not in itself a sufficient reason. Reports may contain inaccuracies – perhaps because of change of social worker, or lack of contact between headmaster and child in a large school – and so it is extremely important that the family should have a chance to refute erroneous information. Members perhaps through embarrassment, can be too timid about revealing facts which are material. Examples observed are:—

(1) *The school report states that the child has been suspected of theft. If this is mere suspicion, the child ought to be allowed to refute the allegation.*

(2) *The social background report states that the father is an alcoholic. This is a factor that is likely to be material to the manner of disposal, and highly unlikely to be unknown to the child. On what basis would non-disclosure serve the child's best interests?*

It is not uncommon for children to be referred on what may appear trivial grounds and the decision as to disposal taken on the basis of the background report. If information in the background reports is not disclosed at the hearing, it may be difficult to provide adequate reasons for the disposal – thus there is a wide loophole for appeal. If there is disagreement over a fact, the hearing must either ignore the disputed fact in considering the case, or, if it is important, continue the case to a subsequent hearing while further investigations are made regarding the child and his history (S.43(3)). For the purpose of this kind of investigation, the hearing may require a child to attend or reside at any clinic, hospital or establishment during a period not exceeding twenty-one days (S.43(4)).

When the case has been fully considered, the chairman states the decision which seems most appropriate. Basically, three options are open – (1) continuation of the case, (2) discharge, (3) a compulsory supervision requirement. The chairman should ensure that fellow members have been given an opportunity to state their views. At one hearing, the chairman, on announcing the decision, found himself in the embarrassing position of having to retract as the other two members did not agree with him. Decisions should, preferably, be unanimous, but failing that, the majority view will prevail. The chairman has no more authority in deciding the appropriate action than the other members and must be careful not to override their views. Rule 17(4) requires the chairman to inform parents and child of the decision, the reasons for the decision, the right to appeal, and the right to receive notice of the reasons in writing. The stating of reasons is important as the family is entitled to know *why* a certain decision has been reached. The reasons must be adequate ones, justifying the decision. In the case of *K. v. Finlayson*[1] the reasons given stated the procedure which was followed in reaching the decision. This case makes it clear that failure to give valid and accurate reasons provides grounds for appeal. Thus, the best and most appropriate decision might be overturned if reasons are not correctly stated. A point sometimes missed is that it is the *chairman* who is responsible for stating reasons (Rule 9(3)). Too often, the reporter notes down various facts throughout the hearing and the chairman signs these at the end. It is *not* the reporter's job to decide the reasons.

It is a common error to forget to tell the family *clearly* of their right of appeal. Generally the right of appeal is to the sheriff within three weeks (S.49(1)). Where a supervision requirement has been made, there is a right to make an application to a hearing for suspension of the supervision requirement pending appeal (S.49(8)). The chairman should also inform the family that there may be a right to legal aid. Parents may be referred to the reporter for further details. It may be noted that these rights of appeal are only against 'a decision disposing finally of the referral' (*H. v. McGregor*),[2] or the issue or renewal of a warrant for detention (S.49(5)(a)). Where the decision relates to procedure – e.g. a referral to the sheriff to establish grounds which have been denied, or a continuation of the case for further investigation of a disputed fact – there is no right of appeal, because there is no final disposal.

Observance of these rules should not be regarded as an unduly onerous burden. There is a purpose behind each and each should be carefully observed, for no more than other members of society do panel members have the right to act arbitrarily, illegally or unjustly.

REFERENCES

1. 1974 *Scots Law Times (Sheriff Court)* 51.   2. 1973 *Scots Law Times* 110.

12

INTERVIEWING, COMMUNICATION AND DECISION-MAKING

JANET HASSAN

COMMUNICATION as a concept is so widely used and taken for granted that we find great difficulty in defining and examining its elements. We recognise there are skills involved, but our experience of slickness and manipulation in the mass media may lead us to have serious reservations about the moral standards of the 'good communicator'. This element of insincerity however is an accretion; it is important that we strip this irrelevancy away and recognise that the basic philosophy of the hearings system can never be given expression in practice unless it is possible to achieve good communication at varying levels. Elsewhere in this book communication with the community, with the courts and the police, with the school systems, and with the interested allied professions, are examined. In the present chapter, communication is considered only within the boundaries of the actual hearing.

It is easy to assume that the participants in a children's hearing come together with a shared purpose. But is this indeed the case? On one side the community and its representatives are perturbed by certain behaviours or symptoms. On the other, the 'grounds of referral' have to be accepted, otherwise there is no hearing. Even at this initial stage, there are slender links of communication – to work towards a shared agenda, a shared purpose based upon a common understanding and thence hopefully together reach a decision. Given the agreement on the grounds of referral, either party may have very personal views on the possible boundaries of the necessary exploration. 'What's that got to do with it?' is a legitimate protest which should be capable of answer or withdrawal; the adolescent will tend, at his protesting age, to voice this or indicate it; many parents indicate such boundaries very succinctly in monosyllabic or gestural 'hands-off' signs; younger children may be more openly honest and opt out of participation altogether. Such boundaries and the areas between the grounds of referral and the boundaries have to be worked at mutually and with consent. To demand an answer is to negate the thesis of the hearing; nevertheless lies, half-truths, evasions, distortions, may be 'communication' when understood as such.

The possibility of communication may be decided in the first minutes of the hearing. The setting and seating say things to all of us in any situation. The degree of formality demanded and given can be crucial. No formality is insulting and diminishes purpose; over-formality is disconcerting to some adults and many teenagers. It is often overlooked how seldom children meet courtesy and respect from authority figures in our culture; this takes varying times to digest, to come to terms with. To be asked for an opinion is difficult for a young person who has been trained to parrot adult answers as the only acceptable views; he needs time and encouragement and we need skill in questioning in order to elicit a response. 'What do you think about it?' is not just words but intonation, encouragement, acceptance, 'equality', interest, empathy; none of these negate or detract from the real authority of 'holding to purpose'. The 'I don't know' in response is seldom without some communication or refusal of communication which can if understood open up new avenues of discussion. The more common response of gesture and movement is also a form of communication and should be understood as such.

We talk as if communication were purely and solely verbal, whereas we know that our sensory apparatus, especially seeing and interpreting movement, is part of our common heritage of shared skills. We use observational skills in our normal communication, we watch and pick up the flickers of eye movements, the intonations of speech, the large and small muscular movements of dissent, agreement, aggression, sympathy, respect, liking and so on. So potent is this 'signalling' that most of our social intercourse allows preliminary time to tune in to the other's signals; comments on the weather, for example, say the obvious but allow communication at these levels. This level of communication is part and parcel of the hearing situation although it should be noted that since the agenda is agreed, fill-in talk can be off-putting and subtly insulting especially for children who are more blunt and less circuitous than socialised adults in demanding that we get to the point. In these preliminary stages of interaction and searching for common ground, assessment is going on on both sides of the table. Children, without the screening barrage of words and wordiness are very frequently very skilled in their assessment of the adults involved, especially panel members. Their assessments may be loaded with prejudice but from their individual stance, they observe the minutiae of behaviour with very sharp skills; being unable to communicate well, being unable in effect to check on the validity of their observations, their non-responsiveness can be understood as a 'blocking' mechanism.

Given the agreed agenda, namely the grounds of referral, both sides have responsibility for communication; good communication can only be facilitated, it cannot be ordered or demanded, even with all the skills in the world. It is time and purpose bound; its purpose is to facilitate exchange and interaction which will throw light on motivations, responsibilities, maturity levels, expected outcomes, capacity for parental support, possible interventions and help.

In holding these 'ends' and possible 'means' what qualities are involved in being a good communicator?

Human curiosity is an essential ingredient, as is a genuine interest in the lives and struggles of children and adults alike. This kind of curiosity is neither prurient prying nor vicarious scandalising, with judgemental stances and the satisfaction of 'holier than thou'. Rather it implies modesty, humility, sympathy and respect for the universal human dilemma of our common frailty. There must be a real appreciation of people in their unique human struggle. Given this background of communication, there will be no conveying of attitudes that the people concerned are types or categories such as 'inadequate' but rather an affirmation of their possibilities however limited by some standards and a belief in continuing human growth.

Satisfaction in listening to people and reaching some shared understanding with them is no less important. Such satisfactions of communication are sought and worked for as skills; self-criticism of failure in communication will be a constant feed-back which does not discourage but sharpens communication tools. Such feed-back may be sought from the other side of the table with the ability to ask or comment on feed-back – 'You are not understanding me – I'm not being very good at this question' – and listening to and using the answers. This ability to revise one's original statements and beliefs, to keep wondering what is going on, to accept misunderstanding, to be open to correction, to reflect without rancour on one's rôle as others see it, is fundamental to good communication.

Words disguise or clothe very naked primitive feelings; feelings may be so overwhelming as to be wordless and can be suddenly translated into tears, aggression, shock. Good communication will not forestall such breakdowns but will, if the response is appropriate and early enough, forestall the paralysis and guilt of total breakdown. The good communicator here is a person who is aware of his own personal dimensions of feeling and can through this awareness either forestall or handle emotional scenes in the ways most likely to advance the understanding and decisions of the hearings. Very real personal feeling may be aroused in panel members – by insolence, refusal to communicate, challenge to their authority, the nature of the offence, feelings of futility and depression in face of the impossible. To be sensitive to these feelings while yet controlling their destructive manifestations is both a personal and a team effort. The supportive understanding of co-partners in the enterprise can and does maintain boundaries for control and self-examination which enhance insights and personal learning.

DECISION-MAKING AND ITS PROCESSES

The sequence of the hearing may conveniently be seen in consecutive steps.

Interpretation of reports

Social experience as a citizen, relevant training experience and personal sensitivity will highlight certain features of this data with strong emphasis, danger signals, significances; whether these signals are 'social' or 'personal' or both, there must initially be a more or less conscious jockeying for attention and significance of the many factors involved. Reading 'good' reports opens such options, brings them to attention, helps the hearing to weigh them, does not allow the easy option of too early foreclosure, too simple an answer. Panel members must assess reports and what is conveyed and communicated in them; no valid report is without communication and this has to be read and 'assessed' by panel members.

Introduction of hearing

The initial stages of a process can wreck, facilitate or divert each further stage although it must be stressed that with honest appraisal, mistakes are seldom irrecoverable, especially if they are admitted. The crucial area of observational skills has already been pin-pointed; we need our hands, our eyes, our grimness or grimaces, our shrugs, shufflings and shiftings; these are of course, more controlled when we are at ease in our rôle or sustained by the rôle, an advantage which is always enjoyed by panel members during hearings.

The blandness of authority figures as they play their rôle can be very disconcerting, for it tends to prevent access to information needed to establish where one stands in the discussion. For adolescents, this blandness can be particularly disconcerting but it can also be a valuable learning experience in how to convey purpose and intent, and how to respond to purpose and intent. This lesson can take time, time which cannot be timed by a clock for it will vary with different people. Softening-up processes which occupy this interval should be carefully scrutinised for they may be interpreted as irrelevant patronage; and young people, in their clear sighted honesty of assessment, may interpret such processes as 'phoney'.

One of the acquired arts of this situation lies in explorations which affirm the person and yet in so doing, will provide knowledge which throws light on factors in the child's background. His home address is such an opener when properly used: where is that exactly? – is it near so and so? – did you have to get the bus to get here? All such openers are more valid than pseudo-relevances such as football allegiance, 'inside' information which is designed to affirm that I, the adult, know this as well as you do. Topics introduced must be timed, relevant, direct, open and not uninvolved, uncaring or patronising.

In the initial exploratory 'searching', parents may welcome conventional moral judgements and condemnation of offences. They may with alacrity agree on such condemnation as the agenda which they will share as a screen against more searching, more uncomfortable probings and evaluations of attitudes and social values; what is at issue here is the many and varying moral and social attitudes which are held by differing communities and even within one community. Unless these are explored – or at least embarked upon as an open topic for relevant discussion among adults, the first principles of the hearing thesis will have been avoided. What are the equivalents in offences – how do children acquire a moral sense rather than a code of crimes and relevant punishments? Without such explorations, panel members will be seen as exclusively concerned with the negative issue of offences. Taking such exploration as one aspect of their rôle and function in the community, panel members may begin to harness a sense of thoughtful responsibility within a community leading to a development of inner disciplines and a concern for its children and young people.

Detracting from these primary purposes of communication is an over-preoccupation with the papers; this can be inhibiting and a disguised threat, invoking the unseen forces ranked behind the hearing situation. Deadpan responses are the only answer for such unknown hierarchies.

Information-gathering and clarification

The impetus of the hearing should be towards sharing of information, of attitudes and of awareness. It should be noted that lying at any level is a matter of communication and perspective – not a matter in this instance for moral judgement. The fact that offences begin the interview creates a temptation to dwell on them unnecessarily or opens up the equally tempting prospect of taking flight from them. What is required are bridges, bridges of relevant discussion and interest; open rather than closed questions become important. Closed questions predetermine the answer or hint at the acceptable answer, 'That's a good school isn't it?' Openness suggests expansion, 'Tell me about it.' When? Who? Where? Why? predetermine answers or at best reduce the areas of expansion of possible answers, while colloquial forms of speech which cover the same purpose open up the discussion to incorporate a range of inter-pretations and explanations. 'How was that?' 'How do you feel about it?' do not circumscribe affect, purpose and attitude in the same way. The closed question can be answered by 'Yes' or 'No' and hence lead frustratingly into a series of affirmations or denials; 'Tell me more about it' is an acceptance of willingness to listen, to accept feelings, opinions, even prejudices and hates, as valid. 'Is it any good?' asked in relation to a school, for example, allows the child to elaborate his own opinion as opposed to stereotypes. Closed questions have fixed alternatives – 'It's very good isn't it?' Such closed questions can make adults feel good; their views are confirmed and in this pseudo-agreement there is the shadow but not the substance of communication.

To sustain a relevant flow of purposeful talk is rarely easy. To remember and pick up connections, the relative antecedents which provide links in the dialogue needs to be worked at as a skill. Continuity without purpose may be driven by the panel member's anxiety, his concern to hang on to his own theme, his personal direction, his internal orientation. The respondent in this situation will quickly be aware that in this communication he is minimally relevant, the agenda is pre-arranged, questions and answers pre-set as in an examination. In such instances communication is confined to the internal dimensions of the panel member and does not help the total process.

Communication of ideas

The hearing situation it may be argued, was conceived as a learning experience for all concerned, not only for the young person in trouble. This aspect tends to be forgotten in the urgency of trying to arrive at good or right decisions. The hearing is a pause – an opportunity for the reflection of challenge, for listening, for the exercise of responsibility and accountability. In this exercise the mirroring and/or reflecting back of the respondent's own words can facilitate these processes. Such reflection must avoid sarcastic or ironic intonations if it is not to be insulting and counter-productive.

At this later stage, the child in trouble should be moving towards the possible decisions and beginning to be aware of the alternatives. His views should be sought, listened to attentively, considered with seriousness as valid possibilities.

Decision-making

These foregoing processes should be seen as affirming the uniqueness of the individual however commonplace the symptom. In this affirmation, clichés of punishment and ritual disposal will have no place. There is, however, no escape for either parents or child in easy answers. Decisions should arise out of the total sense of the process which has constituted the hearing; it must make sense, be a summation of the on-going themes of the hearing. The rationale of the separate themes and the preoccupations of the separate members of the hearing must be seen to be open to question, discussion and justification. Disagreements between members of the hearing can, with profit, be open if these differences of view are rational and free from primitive prejudice. Open disagreement may be preferable in its effects to collusion in an authority-saving exercise. If the child and his parents are to be seen to be accountable to the hearing, it is equally necessary that the hearings system be accountable to the community for its decisions.

Section IV

RELATED SERVICES

THERE IS SOMETIMES a marked contrast between the detailed and complex information available to the hearing from reports and from its members' own observation, and the limited range of disposals available to it. If any action at all is to be taken it has to be in the form of a supervision order; either the young person will remain at home and come under the supervision of a social worker or, less frequently, he may be required to stay in a residential institution.

A supervision requirement differs in many ways from a probation order, though the two are often confused. Essentially it is an opportunity for a young person to form a relationship of trust with a social worker, and for the latter to use that relationship to help bring about greater self-awareness and a move towards more mature attitudes and more responsible behaviour. The difficulty of the task and the challenge to the social worker's skills should not be under-estimated.

The decision to place a child in a residential institution brings out in sharp relief the possibility of conflict between the rôle of the hearings as a welfare system and their rôle as a system of juvenile justice. The decision does not rest upon the consent of the child and it is commonly seen by him as punitive; yet panel members, as adherents of the welfare conception of their rôle, will wish to see the disposal as therapeutic in intent. The moral uncertainty of panel members is however but a magnified form of the prevailing general confusion as to the objectives of residential care for young delinquents. If more systematic and sensitive analyses were available of the régimes and environmental qualities of List D schools, and of their effects on those who are committed to them, it would at least be possible to validate the intentions underlying a decision against its likely consequences.

A number of public services concerned with the welfare of children and operating for the most part independently of the hearings system, may be drawn upon for distinctive contributions. Guidance teachers within the schools are most likely to be brought into contact with the hearings system at the stage of assessment, but can also be involved in the supervision process. The child guidance service – the similarity of names is unfortunate – is in Scotland part of the educational system and offers specialist help for children with serious educational difficulties. Such difficulties are disproportionately common among the young people who appear before children's hearings, as are deep-seated disturbances of personality and relationships. For children in the latter categories, psychiatric help may be offered while under social work supervision or in residential care.

Intermediate treatment differs from the services discussed in the previous paragraph in having been designed primarily for children in trouble with the law, though drawing upon long-established models of youth activity. The keen interest that it has aroused reflects the concern of panel members and social workers to find programmes for young delinquents which while more exacting than supervision alone do not involve removal from home. To say that as yet we have little information as to its effectiveness in practice, as distinct from its intention, is not to single out intermediate treatment for criticism, for it is no more vulnerable in this respect than other and longer-established services.

13

SOCIAL WORK SUPERVISION

SUE SPALTON

SINCE THE IMPLEMENTATION of Part III of the Social Work (Scotland) Act 1968, there have been numerous questions, complaints and uncertainties about social work, social workers and their departments, and about the meaning and usefulness of supervision. It is scarcely surprising that reporters and panel members have felt trapped by being on the one hand expected to be a party to the administration of what was intended to be a liberal programme of child care practice and community concern, and being on the other hand denied the resources for that programme.

In this situation, the most immediate and obvious scapegoat is the local social worker and his social work department, which is seen to be the agency with total responsibility for the delivery of services, reports, supervision – residential or otherwise – the recruitment of volunteers, and the development of inter-mediate treatment programmes. Social workers at all levels experience constant frustration and a recurrent sense of impotence. In addition to the disparity between demand and resources, there are problems which arise from the fact that social work's rôle and status as a profession are not yet fully developed, although the responsibilities imposed on it are extremely exacting. The ratio of qualified to unqualified social workers is still too low, and those who are experienced as well as professionally qualified have tended to be drawn away from fieldwork into management in a period of expansion and reorganisation.

Discussion of the possibilities of working with individual children on compulsory supervision must first take account of a number of internal and external questions relevant to current social work practice. The existence of the Social Work Act has undoubtedly raised the level of community expectation. The social work department is now expected to assume responsibility for a vast range of human problems, some of which can be dealt with comparatively routinely while others are of extreme complexity and subtlety. Most social workers feel now that there are few areas of human life and death for which they might not be held responsible. With the dissolving of the old boundaries which defined the limits as well as the extent of responsibility, has come the feeling that if someone else is not explicitly responsible, then the social worker may be. If the housing department evict, or the school excludes, or the Depart-

ment of Health and Social Security refuses benefit, then what was their responsibility is all too easily transmuted into the responsibility of the social
worker.

Social workers are called upon to operate in ways which take account of
people's differing needs and the rules under which they work demand the use
of discretion and judgement. This makes very different demands from the kind
of proportionate justice which treats everyone alike as in the Department of
Health and Social Security contributory benefits system. However there is a
sense in which discretionary distribution of services must always be unfair. A
group of children on supervision have very different needs and each will not be
given an equal amount of time. If this kind of choice is multiplied over the range
of any social worker's case load, and has added to it the characteristic commitment to attend to the needs of the underprivileged, it gives some idea of the
dilemma which is central to social work in society.

Choices in social work in some ways become more difficult as they become
more informed and more conscious, and as they have to be made over a wider
range. All kinds of choices are made not only by directors and committees, but
also by individual social workers with individual cases. A problem would arise
for instance where the choice lay between an intermediate treatment programme, an alarm system for old people in bungalows and a fostering
programme for hospitalised mentally handicapped persons. Given that there is
only so much jam and that it is useless to spread it to the point of invisibility,
where does one spread it so that it can be seen and tasted? Whom does one
choose? If one does make a clear choice, it is bound to be a choice against others
who are equally jam-needing or jam-deserving.

Social workers may have difficulty in deciding whether they are in the
need-meeting or the demand-meeting business. Every consumer of social work
time seems inevitably to see himself as *the* priority – the matron of a children's
home, the superintendent of a day care centre for mentally handicapped, and a
reporter each said recently to social work students that his claim on social work
time should be given top priority. Priority indeed has become an almost
meaningless word – rather like the headmaster who wrote on each of three
school reports on three co-accused, 'this is the worst boy in my school'. Whose
needs and whose demands have the prior claim on a social worker: a three-
months-old-baby in long-term care who desperately needs a foster home; a
parolee who killed; an old lady over 80 with a spastic daughter of 60? Should
the sheriff, the councillor, the reporter, the Spastics Society, the Secretary of
State, by their demands be able to determine the level of response to needs?
Should the anti-social nuisance value, or the disgust value of a client be the
arbiters for the time we spend? Should the demand the client makes or his
co-operation clinch the issue? Rationing is done in many ways: some feel that
those with no votes and literally no intelligible voice should perhaps be first
– others feel that because the elderly are not by and large an anti-social nuisance
they are ignored for that very reason, and their priority should be reassessed.

In attempting to allocate resources of time and money on the basis of need
rather than demand, social workers at all levels know that they cannot even

identify, let alone quantify, all the variables that exist in each individual need, or in each group of needs. There is no clear consensus between social workers, their clients and the majority of taxpayers and their representatives as to what values should inform decisions about priorities. In most circumstances, as a general rule, social workers believe that all young children should stay with their parents except in dire cases. By contrast, some people take the view that children are precious and a gift and that bad parents should be punished by having the children removed. A wide range of issues surround the question of whether or not every effort should be made to care for various people within the community rather than in institutions. There is not a consensus view about the desirability of care within the community and the question arises as to how far ahead of public opinion social work and the law relating to it can afford to be, and at the same time remain credible.

It is unfortunate that one consequence of the expansion of social work and its increasingly wide statutory remit is that social workers as well as the general public have become unsure as to where social work ends. Indeed, some definitions of social work are so wide as to include any helping activity and even any political activity. Social work as well as law or medicine does have boundaries and it cannot cure or legislate for every ill known to man. Bad experiences in a child's or parent's past cannot be obliterated (no more can the good ones): separated parents will not necessarily come together again (nor necessarily should they); poor housing, inadequate schooling, low income, ill health or handicap are not problems to which the social work department has the solution. Social workers will be concerned and involved with people with all these difficulties. Many social workers become politically active just because some of these problems, if they have solutions, will be resolved by political rather than professional activity. It will always remain a fact of life that there are problems which have no solution. So when social workers are expected to do something it is as well for them and for the general public to look at the problem and to ask – what is the something and can any one person or social work organisation achieve it? There may or may not be general agreement between a social worker and a hearing as to what is desirable; what is certain is that there will often be a wide divergence about what is possible. Social workers do not, for the most part, operate in the clear-cut area between right and wrong, but in the uncomfortable shades of grey, and they attempt to choose the least of various evils. It is precisely this situation which in effect defines the essentially limited and finite extent of social work help, or indeed any other kind of help. Needs seem to be infinite, resources are always limited, and when it comes to choice about priorities, there is no clear consensus as to how things should be arranged.

Given this background, what can in practice be undertaken with children on supervision? Perhaps the most important requirement of all is to ensure that the whole area of work receives a fair share of attention. It can very easily be neglected. In an overcrowded work situation in which crises of many kinds make constant and clamant demands, ongoing work with individual children may easily appear a low priority, especially if the social worker already has some marginal contact with the child as a member of a family which is already being visited. Apart from the delinquent or the promiscuous, the nuisance value of the child in the community is small and, unlike the elderly, he has no vote. Provided that the law is not being broken in relation to the child (neglect, ill-treatment, failure to send him to school) then no one has the right to intervene unless the child's actions bring him to official notice.

In this less than perfect world with less than perfect parents, no doubt all children could benefit from regular individual attention from a sympathetic adult. A distinction has to be drawn however between the desirable, which will never be attained, and the possible, which might be worked towards. Consideration should be given not to the impossible task of all the children who could benefit from informed caring, but the almost impossible task of working with those children who are either defined as our clients by law, by themselves or by their parents.

Children are not usually easy clients. Firstly, they do not have the sophisticated defences of the adult which make life easier for the social worker. Secondly, assuming that the need to be needed is a powerful factor in the motivation of social workers and that much of this need is at an infantile level, then working with hurt and needy children is likely to be a painful process. Thirdly, children are brought up not to trust or talk to strangers – and what else is a social worker? Add to this the fact that many child clients will have found in their experience no reason to trust or to like adults. The over-confiding child is just as vulnerable as the sullen one. Fourthly, working with hurt children is nearly always a painful thing. All social workers should not be expected to be equally good at it, and like most skills, it develops slowly.

There are specific advantages that can result from a compulsory social work relationship with children. A compulsory relationship is based upon the external reality of the decision of a hearing which was preceded by certain specific admitted or proved events. These events may signify little or much, but they do provide *a focus on external reality*. Even, or perhaps most especially, with a disturbed or acting out child with a bad history, it is important to hang on to at least some of the facts. Cause and effect are imperfectly understood by both young and immature older children.

> 'Why do you have to come to see me?'
> 'Because the Hearing said so.'
> 'Why?'
> 'Because I did Y, or because Z happened.'

This kind of rather basic preliminary has the essential virtue of reality. Immature clients – and by definition children are that, whatever else – especially need this kind of focus. The fantasies of small acting-out clients are in inverse proportion to their size – this is an indication of the need for a focus on the here-and-now facts. Compulsion can be an important factor in this kind of focus on reality.

A compulsory relationship also offers *a sort of security*. Until a child does something by way of a further reason for referral or the order expires, or something else is done to the child, he is stuck with the social worker and the social worker is stuck with him. There is in this situation the possibility of mutual 'tholing' which can be a very sound basis for beginning a more sub-stantial kind of relationship. Children who have known fragmented and unsatisfactory relationships can benefit in a particular way from being obliged to tolerate a closer relationship than the child has previously been able to experience. There is a kind of security in knowing the worst about one's situation as a client, albeit as a child client.

This kind of security can allow for a further possibility within a compulsory relationship, which may be identified as *freedom to hate*. 'Hate' is perhaps a strong word, maybe 'freedom not to like' is a more accurate expression. Many children placed on supervision by hearings are those who act out and act up and who do not easily relate positively to adults in authority. They are not likely to make an instantly positive response to a social worker. Mistrust, dislike, uncertainty and passive or active hostility are very likely responses, and it is important that they are acknowledged and worked with, rather than avoided by attempts by social worker and child to deceive both themselves and each other in a spuriously cosy relationship.

A consequence of accepting the negative feelings in this kind of relationship is that allowance can be made for what such children experience as much more overwhelming than hostility, and that is their *need for dependence*. In accepting the overtly bad side of someone, the social worker can begin to work with that helpless side which belongs to early childhood. Many children on supervision have experienced erratic parenting and need a quasi-parental kind of social work help. Sometimes this means that even children can come to understand the feelings that arise from past experiences which sometimes erupt in behaviour which the child, unaided, can neither control nor understand, much less explain.

Much inexplicable and ultimately self-destructive behaviour is rooted in the lack of a sense of personal worth. It is pointless to expect people to be able to love their neighbour if they do not love themselves. The development of a proper sense of self-esteem is dependent on the experience of having been loved oneself. The capacity to love depends at every level upon having first been loved oneself. Some social workers are uneasy about using a word like love in relation to their work, but it remains true that where people have not had adequate primary care, then without it, they will be most unlikely to resolve their problems which so often become society's problems as well.

The important counter-balance to this is that a compulsory relationship provides the possibility of control. 'The most important and influential relation-ships in any person's life are those which are, in their very nature, enforced. A child is born into a family whether he likes it or not, and with very few excep-tions, there are no opportunities for the child to evade the necessity to make some adaptations to the demands of the parents and *vice versa*'. Now it is pre-cisely this kind of reciprocal adjustment which so many children in difficulty have not been able, or had the opportunity to make. The driven quality of some acting out behaviour is a clear cry for help that is controlling as well as caring. The person (whether adult or child) who is unable to set limits for himself and who is unable to conform to the demands that society makes on him in the interests of its other members is a very unsafe person. An absence of internal limits and an incapacity to live within externally defined limits, not only means that a given individual may *do* anything, but also that anything may *happen* to him. Consistent control in the context of a personal but compulsory relationship can begin to construct limits which may become in time inside instead of just outside the individual. For example, a persistent juvenile nuisance who, prior to the implementation of the Social Work (Scotland) Act 1968, appeared in court every month, either for a fresh breach of the peace or minor assault, or non-payment of a fine, or maybe a deferred sentence, finally broke into the big time and opened up a telephone coin box with a consequent appearance before the sheriff. When it was suggested that probation had been of little use, this normally monosyllabic youth replied 'I widnae say that. It makes ye think!' He went on to convey, in his own fashion, that there had been times when he had refrained from certain activities, not because he did not fancy them, but because he had to face his probation officer regularly on Friday nights with his pay packet.

It is imperative, if any attempt to exercise control is to be meaningful to a child or to any client, for it to be rooted in a demonstrated concern for the basic essentials of life: food, shelter, clothing and money. The more outrageous and at risk any child is, the more concern there should be in these areas. The feeding, holding, clothing, cleaning activities are the ground upon which mother and infant relate. Where early relationships have not adequately met these needs, and where an individual of whatever age is acting like a toddler, the primary care is the first priority. The experience of and response to warm, predictable, caring control is a necessary stepping stone on the way to both independence and responsibility. This kind of perspective is not needed by all children in difficulties but it is very necessary to those most severely at risk.

Face to face work with individual children and their families takes place in a particular context which also needs to be understood. The decision to concentrate on work with individual children was deliberate – so often it is not that this method of work has been tried and found wanting; rather it has been found difficult and not tried. There is a range of other methods of social work intervention which need to be employed in working with children on supervision and these are discussed elsewhere.

REFERENCE

1. Hunt, Arthur (1966), Enforcement in Probation Casework. *New Developments in Casework*. Ed. Eileen Younghusband. Allen and Unwin.

14

RESIDENTIAL PROVISION

KATHLEEN MURRAY

IN RECENT YEARS there has been an active and continuing debate about the aim and purpose of residential provision. The issues have been sharply focussed by legislation which has required increasingly that children be placed according to their needs and also that delinquent and non-delinquent children be treated within a unified and flexible system of residential child care. Those responsible for requiring the compulsory removal of a child from his family look for criteria on which to base their decisions. Yet very little information is available on the aims of residential living and on the long term effects of the experience.

In order to understand fully the current dispute about residential care, it is necessary to review the complex and somewhat obscure history. In the early years of the nineteenth century children convicted of an offence became subject to the same punishment as an adult. Young offenders were liable to be sentenced to death, transportation or imprisonment and little attempt was made to do anything positive or constructive about their situation. It took Parliament nearly fifty years to change this and to commence the adoption of a policy which was directed toward reform rather than merely punishment.

The first real attempts to care for children outside the prison system were made in the reformatory and industrial schools. These were founded by philanthropic organisations but owed much of their impetus to a number of liberal reformers. One significant figure was Mary Carpenter whose mission was to save the children of the 'perishing and dangerous' classes. The former she described as, 'those who had not yet fallen into actual crime but who were almost certain from their ignorance, destitution and the circumstances in which they were growing up, to do so, if a helping hand be not extended to raise them', and the latter, the 'dangerous' classes, those 'who had already received the prison brand, or if the mark had not yet been visibly set upon them, were notoriously living by plunder – who unblushingly acknowledged that they could gain more for the support of themselves and their parents by stealing than by working'.[1] She made every effort to persuade the State to use industrial schools for the children of the 'perishing classes' and reformatory schools for those of the 'dangerous classes'. This led in 1854 to the passing of the Reformatory School (Youthful Offenders) Act relating to the use of reformatories and the Industrial Schools (Scotland) Act dealing with industrial schools. While remaining under voluntary management both the reformatories and the industrial schools received legal powers to detain children and were subject to government inspection. Although by today's standards these schools would be considered rigid and disciplinarian, their emphasis was on helping rather than punishing children. For the first time children in trouble began to be seen officially as being the victims of society and their poverty, rather than as the performers of evil deeds.

In the early 1930's the distinction between reformatory and industrial schools was abolished and under the Children and Young Persons (Scotland) Act of 1932 they became 'approved schools' meaning schools approved by the Secretary of State for the purposes of the Act. Since that time it has been possible to commit children found to be in need of care or protection to the same schools as those found guilty of offences. The distinction between the wicked or naughty child and the neglected one, between the depraved and deprived was abandoned at least in theory. In reality the institutions charged with looking after children who came before the courts still reflected the attitude of Victorian society. The voluntary bodies controlling many of the schools seemed unable to accept the change of thinking and encouraged the maintenance of a disciplinary and authoritarian tradition. The neglected and delinquent were inextricably involved with each other and this tended to make those in need of care resentful and suspicious that they were being punished under the old theories rather than treated under the new. The institutions have continued to live with this confusion about their position and in fact it may never be resolved.

The Kilbrandon Committee expressed the same dilemma when they interpreted the difficulties arising under existing residential arrangements as reflecting

(a)   the effects of lack of a unifying principle within the existing services concerned with education and child welfare;

(b)   a tendency in some quarters to regard children coming before the courts – at any rate delinquents – as a class apart; and

(c)   problems (financial and other) affected by the size and number of local authorities.[2]

It was recommended that existing statutory distinctions between certain types of establishments should be abolished and replaced by the creation of a continuous and varied range of residential provision. The White Paper then proposed that 'the range of residential establishments to which the panel will have power to send children will include children's homes and hostels and the present approved schools which will no longer be a separate category of establishment to which a child should be sent but will become an integral part of a range of establishments providing a variety of regimes and special treatments'.[3]

Since April 1971 when Part III of the Social Work (Scotland) Act was implemented, all residential facilities have been open to all children according to their needs and the children's hearings have been free to call upon any one of the total range. However the concept of a comprehensive range of residential care has been extremely difficult to implement. In reality the variety of existing provision was severely limited, the management and staff were eager to cling to traditional models of residential care, and the dilemma about the needs of delinquent children continued to obscure the objectives of the facilities.

List D schools

'List D schools' is the composite name currently given to the group of establishments formerly known as 'approved schools'. The term is derived from their classification on the Scottish Education Department lists but it is hoped that a more appropriate title will be adopted in the very near future. There are 26 List D schools in Scotland of which 6 are for girls. The provide accommodation for 1,500 boys and 260 girls between the ages of 8 and 16 who are sent there by children's hearings as being in need of compulsory measures of care or who are placed there by the Secretary of State as a result of court orders. The schools are classified according to the sex, religion and age of the pupils. A number of schools which have opened in recent years are relatively functional and modern in design but the majority came into being during the last century and have required substantial modification to meet present-day requirements. Some accommodate as many as 100 pupils while others deal with little more than 20. The location varies from city suburbs to rural countryside but three regional authorities – Borders, Dumfries and Galloway, and Highland – have no List D schools. The average length of stay is about ten to fourteen months but within each school there is considerable flexibility.

The List D schools are at present dependent on the direction and financial support of the Social Work Services Group within the Scottish Education Department. Two are run by a regional authority social work department and the rest are under voluntary management. In 1972 the Secretary of State announced that List D schools should cease to be a central government responsibility once the new regional authorities had come into being. This would enable the schools to develop closer links with social and educational services. Following this decision there has been a good deal of debate about the appropriate location of control over the schools within the regional structure. Much of the dispute has been over the relative advantages of an education based and a social work based setting for the List D schools. The dispute is certain to be resolved by administrative decision in the very near future but what is of continuing importance in the record of that debate is the way in which the arguments in favour of different arrangements imply varying and to some extent conflicting views as to the proper function of these institutions.

Those in favour of control by an education committee are inclined to stress the traditional goals of the schools. Their primary purpose is seen as the meeting of the educational needs of children within the broad framework of a comprehensive system. As the majority of children are educationally backward the provision of remedial help is a basic ingredient which may be met more readily if the schools were part of the educational system. The recruitment, retention and interchange of good teaching staff would be easier and back-up educational resources and professional services might be more readily available if the schools were under education committee control. In further defence of this argument it is claimed that segregation of a minority of children in another system inevitably increases the chances of labelling by society.

There is also a strong body of opinion in favour of control by social work committees. Because the children are committed mainly on account of social failure and are in need of an opportunity to form secure and supportive relationships with adults and with other children, the schools are seen as serving a social rather than an educational need. The residential experience may be a brief episode in the life of a child who comes from and returns to his family and community which exercise the strongest influence upon him. It is appropriate therefore that he should experience the continuous support of a family-based and community-based social work service.

Commenting on the future administrative structure of the schools, the List D psychologists point out, 'There is no *one* reason why children are sent to List D schools and there is no one defining characteristic of List D populations which sets them apart from their contemporaries in a way that would argue the relevance of one administrative structure rather than another. . . . The question it seems to us, therefore, is not so much "Social Work or Education?" but "Who wants List D schools?" Who is prepared to provide a structure within which the multifarious handicaps of the population may be tackled hopefully and purposively . . . who will trust the List D schools to pursue the challenge of helping growth in these children and in turn sustain them through their certain disappointment and failure to attract public support in what they are attempting to do?'[4]

In practice it is often difficult to be clear as to the purpose of individual institutions, not least because those who run the system and those who are subjected to it define the situation in different ways. A staff member may see his contact with a boy as essentially warm and permissive whereas the boy as a result of previous expectations and anticipations, may regard it as essentially restrictive. Owen Gill[5] examined the views of 77 boys admitted to an English approved school during a five-month period. He found significant differences in the perceived function of the school between staff and boys: 'The boys reinterpreted the residential experience to fit in with their preconceived ideas about the purpose that such a school could serve. They defined it not in terms of their disorganised social backgrounds but primarily in terms of their delinquent activity. This was clearly at variance with the way in which the school was seen by those who ran it.' Gill noted that the boys saw 'good behaviour' as the way to release and that this feeling tended to be reinforced by the grade system. Also he saw a danger that the staff might mistakenly regard the results of boys accommodating themselves to the institutional situation as an indication of a more general progress.

Tony Walter[6] in an unpublished study of the process of interaction between staff and boys in one List D school reported on significant differences in outlook.

The official philosophy was concerned with the personal problems that caused each boy to get into trouble and called for 'individual treatment'. In practice only a minority of boys could be treated according to their personal problems. In general it was impossible to identify these problems and consequently the processing of boys through the school was highly routinised according to their behaviour and age. The boys' own impressions of the purpose as being the correction of bad behaviour was confirmed by the routine life of the school. Their main concern was getting out of the school and when they referred to 'problems' they were really referring to their inability to behave.

As these studies indicate, the régime and purpose of a school may be interpreted in significantly different ways by boys and staff. Similarly panel members and society at large have their own expectations of the schools and these may differ widely from the internal philosophies. For example local residents have been known to object to pupils of List D schools walking through the streets. Some teachers and social workers believe that children in List D schools are locked up after tea-time. One head of a List D school resigned on account of his interpretation of the institution's aims being unacceptable to the school managers.

By attempting to provide both disciplined training and therapeutic care the schools have placed themselves in a situation of considerable uncertainty. The great variety in the régimes of different schools reflects largely a relative weighting of these two objectives. Consequently the selection of a particular school for a particular child could be a very difficult process which is currently avoided on account of shortage of places. Panel members rarely have a choice but should they feel that a child will be damaged by a particular régime, the hearing may decide to keep the child at home. A number of headmasters adhere to certain admission criteria which are related to the rôle and function of their schools and all schools have freedom to select and reject among the children put forward for places. The assessment procedures are still crude and only in the most obvious cases will the suitability of a régime be apparent. There are however a number of objectives which are manifestly clear in the régime of many of the schools. These are mainly the provision of remedial education, instruction in vocational skills and the opportunity for creative self-expression.

The majority of children admitted to List D schools suffer from considerable educational neglect. Particularly in the junior schools much attention is given to remedial work so that the child will return to day school with improved skill in the basic subjects. In senior schools there is considerable emphasis on preparation for work and every opportunity to explore a number of vocational possibilities. Training in a trade can provide an important introduction to the world of work as well as counting toward an apprenticeship. Most senior schools encourage young people to find employment and to experience the routine of work before leaving the security of the institution. In recent years it has been noticeable that creative activities have assumed some importance in the life of List D schools. Art specialists are commonly on the staff and their work and influence can open up creative possibilities for the young people. Participation in artistic activities can lead to more constructive use of leisure, to the development of new skills, and to the discovery of a significant medium of self-expression.

The provision of remedial education, vocational training and the opportunity for realising creative potential are easily recognised in the schools and their value should not be underestimated. The acquisition of skill and the restoring of self confidence are significant benefits for the majority of children. However few List D schools would claim these as their sole objectives. Most schools would assert that they make some attempt at 'individualised treatment'. This provision is much harder to identify and define, and it can be the focus of varying interpretations.

One model sometimes adopted is that of the 'therapeutic community' which was created first in the mental hospital setting by Dr Maxwell Jones.[7] The intention of the 'therapeutic community' is to alter the traditional passive rôle of the 'inmate' through a process of active resocialisation in which rôles are broken down and relationships become more equalised among staff and residents. This approach places great strain on staff and many who adhere to traditional rôles find the concept a threat and a challenge to their authority. This régime can also collapse quickly and to the detriment of youngsters if there is any change of leadership.

Other régimes attempt to individualise the approach and pay attention to the particular reasons why a child is felt to be in need of residential treatment. Children are encouraged to discuss their individual problems and to 'act out' their aggression and insecurity. In this process particular importance is placed on the production of warm and accepting relationships between the individual staff member and the individual child. It is hoped that through this the child will come to be influenced by the adult at a significant emotional level.

Panel members are particularly interested to know the effects on children of the residential experience. Prior to the commencement of the hearings system, the reconviction and recommittal rates for boys within three years of their release from approved schools was remarkably constant from year to year and throughout the UK. (In 1962 the reconviction rate was 62%, in 1965 it was 65% and in 1966 it was 63%.) Unfortunately it is not at present possible to say what proportion of children placed on social work supervision are subsequently admitted to List D schools or what proportion of those entering junior residential schools later graduate to senior schools, let alone to identify factors associated with a favourable response to residential care. This lack of elementary analysis cannot be excused in a system now more than five years old.

One Scottish study which commenced prior to the introduction of children's hearings found that even when the population was specially selected and the régime enabled the development of close and supportive relationships between staff and boys, the results differed little from the national 'failure' rate.[8] In her report of the research the author comments, 'perhaps it is asking too much of List D schools to expect them to resocialise young adolescents and send them back to the community inoculated against further transgressions since they return at an age when the offence rate has not even reached its peak. They are adolescents meeting the crises of entering work and forging new identities for themselves. At the same time they have often to cope with the problems of disturbed family life and the making of new friends if they are to reject their old way of life. It would seem essential that such a return to the community should be eased by methods of after-care which seem to continue the concern displayed within the school.'

The 1968 Act transferred responsibility for after-care from welfare staff based in the schools to staff of the regional social work departments. It was hoped that such an arrangement would result in greater continuity of care for the child and his family in need of help. The confidence which could develop between the child and social worker would result perhaps in a successful re-habilitation. Research findings raise some doubt as to whether this may be possible particularly while social workers remain under heavy pressure of work.[9]

The shortage of residential accommodation for children has been from the outset a source of concern to panel members. Children are being held for long periods in assessment centres and others at great risk are sent home. A recent survey showed about 70% of the children in Glasgow assessment centres were awaiting List D places. A new quota system is being considered whereby vacancies will go to the children in greatest need rather than to those who have been waiting longest. However, the important questions which arise from this situation are whether more residential places should be provided or whether measures should be taken to reduce the demand.

The population in List D schools continues to reflect the poverty of appropriate educational and hospital provision. All schools are containing and giving help to a number of extremely difficult children many of whom have been transferred from in-patient psychiatric units. In order to help the management of these very difficult young people there has been a deliberate increase in the amount of consultation, support and advice available to the List D schools. There are now thirteen psychologists working in the List D service and many schools have access to psychiatric advice and consultation on a regular basis (see chapter 17). None-the-less there are some young people who are unsuited to the relatively open régimes and short-term treatment provided by List D schools. In their study of the residential provision for children in the east of Scotland, Newman and Mackintosh[10] identified two groups who ought not to be placed in List D schools:

    (i) *those needing security and long-term treatment;*
    (ii) *those without a home or family care.*

The emphasis in recent years has been on the development of secure accommodation. A considerable number of young people have had to be placed in penal establishments on account of absconding or unruly behaviour. Until recently there were only two schools providing a total of 52 places of maximum physical security. Additional places are planned both for schools and for assessment centres.

A secure treatment unit called the Scottish Youth Treatment Centre will open shortly. Although situated in the Lothian Region, it will serve the whole of Scotland. The primary aims of the Centre have been summarised as follows:—

    (i) *To provide long-term care for seriously damaged young people, especially those whose development has been so grossly impaired that they cannot function in the community and those who give rise to major concern in present open establishments and hinder the care and treatment of their contemporaries.*

    (ii) *To achieve for these young people some degree of adjustment to themselves and their environment satisfactory to themselves and to society.*

    (iii) *To prevent further personality damage to these young people who have already suffered so many rejections.*

There would appear to be general agreement confirmed by the Newman and Mackintosh study that although the gaps in treatment resources result in a clamour for List D places, development should be towards filling the gaps rather than providing more residential schools. It already costs at least £100 a week to send a young persen to a List D school and this rising figure can only be justified if it is the most effective form of provision. More attention might be given to preventive action through earlier recognition of difficulties and a much broader range of alternatives in social work and in education, in day care, in intermediate treatment and in local residential facilities. The List D school will continue to have a significant rôle in work with deprived and delinquent children but it should be part of a wide spectrum of facilities which can offer a programme of care appropriate to the needs of an individual child.

Residential assessment centres

The greater the range of treatment provision the more important it becomes to establish what sort of child can benefit from a particular form of care. Adequate assessment facilities should be available in the community but occasionally it will be necessary to remove a child from home for this purpose. The Study Group set up by the Social Work Services Group in 1971 identified two groups of children who were likely to require residential assessment:

    (i) *children who will continue to offend or create difficulty in the community if they are allowed to go home;*

    (ii) *children who because of emotional or temperamental instability need such security for their personal well-being, including children who would be likely to abscond.*

In practice a very large number of children who fall into the above categories cannot be admitted because the demand for places so far exceeds the supply.

The residential assessment centres have been accommodated in the former remand homes and in recent years there has been pressure on local and regional authorities to improve and extend the provision. Their function is both to detain children and to offer assessment by the members of the centre staff as well as consultation with medical and educational specialists.

Newman and Mackintosh found that at any time during 1973–74 at least half the children in the regional assessment centre in Edinburgh were waiting for placements and the presence of these waiting children prevented others from being admitted. The majority of children waiting for placement went to List D schools and most stayed for more than three weeks in the Centre. The situation elsewhere is certainly no better and may indeed be worse (cf. p. 145). Obviously none of the centres will be able to work effectively until there is a variety of appropriate placements for children once they have been assessed.

Children's homes and hostels

One of the principal assumptions behind the new system is that many children formerly committed to approved schools would benefit from a very much wider range of treatment provision. In the past children tended to revolve around the symptom-orientated services to which they were originally referred. A child who appeared before the juvenile court might have been committed to approved school or to borstal whereas a child received into the care of a local authority might have been admitted to a children's home or to a hostel. The 1968 Act made the same range of child care provision available for all children whether or not they came under compulsory procedure. Delinquency is recognised therefore as one manifestation of underlying conflict between the child and the community, springing from a variety of personal and social factors. Its management is seen as parallel to every other type of social breakdown and requiring a broad range of provision, flexibly organised and readily adapted to meet the needs of individual children.

There is a disappointing lack of information on the extent to which existing facilities are now making provision for a wider range of children. Newman and Mackintosh[12] noted that in the east of Scotland about a quarter of the children in homes and hostels were admitted under section 44 of the 1968 Act having been made subject to a residential supervision requirement by a children's hearing. Well over half were in care under section 15 – that is they had been received into care with the agreement of their parents – and the remaining quarter were under section 16 which meant that the local authority had assumed parental rights. It is not known how many of those admitted under section 44 were delinquents.

The same study reveals the startling fact that the local authorities in the south-east had 233 boys in List D schools on 'Census Day' and themselves provided only 6 hostel places especially for boys over 12. The corresponding figures for girls were 34 and 25. Fife provided another 17 places which were shared between boys and girls. Additional places were provided by voluntary bodies.

In general residential accommodation in homes and hostels is provided by the regional authority social work departments and by voluntary organisations. Children's homes vary in size from the large mansion house in the affluent city suburbs or in isolated country areas to the purpose built 'family group homes' in the heart of housing schemes. On account of the great range in the quantity, quality and training of their staff, the homes vary in the quality of care given to children. The majority give good nurturing care but not all provide remedial care and few can cope with delinquent children.

The churches and voluntary organisations in Scotland command a great deal of experience and resources and they play a major part in meeting the social welfare needs of communities. Over half of the children in residential care in Scotland are in voluntary homes and hostels. Indeed most of the specialised care is provided by voluntary organisations such as Dr Barnardo's, the Order of the Good Shepherd, the Salvation Army and the National Children's Homes. Unlike the regional authority homes, they can be selective in the children they admit and are in some instances better able to tolerate troublesome delinquent behaviour.

Newman and Mackintosh[13] looked at the staffing of children's homes and found high turnover, low morale and workers who felt isolated and unsupported. They confirmed the need for improvements in pay, training, conditions, accommodation and in the links between residential and other workers.

By now it will be very clear that the breadth of residential provision for children has scarcely developed since the introduction of the hearings system. Many more children are being removed from home than occurred in the past but the effect has been to create a demand for residential places which cannot be met and to place intolerable pressure on the List D service. On account of the rising cost of keeping a child in a List D school and the doubt being expressed about the value of the experience, the emphasis is now shifting to the possibility of developing preventive and alternative services in the community.

Some demand, however, will always remain for those residential places which have the staff and the facilities to cope with a carefully selected group of young people. Newman and Mackintosh advise, 'We should aim for a situation where residential care is readily available for children for whom it is thought best, but where the decision to place a child in residential care is never forced by lack of alternatives. For we are not suggesting that residential care is never right, but rather that it should be used with discrimination.'[14]

Panel members inevitably seek guidance on the 'right' use of residential care. In time research may offer more detailed information on the most appropriate residential situation for an individual child. Until then, panel members will have to depend on the guidance of professional workers, on their own knowledge obtained from experience of visiting the schools and from their discussion at hearings with staff and children.

The basic problem is one of determining whether the residential experience will have any relevance to the child's home situation to which eventually he will return. The material provision and routines are generally considered beneficial but the child from a deprived city area admitted to a school in the country may regard the experience as largely unrelated to his pattern of living. Cultural horizons may be enhanced, skills may be developed and a whole variety of sporting and social activities may be encouraged but these will often have little connection with the child's real world. Less able children will learn more quickly and profit considerably from intensive remedial programmes. Relationships with adults and other children may be improved. None-the-less the full extent of an individual child's needs cannot be satisfied in any single régime. Because the majority of residential schools and homes are single-sex there is little opportunity for an adolescent to develop and learn to handle his complex and intense emotional life. Few institutions provide an opportunity for privacy or for indulgence in individual activities. Nor can they be expected to provide the unconditional love experienced in family life.

It is both morally unjustifiable and uneconomic to use residential provision for children whose difficulties could be resolved by other means. Responsibility for meeting the needs of children must be shared by different disciplines, departments and organisations. The collaboration of social work, education, health, employment and housing services would enable more effective planning for individual children and more controlled and constructive use of residential places.

REFERENCES

1. Carpenter, Mary (1851), *Reformatory Schools for the Children of the Perishing and Dangerous Classes and for Juvenile Offenders.*
2. *Children and Young Persons Scotland* (1964), Cmnd. 2306, HMSO, para. 169.
3. *Social Work and the Community* (1966), Cmnd. 3065, HMSO.
4. Forrest, A. R., Hassan, J. and Vallance, R. C. (1975), List D Schools: A Comment. *Focus*, April.
5. Gill, Owen (1974), *Whitegate: an Approved School in Transition.* Liverpool University Press.
6. Walter, Tony (1975), *Delinquents in a Treatment Situation: the Processing of Boys in a List D School.* Unpublished thesis. University of Aberdeen.
7. Jones, M. (1968), *Beyond the Therapeutic Community.* Yale University Press,
8. McMichael, Paquita (1974), After-Care, Family Relationships and Reconviction in a Scottish Approved School. *Brit. J. Criminology*, vol. 14, no. 3, 236–247.
9. Ibid. 236.
10. Newman, Nancy and Mackintosh, Harriet (1975), *A Roof over their Heads.* University of Edinburgh, Department of Social Administration.
11. Ibid. 65.
12. Ibid. 5.
13. Ibid. 191.
14. Ibid. 187.

15

SCHOOL GUIDANCE

PATRICIA THOMAS

THE INTRODUCTION of guidance into Scottish secondary schools resulted from the deep concern, expressed by many people, about the loss of the individuality of a pupil in the expanding and increasingly less personal secondary school situation. Apart from the informal care offered by the form teacher, no one in school had responsibility for co-ordinating all the different aspects of a pupil's life and for offering a consistent measure of support. The stresses and strains of modern living arising from earlier maturity, greater sexual freedom and the pressures of advertising, together with the effect of the raising of the school leaving age drew attention to the need for the provision of support and guidance.

In 1968 the Scottish Education Department published 'Guidance in Scottish Secondary Schools'. This paper encouraged the development of guidance and defined the main areas of pupil guidance under three headings – personal, vocational and leisure. It was also implied that one teacher should be able to deal with all three aspects so that the individual pupil had to refer for guidance to only one member of staff. Further deliberations led to the publication by the Scottish Education Department in 1971 of 'The Structure of Promoted Posts in Secondary Schools in Scotland' (The Green Paper). This recommended a fundamental reorganisation of promoted posts and included a number of new promoted posts for those who would be involved in guidance work as well as a new type of post in the management structure, namely the 'assistant head teacher'. The Paper further recommended that assistant head teachers and guidance staff should have teaching commitments thus keeping them in touch with the classroom situation as experienced by the other members of staff.

Guidance structure

There are no rules which state how guidance staff should be deployed in schools. Each school uses a system which is suitable for its particular requirements and environment. There are two structures which form the basis of all arrangements – the vertical and the horizontal.

In a vertical system a guidance teacher will have responsibility for a group of children in each year group, that is pupils from 12 to 18 years. This system has the advantage of providing a continuity of interest. A pupil remains with the same guidance teacher all through school and all members of the family will be with the same guidance teacher.

In a horizontal system a guidance teacher will hold responsibility for approximately half a year group and ideally the pupils will remain with the same guidance teacher throughout school. As there are only two guidance staff for each year group this system makes it relatively easy for members of staff to refer pupils.

A combination of these two basic systems is called a 'hybrid structure' in which an assistant head teacher or a member of the guidance team may have responsibility for a year group, while the guidance work is on a vertical structure.

Guidance staff

Initially there were few guidelines for selecting guidance staff. The qualities required are not dependent on academic qualifications and good subject teachers will not necessarily make good guidance teachers. The qualities required are basically those of personality, such as a concern for children and an ability to communicate with them, an understanding of and a sympathy with the problems of young people, an ability to offer advice and give support, a willingness to become involved in the lives of children in trouble at a non-emotional level. The list is endless. These are qualities which are difficult to identify and assess.

Guidance staff have a teaching commitment in their own subject. This makes it very difficult for head teachers who may be very short-staffed in a particular department. The 'ideal' applicant may be a subject teacher in a department which is overstaffed. The conflict is obvious.

Social education and guidance

An important distinction is drawn between social education and guidance. This may be illustrated by reference to a table (see p. 152) suggested by Daws of Keele University:

Section A: Social education includes the acquisition of knowledge regarding social and community life; basic health education such as personal hygiene, accident prevention, first aid and so on. These aspects should be the responsibility of all members of staff, although some subjects, such as English and Modern Studies, do provide more facilities for social education than most.

Section B: There is sometimes failure to realise that guidance is for all pupils. This section relates to all the on-going aspects of 'growing up'. This would include changing attitudes, formulations of standards, relationships with adults and peers, attitudes to sex, selection of a career and so on. This section would also contain a considerable amount of self-assessment by the pupils, when they would be expected to develop a self-awareness and an acceptance of themselves as people.

Section C: Pupils coming into this category will take up most of the guidance teacher's time. This involves giving support to children under stress which may be either permanent or temporary.

Section D: This concerns pupils who need specialist help because of extreme problems. The guidance teacher is required to identify these children and refer them to specialist resources. Very often expert help is not available or parental co-operation is not forthcoming. The guidance teacher is then left to cope the best he can, often as amateur psychologist or psychiatrist.

Work in sections A, B and C is impossible to carry out effectively without the support of the whole staff who are able to give information to the guidance teams and so act as an 'early warning' system. All staff are often involved in giving support to a pupil under stress.

Record keeping and the provision of references and reports

The keeping of records in a school presents many difficult problems. No one objects to academic records of progress being filed away for future reference but problems arise when the records contain personal details about pupils. These may include comments about their home circumstances and their parents' attitudes towards the school, crimes committed in the school and opinions of teachers on behaviour in the school. Many of these observations will be subjective. It is essential that written records be kept as the rate of staff turnover in many areas does not ensure continuity. A guidance teacher may deal with 200–300 pupils, which makes reliance on memory very uncertain.

Guidance staff are also faced with the problem of confidentiality. Their

| | | *Guidance* | | |
	A	*B*	*C*	*D*
Area of interest	Social Education	On-going aspects of 'growing up'	Children under stress	Psycho-therapeutic
Which pupils?	All	All	10–20%	5%
Who deals with this?	All staff	Guidance staff	Guidance staff	Specialists

attitude towards this has a bearing on who has access to these records. Some regard confidences given by the pupil in a one-to-one counselling situation as strictly confidential. Other guidance staff make no such undertaking to the pupil but use their own judgement to decide what is 'in the best interests of the child'. An example might be a boy informing his guidance teacher that he was taking drugs. The 'confidential' approach would be to try to persuade the boy to seek help, but if this failed no further action would be taken. The other approach would be to seek expert help outside school and while the reason for this would be explained in great detail to the boy, it would nevertheless be taken even if the boy did not agree. The majority of guidance staff are inclined towards the second approach, although it is important to realise that 'confidentiality' may present difficulties occasionally. The accessibility of records is a problem which few schools have resolved satisfactorily. Is it really necessary or desirable for all members of staff to know of, say, the home difficulties of particular pupils? Should parents, or indeed the pupils know what is written about them in the records? Should the head teachers have access to all records? These, and many other questions are difficult to answer and each school will find solutions which apply to their own situation. At the same time the rights of the individuals, both parents and child, must be protected. Guidance staff have to examine very carefully their reasons for requiring information about a pupil, making sure that it is contributing towards the helping rôle 'in the best interests of the child'.

The writing of references and reports must depend on someone's knowledge of the pupil. In addition to the general school report which is sent home and indicates academic achievement with occasional comments on classroom behaviour, there are references for employers and reports for children's hearings. The writing of references for pupils leaving school is a serious aspect of a guidance teacher's job, which may have far-reaching consequences. Serious consideration has to be given to the question as to how much information an employer may be entitled. Generally staff are torn between a desire to be fair to the employer and the desire to give the young person every chance to do the best he can. Every teacher can quote instances of disruptive pupils who were rude and insolent and nearly always late and often truants who, within weeks of leaving school, become responsible citizens arriving on time for employment and working well. Is it fair to condemn a pupil because of be- haviour which was undoubtedly aggravated by the school situation? This is something that a guidance teacher has to resolve in each individual case.

Reports for children's hearings are generally prepared by a member of the guidance staff although there are still a few schools where the head teacher writes the report with very little consultation with the guidance team. Most guid- ance staff recognise the need for a full report, especially regarding the attain- ments, behaviour and attitude of the pupil in school. The usefulness of a report will depend on several factors, one of which may be the attitude towards 'confidentiality' in the school concerned.

In the ideal situation the guidance teacher will collect and collate the opinions of all the members of staff involved with the pupil concerned. The final version will be a composite report from all the staff even though it will be signed by the guidance teacher. There is often conflict when the majority of the staff consider the pupil to be disruptive and unco-operative in class while the guidance teacher may have an excellent relationship with the pupil at all times.

It is important for panel members to know how the reports are composed in the schools they serve. Members should also be very careful about quoting the name of the signatory to the report to pupils and parents. All too often panel members have quoted the guidance teacher as having certain opinions on the pupil's behaviour and attitude whereas this is not the opinion of the guidance teacher but a consensus of opinion of the staff as a whole. This type of action may result in the breakdown of a meaningful relationship between the guidance teacher and the pupil which has often taken a long while to establish. A consequence of this has been that future reports to the hearing are more restrained and full co-operation and confidence is no longer given to the hearing. It is far more accurate and equally effective to quote comments as coming from 'the school' or 'your teachers' rather than attributing the comments to the guidance teacher who, in most cases, is merely acting as a spokesman for the rest of the staff.

Provision of a planned guidance programme

Usually a guidance programme is administered as weekly periods of group discussion with 12–15 pupils, generally of mixed ability. The group leader (guidance teacher) is expected to participate in a non-directive capacity allowing the group to come to their own decisions and conclusions while making sure that they do so with the knowledge of all the facts in a situation. Special skills and techniques are required to handle this kind of discussion which differs from the traditional pattern of classroom communication between teacher and pupil.

While discussion can sometimes be completely unstructured and based on topics introduced by the pupils, the majority of guidance teams prefer a planned programme which broadens the pupils' perspective and at the same time allows for consideration of local and topical items. A guidance programme will cover three elements:

(a) *guidance for leisure;*
(b) *careers or vocational guidance;*
(c) *personal guidance.*

Into all these areas will come an element of self-assessment, especially in personal and vocational guidance. Pupils learn to come to terms with themselves as they are and as they would like to be. They also learn to understand and accept each other. There are many approaches to self-assessment both through simple games as well as through use of the 'interest guides' which require special training for their administration and interpretation.

(a) Guidance for leisure is becoming increasingly important in schools. Leisure activities have broadened to include many interests outwith those normally associated with the physical education department.

Hobbies afternoons are a common feature in many schools and it is hoped that pupils will find an interest which may continue into adult life.

(b) Careers and vocational guidance play an important part in any guidance programme. Details about careers and their entry requirements are available and discussion ranges over a broad series of topics concerned with the world of work. Most schools have a specialist careers officer available at specific times in school for advice on job opportunities and entrance qualifications for further education and training. Parents also have an opportunity to consult the careers officer.

The selection of a suitable course at the end of the second year is a most important part of vocational guidance. Correct advice at this stage will ensure that each pupil follows a balanced course within his own ability. Disruptive behaviour in schools can often be directly attributed to the fact that some pupils are on courses which are beyond their ability and as a consequence they become bored. In many schools, because of staff shortage in certain departments, there is very little the staff can do to remedy this situation.

(c) Personal guidance as part of a planned programme is of major importance. Pupils are given an opportunity to examine their own problems and attitudes by looking at hypothetical situations. When confronted with the question 'What would you do if your parents discussed you with other adults in your presence?' pupils reacted very unfavourably. Transferred to the situation of a children's hearing this has implications for panel members.

Liaison with outside agencies

Guidance staff in school are expected to liaise fully with parents, social workers, children's panels, police, primary schools, medical services and many other agencies. Liaison with parents is an important part of a guidance teacher's job. Many schools make sure that parents are aware of the non-teaching times of the guidance staff so that appointments can be easily arranged. In other schools, guidance staff may make themselves available during the evenings. Parents are being informed far earlier than previously when problems occur with their children in schools and are given every opportunity to visit the school for discussion. This applies particularly to poor attendance and disruptive behaviour in the classroom.

Liaison with social workers is especially important when children are on supervision. It is also important to have this link in schools where the guidance policy does not encourage home visits. There are mixed feelings about teachers visiting the home when awkward situations can be created for the pupil and his family. On the other hand there are many parents who resist visiting the school and will not be seen unless by the teacher going to the home.

Most schools have an excellent relationship with the local police. Many 'incidents' are dealt with most successfully at police/school level and two-way consultations about pupils are frequent.

Close contact is also maintained with the 'feeder' primary schools. Guidance staff visit these schools to see the pupils at work and to discuss pupils individually with their teachers. Arrangements are sometimes made for the pupils to visit the secondary school before their transition date.

There is a significant liaison between the school and the children's hearings system. The position regarding reports has been examined. In some areas the guidance staff are invited to attend hearings with the proviso that the parents or the child have the right to object. More and more guidance staff are finding parents and pupils requesting their support at hearings. The experience is valuable for guidance staff and improves their relationship with the pupil and his family.

In some areas where the social work departments are under great pressure, responsibility for supervision has been given to the guidance teachers. All pupils under supervision will be seen regularly by the guidance staff and at the same time close consultation is maintained with the responsible social workers. In school a child can be 'supervised' and given support for the whole of the school day as required.

Guidance staff can also make a valuable contribution to the hearing situation by explaining to all pupils the underlying philosophy of the system and by ensuring that they understand the procedures at the hearing. It is helpful therefore for school staff to have previous warning of the dates of hearings as well as some notice of the decisions made at a hearing.

Panel members are often unaware of the rôle played by the guidance staff in a school and perhaps more time should be spent on this aspect in their initial training. Equally, in some schools, guidance staff are unaware of the aims and methods of the hearings and would welcome the opportunity to attend hearings as observers. Guidance staff and panel members should meet regularly for discussion of their common concerns. Much practical help and assistance can be offered by the guidance teacher to children appearing at hearings and particularly when little or no support is coming from the parents.

Provision of a support system

Although guidance is for all pupils the provision of a support system is the most consuming part of a guidance teacher's time. All pupils are interviewed regularly and children with problems are seen more frequently. The early identification of pupils 'at risk' is an important part of the guidance teacher's remit. The following children would be included:—

(a) *Those from single parent families. In general children cope better with a parent's death than with apparent 'desertion'.*

(b) *Those from large or socially deprived families.*

(c)   *Those children often described as 'invisible' – the shy, the timid, and the friendless who are an easy target for bullies.*

(d)   *Those children who are 'different' may be subjected to teasing or other indignities which can be so traumatic for an adolescent. These may include children who are overweight, coloured or least able and also those who have a different accent or special medical disabilities, e.g. epilepsy.*

(e)   *Those children from families with plenty of money who have 'everything' – except love and affection.*

The support given to these children may be temporary or permanent. In all cases the aim of the guidance support system is not to remove the stress but to reduce it to a level which is tolerable for the child.

The period of secondary education coincides with the onset of adolescence and the influence that a school can have on young people during this time must not be underestimated. Guidance work, dealing with children and problems is a long-term exercise in which there are no instant reformations or cures. Its effective operation depends on the co-operation and understanding of the whole staff, especially the head teacher. Research work in England has shown that in schools with good guidance systems there has been a reduction in truancy and vandalism, pupil/teacher relationships have improved and pupil satisfaction with the educational provision has increased. Without doubt a good guidance team is essential to the well-being of any school and is here to stay.

16

CHILD GUIDANCE

DOUGLAS A. F. CONOCHIE

CHILD GUIDANCE is an essential element in the structure of social, educational and medical services and its importance is recognised by all those whose work brings them into contact with children. The historical origins of the service in Scotland and in England account for the very different structure and development. The English service evolved from the American pattern which had been established in 1909 by William Healy as a service to the Chicago Juvenile Court. This stressed the interdisciplinary approach with a team of workers carrying out the medical, psychiatric, psychological and social investigation of individual children. The team leader is a psychiatrist in most instances.

The Scottish provision emerged a little later from the efforts of a group of voluntary workers who maintained two clinics, one with an educational bias and the other with a medical approach. The first clinic established in 1927 later became the joint responsibility of the education department and the school health service. The orientation has remained educational and psychologists with teaching experience form the majority of staff. Medical consultants and social workers are part of the staff group but the emphasis is clearly educational. The Education (Scotland) Act 1946 gave local authorities statutory powers to provide a child guidance service in clinics or elsewhere. By 1964 a service had been established in 27 out of the 35 administrative areas.

The Education (Scotland) Act 1969, Section 3a,[1] took the final step in the establishment of child guidance services by making their provision mandatory on each local education authority. This Act stated:

> It shall be the *duty* of every education authority to provide for their area a child guidance service in child guidance clinics or elsewhere and the functions of that service shall include –
>
> (a)   the study of handicapped, backward and difficult children;
> (b)   the giving of advice to parents and teachers as to appropriate methods of education and training for such children;
> (c)   in suitable cases, the provision of special education for such children in child guidance clinics;
> (d)   the giving of advice to a local authority within the meaning of the

Social Work (Scotland) Act 1968 regarding the assessment of the needs of any child for the purpose of any of the provisions of that or any other enactment.

The same Act also extended the statutory duties of the child guidance service by requiring that the ascertainment of children for special education should include a psychological as well as a medical examination.

The reorganisation of local government in 1975 made it necessary for each of the new regions to consider how best to implement the 1969 Act. The Paterson Report on the management structure of the new authorities[2] had advised in para. 6.8 'Headquarters would lay down professional and administrative guidelines and provide specialist or advisory services on such matters as care of the homeless, family casework problems, education advisory services and child guidance'. The Scottish principal educational psychologists suggested a staffing ratio of one educational psychologist to 3,000 pupils as a realistic minimum for the provision of an adequate service.

The medium sized authorities – Grampian, Tayside, Fife, Central, Highlands, and Dumfries and Galloway – have appointed regional principal educational psychologists with administrative oversight of their child guidance services though these differ in their internal structures. The Lothian Region has a division of special services, with an educational psychologist in charge as head of the division; this region currently also supplies a service to the Borders. Strathclyde does not have a psychologist in charge of a regional service. Instead, each of the five divisions continues to have a relatively large service under a principal psychologist, the services being administered at regional level by a depute director of education. The three island authorities have appointed principal psychologists to carry out the functions of the child guidance service.

Although the staffing ratio of one psychologist to 3,000 pupils has been accepted as that required before an efficient service can be offered, most regions are a long way from achieving this mainly because of a lack of trained staff. In 1973 there were just over 200 educational psychologists, full-time and part-time, employed by local authorities. The principals' report[3] estimated that 346 were needed as a minimum, and that 383 would be a more satisfactory figure at which to aim. Thus the national picture indicates that child guidance services are at least 40% understaffed as far as psychologists are concerned. This restricts much of the work that can be undertaken and has an adverse effect on the quality of work, particularly when statutory duties exist in respect of special education and children's hearings.

As distinct from practice in England, the initiative for establishing child guidance services has been taken in Scotland by the education committee of the local authority, and the service is organised and administered by an educational psychologist responsible to the education committee. Nevertheless, close liaison with the child health service is maintained. The establishment of the social work department resulted in a single agency becoming responsible for those referrals which, prior to 1968, had come from courts, from probation officers, from children's officers and from welfare workers. For those children who require psychiatric help, links have been built up between the child guidance service and the psychiatric services of the area health boards. Referrals to the consultant psychiatrist are often made directly but none is made without prior consultation with the school medical officer and/or the general practitioner and on some occasions the referral is made through their agency. Consultation may take place at the hospital, in child guidance clinics or even in the schools. The method of referral and the venue are determined by what seems to be in the best interests of the child and family.

The child guidance service is an educational provision and children are referred because they have educational difficulties which may result from intellectual, emotional or social causes. But the educational psychologist has come to be recognised not only as the person who should deal with educational difficulties of any sort, particularly backwardness and learning difficulties, but also as a person who deals with problems of behaviour, personality or emotional disturbance.[4] In addition to his academic training the educational psychologist must have a recognised teaching qualification. Appointment to a post is followed by a period of in-service training supervised by the principal. The experience derived from the academic discipline in psychology, from the professional training and from the practice of teaching in the classroom is invaluable in differentiating between behaviour which may be sufficiently abnormal to merit further investigation and conditions which are little more than normal reactions to abnormal situations and which are common features of the emotional and social development of children. At the same time, the psychologist has first-hand appreciation of classroom conditions and of the many difficulties which may arise there.

The breadth of approach of the child guidance service and its function as an essential part of the educational system bring the eductional psychologist into constant contact with other persons who have responsibilities for children. It is not just the handicapped, the deprived, the disturbed or the delinquent children with whom contact is made, but also the great number of healthy and academically successful children who are under the care of their parents and teachers, youth leaders, counsellors and career masters. National research projects, transfer examinations and gradings also bring the psychologist into direct contact with the normal child. The development of advisory services for primary as well as secondary schools, for general curriculum development as well as specific subjects allows for the co-operation of psychologist with agencies whose working relationship is with the whole school population.

When making an appraisal of a problem, whether it concerns a handicapped, a backward or a difficult child, the educational psychologist will carry out an assessment. Such an assessment will take into account the intellectual, physical, emotional and environmental factors which have contributed to the child's present development stage. It will not necessarily be completed in the course of one interview nor will it necessarily provide an all-embracing solution. The child is seen as often as is necessary and possibly in different contexts, the classroom, the clinic and the home, alone and with a group. The level of his potential for intellectual development, his present educational attainment, and the extent of his social and emotional difficulties are all considered and measured where appropriate. The results will be discussed with parents, teachers and others, if necessary. This comprehensive approach emphasises the importance that the psychologist attaches to treating the child as a total personality to be developed rather than as a patient with an illness which can be quickly cured.

Much confusion surrounds the concept of intelligence which psychologists tend to use in a specialised sense. How the psychologist measures intelligence and what the 'IQ' really tells one about an individual are often misunderstood. Most people would agree that intelligence has something to do with the way a person tackles a problem, how he acts – which one can observe directly – and how he thinks, which one can observe only indirectly by inference from the actions he takes or the thoughts he expresses. A helpful distinction was introduced by Hebb, a Canadian psychologist who studied the effect of brain damage on intelligence.[5] He postulated the concept of 'Intelligence A', the innate potential determined by the genetic inheritance of the individual. This was developed as 'Intelligence B', the capacities acquired during early childhood, which cannot develop in the absence of suitable environmental stimulation. Vernon[6] further suggested that there was an 'Intelligence C' which was represented by an IQ score or some other test score which was only a sampling of 'Intelligence B', which in its turn was not a perfect reflection of innate potential.

Many schools submit reports on pupils and quote an IQ. This is generally derived from a verbal reasoning test administered at age 9 or 11 as a requirement for transfer to secondary education. This is a group test, given to a whole class at one time and is of a pencil-and-paper type. It has been found to be a good predictor of success in an academic type of education but it has been shown to be too dependent on reading ability so that this 'IQ' or rather verbal reasoning quotient may easily underestimate the potential of the child.

The most accurate assessment of a child's potential and attainment will be obtained by an educational psychologist who will administer a wide range of individual tests. Intelligence will be assessed using verbal items covering vocabulary, comprehension, information, analogies and number and also using performance items such as construction of designs from coloured blocks, coding, mazes, sequential arrangement of pictures and simple jig-saw puzzles under strictly standardised conditions. Reading and arithmetic attainments will also be checked using standardised tests so that the performance of the individual can be checked against the average child of similar age. During the administration of these tests, which may take two or more sessions, the educational psychologist will also make subjective assessments of the level of concentration the child shows, the general attitude and level of anxiety. Further investigation of personality or of perceptual problems may also take place but all the time the psychologist will be assessing the relationship that has been established with the child and whether this can be continued in the form of psychological treatment.

A number of avenues are available for treatment. Treatment can be undertaken in the clinic. This may involve the further investigation of the learning difficulty or the emotional disturbance, continuing the process of assessment into the treatment situation. Specific remedial help may be undertaken and further advice given to the teacher as the effects of treatment become apparent and the child's achievements rise and his attitudes to learning change. Having scrutinised the interpersonal relationships affecting the child and adults in his environment, the psychologist is able to advise parents and teachers on the handling of the child. Treatment may be supplemented by modification of the school environment. The curriculum may be changed or the educational placement varied as in a special class or school, day or residential. Collaboration between the psychologist and the school will extend the child guidance service into the classroom. The psychologist may refer the child for other specialised treatment or advice from the remedial teacher, school medical officer or psychiatrist.

In the primary school remedial teachers are an extension of the child guidance service. It is their responsibility to remedy educational difficulties in basic subjects. Surveys are carried out to ascertain those children needing help and individual programmes of work are supplied. Cases of extreme difficulty, or low ability or poor progress are referred to the psychologist for further advice.

The remedial teacher is a specially trained, experienced primary teacher whose aim is to assist the class teacher with those primary children who have specific learning difficulties. As one of the aims of modern primary education is the social education and social integration of the individual child it is important that children with particular problems are not isolated from their peers unless such a course of action is unavoidable. It is therefore the responsibility of the remedial teacher not only to identify the particular problem of the slow learner but also to show the class teacher how such a problem can be minimised or overcome.

The child guidance service has much contact with the child health service. The investigations of the school medical officers are important in that they can indicate whether physical defects or ill-health do or do not exist and to what extent they contribute to the child's difficulties. The school medical officer also plays an important rôle in bringing to the notice of the educational psychologist children observed as a result of routine medical examinations at which problems other than the purely physical are noted. The relationship between the two departments is at its closest in the ascertainment of the various categories of handicapped children where each submits reports and recommendations to the Director of Education.

Psychiatric referral often results in treatment being undertaken at hospital clinics. The psychologist may have a part to play in the transmission of information to the teacher, and the modification of the school situation to ensure the efficacy of treatment.

In respect of guidance and counselling in secondary schools, educational psychologists have long advocated the need for a broadly based system. The educational psychologist has always studied the abnormal individual against a background of normal growth and development. Educational psychology has emphasised social factors, and has promoted remedial training and re-education rather than treatment on a one-to-one basis, analogous to the relationship of patient and doctor. For this reason the child guidance service welcomes and is at pains to promote the establishment of counsellors in schools. But it would be wrong to consider the latter as an extension of the educational psychologist on to the classroom floor. The rôle of the counsellor is to take an overall view of the child's educational experience, involving processes of social and emotional as well as intellectual development, and to help pupils with the decisions that have to be made at significant stages of their school careers. From time to time he will come across children who seem unable to respond to normal methods of help, or where the degree of abnormality is such that the resources of the school are manifestly inadequate. It is at this stage that counsellors must be prepared to call on the specialist services available, and in particular on the child guidance service.

In 1971 Aberdeenshire Education Committee published a report on *Guidance in Secondary Schools*.[7] To quote that report on the subject of guidance and counselling: 'Guidance is a total school responsibility. The educational psychologist has a vital specialist rôle to play in the guidance of pupils. In addition to the specialist skills which they can lend in support of the school guidance staff, educational psychologists have the advantage of being trained teachers who have transferred to the psychological service only after successful experience in teaching itself. More than any other teachers they are already experienced and active in the guidance field through their work with the increasing number of pupils who are referred to them by head teachers when the resources of the school cannot provide the specialist assistance which these pupils need. They have a wealth of experience of home visitations and of the problems of parents as well as children. They have well-established contacts with social workers and social service agencies, with medical officers and psychiatrists and with other agencies whose assistance they can enlist in helping pupils and parents who find themselves in situations of difficulty. The liaison with schools and educational psychologists is already well-founded, and their co-operation will be more than ever necessary when schools have their own guidance organisations. In the initial stages of the introduction of guidance in schools they can be expected to play a major part in the in-service training of housemasters.'

The Education (Scotland) Act 1969 gave child guidance services a specific remit to provide advice regarding the assessment of the needs of any child under the provisions of the Social Work (Scotland) Act 1968. This meant that links had to be established between social workers and educational psychologists. In 1973 the Scottish Division of Educational and Child Psychology of the British Psychological Society carried out a review of Scottish services in order to determine trends in the changing rôle of educational psychologists.[8] An analysis of sources of referral showed that those from a social agency rose from $2 \cdot 3\%$ in 1971 to $6 \cdot 6\%$ in 1972 and to $7 \cdot 7\%$ in 1973.

A supplementary questionnaire completed by 22 Scottish child guidance services elicited the following information:

Referrals from Social Work Departments during the session 1972–1973

Referrals	Number of cases
For exchange of information	889
For treatment	283
For assessment for the reporter	953

Contact with the Children's Panel	Often	Occasionally	Never
(a) Through the reporter	14	7	1
(b) Through the social worker	11	11	–
(c) By attendance at hearings	–	3	19

'All counties' it was noted 'anticipated receiving increased demands for their services and would be prepared to receive more referrals for the assessment of children before the stage at which the children's hearing is held.'

Through the network of services in which they are involved educational psychologists are in close contact with the teachers of all those children who may appear at hearings. In the primary school this will be the class teacher, remedial teacher and head teacher; in the secondary school it may be the form teacher but more likely the guidance teacher or year master and head teacher. Access is available to a wealth of information about a child's educational development. In addition, many children have been seen by child guidance services and reports are available. In some authorities, a routine has been established whereby those children who have been brought to the attention of the reporter are automatically notified to the child guidance centre; records are then searched and up-to-date psychological assessments are provided. Where a child is receiving treatment, the educational psychologist may not be aware of the possible delinquency and the information is welcomed. If the matter is pursued by the reporter and school reports are sought by the social worker, copies of these are routinely received by the child guidance service.

The process of ascertainment for special education is often misunderstood, the educational psychologist being seen as the person who 'puts them away'. Nothing could be further from the truth. The education committee is the only body which can statutorily recommend that a child receive special education and this can only be done after psychological *and* medical examinations have been carried out and the results of these considered by the committee along with any other relevant information that is available. The type of education required will be determined by the nature of the learning difficulty experienced by the child which may be caused by deafness, blindness, physical handicap, mental handicap or maladjustment. Social or emotional factors will determine whether the appropriate setting should be a day school or a residential schoool. A wide range of facilities is available though in many cases the number of places available is insufficient. While the request for consideration may come from many sources, day school, parent, psychiatrist, paediatrician, hearing or assessment team, the education committee is responsible for placement, for ensuring attendance and for the financial commitment.

Thus, if a children's hearing receives educational reports on a child and considers that some form of special educational provision is required, the only resource directly open to them at the moment is a List D school. Other resources are at the command of the education department. As this is a serious step, it is likely that in such cases a full appraisal has been requested from the assessment team. If the team contains an educational psychologist and a medical practitioner, it is comparatively simple to provide the necessary reports and recommendations of examinations required under the Education (Scotland) Act 1969. The wishes of parents will have been considered and often the children's hearing can bring pressure to bear on reluctant parents to accept the educational needs of the child and agree to special provision.

Much the same applies to children who may benefit from treatment by the child guidance service. While the hearing can impose compulsory supervision to be carried out by a social worker, there can only be a recommendation that treatment be sought from the child guidance service. The need for this and the willingness of the service to provide it may well be contained in a report by the educational psychologist, but the hearing can only exhort parents and child to avail themselves of the help offered. Psychological treatment such as is offered by a child guidance service cannot be carried out in an atmosphere of compulsion because so much depends on the ability of the child to make positive relationships with the therapist. This places psychologists in a unique position in relation to the hearings. They are required by law to provide assessments, and because of their professional training they are unlikely to present a report which does not give some indication as to treatment; if however the recommendation involves psychological treatment, they cannot be directed to undertake this. Nevertheless, the psychologist will always be appreciative of the pressure the hearing can bring to bear on parents and child to co-operate in treatment.

In the half century that Scottish child guidance services have existed, much progress has been made but there are still many facets of the work to be developed. With an increased commitment to the education of all children irrespective of the severity of learning difficulties, more emphasis will be given to the assessment of pre-school handicapped children. Concern is now being expressed about the problem created by the 'disruptive' pupil. These disturbed children pose a very special problem for teachers, social workers and psychologists and resources must be allocated to dealing with the situations that develop. While welcoming the institution of multi-disciplinary assessment teams and their inclusion in them, psychologists are conscious of the further demands that are made upon their skills. The demand for more educational psychologists puts a strain on the teaching resources of services, particularly at the present time of expansion, but it is to be hoped that this is a temporary phase. The commitment to assessment under the Social Work (Scotland) Act 1968 is willingly accepted because of the underlying assumption that many of the children who appear before children's hearings as having been 'in trouble' are 'troubled' children. A close liaison between social worker and educational psychologist can serve only to promote the best interests of these children.

REFERENCES

1. The Education (Scotland) Act 1969.
2. *The New Scottish Local Authorities: Organisation and Management Structures* (1973), HMSO.
3. *Principal Educational Psychologist: Child Guidance: The Future – A Working Party Report.* 1972.
4. Petrie and Conochie (1975), *Child Guidance*. Macmillan Education.
5. Hebb, D. O. (1949), *The Organisation of Behaviour*. New York: Wiley.
6. Vernon, P. E. (1950), *The Structure of Human Abilities*. London: Methuen.
7. Aberdeen Education Committee (1975), *Guidance in Secondary Schools* (Ferguson Report).
8. The Changing Role of the Educational Psychologist in Child Guidance Services in Scotland (1975). *Bulletin of the British Psychologist Society*, vol. 28.

17

PSYCHIATRIC SERVICES

KEITH WARDROP

PSYCHIATRY is usually defined as the branch of medicine that is concerned with the diagnosis and treatment of mental illness. As definitions go, however, it is not particularly illuminating. To be of use to the inquiring layman, it needs to be supplemented by a series of explanations of most of the terms used in the definition. How far is diagnosis in psychiatry comparable to diagnosis in other branches of medicine? What is the nature of psychiatric treatment? Most important of all, what do we mean when we talk about mental illness? The present chapter attempts to consider these questions, albeit somewhat cursorily, before going on to examine specific ways in which the work of psychiatrists is or can be of use to children's hearings and the other professionals who work with them, in understanding and helping children in trouble.

Before beginning this discussion it may be worth commenting that the one unambiguous part of the definition is that psychiatry is a branch of medicine. This is true in the formal sense that the title of psychiatrist is used only by medical practitioners with specialised postgraduate training and experience, and in this sense there is a clear distinction to be drawn between the psychiatrist and the psychologist. Psychologists are not medically qualified, and their professional interests are not restricted to the problems of the mentally ill. They are concerned both with the systematic study of human behaviour and experience in all their facets, and with attempts to find solutions to human problems in a variety of 'applied' fields – in education, for example, and in the world of employment, as well as in the clinical setting. A considerable number of psychologists do in fact work with the mentally ill, and although the work they do is characteristically different from that of psychiatrists, there is no doubt – if we are examining the tasks that professional people actually carry out rather than the different formal qualifications they have – that there is a fair amount of overlap, which has tended to grow in recent years.

It is often claimed – and with impeccable intentions – that psychiatric illness is no different from other kinds of illness and that the psychiatric patient is no different from any other patient. Although this statement is completely valid as a moral assertion – that is, as implying that the patients of psychiatrists have the same human rights as any other sick people, the same right to care and treatment, the same right not to be blamed for their condition – no wider interpretation should be placed upon it. It ignores the fact that there are some basic and far-reaching differences between the life-situation of the mentally ill and that of other sick people, and between the treatment approaches open to them. To deny these differences is possibly comforting to the psychiatrist who feels the need to have his medical identity reinforced, but it implies a distorted and potentially harmful view of the problems of the mentally disordered.

Mental illness involves, in varying degrees and in varying combinations, disturbances of thought, of mood, of the emotions, of the capacity to form and maintain relationships with others. What makes the scope of psychiatry peculiarly difficult to define and delimit is the very wide range of degrees of severity of such disturbances. The psychiatrist may see patients whose thought processes are profoundly disordered, who experience gross delusions or hallucinations, and who seem to have virtually no contact with the real world as most people perceive it. He may see patients whose disturbance is primarily one of mood, who are lost in a depression so profound that they are almost withdrawn from life and may indeed be in real danger of self-inflicted death, or who alternate between such a state and an opposite extreme of excitement, elation and euphoria. In such cases he is likely to identify something that is unarguably – or almost unarguably – a disease process, even though its root causes may in the present state of knowledge be impossible to determine. The same psychiatrist however may also see patients who are handicapped by their condition without being wholly disabled. Their anxiety, their depression, their difficulties in coping with the stresses of everyday life or with human relationships may cause great pain and much unhappiness; yet many psychiatrists would argue that the patients in question should be seen as people experiencing problems in living and not as suffering from an illness other than in a metaphorical sense. Problems of the latter type are of course several times more common than the more severe or psychotic conditions. But whereas a high proportion of the latter find their way to the psychiatrist, the less profound disturbances are often wholly neglected (in the sense of not receiving any professional attention) or, if they do come into the orbit of medicine, are commonly dealt with by general practitioners without referral to psychiatric specialists.

It is worth adding that some recently fashionable schools of thought have maintained that no mentally ill people are 'ill' in the conventional medical sense and that all of them, even the most deeply disturbed, are searching for solutions to their human predicament. This is a view which has commanded very little support among psychiatrists; but even the more conservative would probably concede that there are real difficulties in drawing the line that divides 'true' illness from unsuccessful grappling with the problems of existence. It may be argued that the distinction is of only academic interest, and that to the patient needing help the categorisation of his problem is of little importance. But the issue is not merely a theoretical one, for the way in which psychiatric problems are conceptualised is likely to influence profoundly one's views as to how the tasks of diagnosis and treatment should be approached.

In fact, the style of diagnosis in psychiatry is in general quite different from that employed in most other branches of medicine. Usually a provisional diagnosis is made on the basis of case-history and clinical examination, subject to confirmation by radiological or laboratory investigation. Psychiatrists however almost always reach a diagnosis on the basis of accounts of the patient's symptoms and his life-history. Personality assessments made by psychologists using standardised tests may provide valuable information, but essentially these help to build up the general picture. The psychiatrist can never solve his diagnostic problem by looking at an X-ray plate or identifying a pathogenic organism or an abnormal cell pattern under a microscope.

Perhaps the most important feature of the history of psychiatric treatment has been the shift in recent decades towards therapeutic methods characteristic of general medicine. The growing use of physical methods of treatment – and in particular the ever-increasing use during the past twenty-five years of psychotropic drugs – has in many respects revolutionised psychiatry. With custodial care no longer its most common feature and with the potential for achieving dramatic improvements even in seriously disturbed patients, psychiatry has not only transformed the scope and functions of the mental hospital, its traditional setting, but has also moved confidently into the general hospital and the out-patient clinic. There have been setbacks as well as advances however. It has been clear for some time that although the new treatments were extremely effective in relieving symptoms and helping patients to cope with their everyday lives, they were rarely successful in eradicating the underlying condition. Relapse rates are high, and many former patients can avoid a renewal of disabling symptoms only if they walk an emotional tightrope. Much psychiatric illness, in short, is quite different from those conditions which can be permanently cured by decisive intervention (for example, acute appendicitis) and much more like those long-term illnesses (for example, chronic bronchitis, rheumatoid arthritis) where skilful treatment can keep symptoms under control and give the patient long periods of adequate health, but where the fundamental pathology is unchanged and there is always a consequent risk of relapse, indeed of deterioration. It might also be argued that an excessive preoccupation with physical treatments may lead to lack of interest in the patient as a person – his life history, family situation, social pressures, emotional tensions – and in possible ways of helping him to understand himself better, to bring about desirable changes in his life, and to come gracefully to terms with those aspects which cannot be changed. This is not to assert an inevitable antagonism: drug treatment and psychotherapy may go hand in hand, and sometimes do. But the former *can* easily make the latter seem neither necessary nor scientifically respectable, and often does.

If we consider the rôle of psychiatry in relation to the work of children's hearings, it soon becomes clear that there are two opposite dangers that must be avoided: either the potential contribution of psychiatry may be undervalued, because of our uncertain ideas about the problems of the age-group to which the children who come before hearings belong, or its importance may be exaggerated, because of our confusion about the causes of the behaviour responsible for their being there. The great majority of the young people seen are in early to middle adolescence. This is now generally recognised to be a period of development involving considerable physiological and psychological demands on all who pass through it, giving rise to stress and turmoil in varying degrees. Since problems about one's identity and one's relationships with family, with peers and with the wider society are so common in adolescence, it is tempting to assume that personal difficulties and abnormalities of behaviour appearing then are bound to be transitory and do not require any professional intervention. Opposed to the view of adolescent turmoil as a phase which is bound to be outgrown is the view that delinquency is indicative of maladjustment and therefore requires treatment of a psychiatric nature. The terminology of the Kilbrandon Report and the Social Work (Scotland) Act might easily encourage us in the latter direction. They emphasise 'treatment', and for most people the term has primarily medical connotations: treatment is what doctors do. Should we see all delinquents as mentally disturbed and therefore in need of psychiatric treatment?

The truth, as Oscar Wilde remarked, is never pure and rarely simple. In the present instance, it lies rather elusively somewhere between the extreme (and admittedly slightly caricatured) views summarised above. Most young people survive the storms of adolescence more or less unscathed – but some do not. Most young delinquents do not suffer from a serious psychiatric disorder – but some do.

As far as adolescents in general are concerned, studies of unselected populations (i.e. all the children in a particular age-group in a particular community) have been carried out in an attempt to determine what proportion have severe or moderately severe psychiatric disturbance. As the earlier part of this chapter suggests, the demarcation of such categories is very much a matter of judgement, and the resulting statistics should therefore not be taken too literally; they do however provide useful indicators. In a study of children aged 10–11 living in the Isle of Wight,[1] 6·8% were found to have a degree of psychiatric disorder sufficiently handicapping to warrant psychiatric attention, with only one in three of these being judged to have a severe disorder. A follow-up study some four years later found only a slight increase in the prevalence of psychiatric disorder, though a marked shift in the presenting symptoms with a greater frequency of depression and school refusal.[2] On the other hand, a survey in Blackburn, Lancashire, using similar criteria, identified severe psychiatric disorder among 6·2% of boys and 2·6% of girls, and moderate disorder in 14·6% of boys and 11% of girls.[3] The Blackburn children were three years older than those in the original Isle of Wight sample, but the author is inclined to explain the difference in findings in terms of the socio-economic composition of the two areas rather than the difference in the age-groups examined. It seems now to be a fairly common psychiatric opinion[4, 5] that most psychiatric disturbance seen in adolescents has its roots in earlier childhood; and that the miseries and strains of adolescence are coped with more or less adequately according to the strength of personality with which the young person is able to confront them.

If somewhere between one in ten and one in five of all young adolescents appear to be sufficiently disturbed to warrant psychiatric attention, it is almost certain that the corresponding proportion is higher among those in the same age-group who come before children's hearings. There is little to be gained from any attempt to calculate a precise frequency. If we bear in mind the multiplicity of social and psychological factors involved in the causation of delinquent behaviour (see chapter 8), as well as the filtering processes which result in only a fraction of delinquents actually appearing before a hearing (see chapter 3), it becomes obvious that no real significance could be attached to an assertion that this or that per cent of the youngsters in question require psychiatric attention. From the point of view of panel members it is much more important to have an indication of the specific types of problem which suggest that psychiatric advice and possibly treatment may be appropriate. The effective use of psychiatric services is very much dependent on the informed judgement of those who make decisions about referral. In this connection, Haldane's list of relevant problems,[6] though intended primarily for the guidance of family doctors, is of great interest. He includes the following:

1. *Disorders related to separation from parent(s)*

> Under this heading, one would think of:
> (a) the child who, following his own or mother's prolonged period in hospital, is unable to relate to mother in a mutually satisfying way;
> (b) the child or adolescent who, about four months after the loss of a parent by death, separation, or divorce, appears still emotionally disabled in one way or another;
> (c) the child entering infant school, transferring from infant to primary or primary to secondary school, or a recent entrant to secondary school who, some months after a death in the family or the continued illness of an adult on whom dependent (remembering here the importance of grandparents and of pet animals), cannot leave home each morning for school; or who, being previously non-delinquent, develops a delinquent pattern of behaviour such as stealing or absconding from home.

2. *Depressive illness in child or members of a family*

> Examples of these include:
> (a) physical symptoms, overt anxiety, or acting out behaviour in the child or children of a mother who is depressed, especially the mother suffering from unresolved puerperal depression, which need not be clinically 'severe' to have seriously adverse effects on the emotional health of her children;
> (b) the child or adolescent who appears depressed. Depressive disorders in children and adolescents are not rare and if not recognised early can be difficult to treat, with a poor prognosis in terms of the young person's capacity to function effectively;

(c)   talk of suicide, threats to commit suicide, or attempted suicide in children and adolescents. While not all such situations are indicative of depressive conditions, they should always be regarded seriously and never dismissed as gestures.

3. *Other conditions*

Other conditions include the following:

(a)   the child thought to be autistic or the adolescent suspected of having a schizophrenic illness;

(b)   the abnormally anxious child or adolescent, however the anxiety is expressed;

(c)   the child or adolescent who shows obsessional, phobic or apparently hysterical symptoms;

(d)   the child or adolescent who shows significant delays or deviations in psychosexual development or who remains anxious about such development after reassurance by the family doctor;

(e)   the child or adolescent whose appetite or sleep rhythm are disordered without apparent cause;

(f)   the adolescent in a state of confusion and panic, desperate in his desire to be away from parents and school, lost in his attempt to 'find his own feet', including those who express such distress in aggressive or delinquent behaviour;

(g)   the adolescent drug taker who seeks treatment or asks for help in giving up his use of drugs;

(h)   the hyperkinetic, retarded, sometimes brain-damaged child, not responding to medication, whose tense, overactive, aggressive, destructive behaviour is so difficult to tolerate and control;

(i)   the epileptic child or adolescent whose behaviour is aggressive, destructive, sometimes delinquent, whether or not seizures are difficult to control;

(j)   the adolescent with anorexia nervosa, who may require emergency admission to a psychiatric unit;

(k)   the obese child or adolescent, provided that he and parents are capable of undertaking both the psychological and dietary work involved;

(l)   children and adolescents suffering from asthma with a major psychogenic component, including severe cases not responding to pharmacotherapy, are in some areas agreed to be appropriate referrals;

(m) some physically handicapped young people (the treatment of whose physical condition is properly the continuing responsibility of non-psychiatrists) who are so unable to accept, live with, or adapt to their handicap as to require psychiatric treatment in the hope of helping them to do so;

(n)   children and adolescents whose learning disabilities may have a significant emotional component and those who appear to be 'under-achieving' at school because of unresolved emotional problems.

Some of these conditions (for example, 3f, g and h) are likely to recur much more frequently in children's hearings practice than others (for example, 3j, k and l) but since for the disturbed child delinquency may be a symptom with many different meanings, they are none of them unknown. In identifying almost any of these however a fair amount of skilled judgement is called for.

The decision to seek a psychiatric assessment may be made on the basis of observations included in the social work report, occasionally of other pre-liminary reports, or of the impressions formed directly by panel members in the course of their interviews with child and parents. Whatever other factors may have been noted, it is always desirable to seek a psychiatric opinion if there is any likelihood that the child will be recommended for admission to a List D school. In such cases the hearing should be continued to allow an opportunity for an assessment to be obtained. Specialists in child and family psychiatry (unlike most medical consultants) do not expect all their referrals to come from general practitioners. There can however be advantages in consulting with family doctors before children are referred to psychiatrists.

There are different ways in which the psychiatrist can be involved in assessment, but the ideal procedure is for each panel to have access to its own assessment team drawn from the relevant skills and disciplines in its area. Each such assessment team should include a psychiatrist among its members; although not involved in every case, he is available to discuss cases and to see personally those thought to require further investigation. Where such assessment teams are in operation, a level of mutual understanding develops within the team and between the assessment team and members of the children's panel which the team serves, which can become of very great value in helping hearings to reach satisfactory decisions. The psychiatrist who works as a member of such a team can contribute from his own particular experience to the discussion of many cases with which he does not need to be directly in-volved. For panel members and reporters there is the additional advantage of receiving comprehensive assessment reports in which psychiatric findings and opinions are included instead of separate reports from different professionals.

Unfortunately, there are few areas of the country in which facilities for an integrated assessment procedure exist. In most places panel members, while continuing to press for better facilities, must make the best use of whatever resources in skilled personnel their area can offer. Most cases requiring psy-chiatric investigation have to be referred to a psychiatric department where the psychiatrist is not a member of an assessment team and in such cases the report will be submitted independently to the hearing. It is undeniable however that in many parts of Scotland the availability of specialist skills is extremely limited. In October 1974 there were in the whole of Scotland only 23 con-sultants, 15 senior registrars and 10 registrars working wholly in child and adolescent psychiatry, and responsible for providing a service of which assess-ments for children's hearings are only one of many components.[7]

It is reasonable to expect from a psychiatric report not only a formal diagnosis of psychiatric disorder (or of its absence) but also a detailed description of the child's personality and underlying problems and some discussion of the motivation of the delinquent behaviour. In addition, assessment should look to the future as well as present circumstances and previous history and make recommendations as to future treatment and management. In particular the report should indicate whether specific psychiatric treatment would be appropriate.

The other major contribution which psychiatry can make to the work of the hearings system is in continued treatment or management. Cases where a specific psychiatric disorder is found should obviously become mainly the responsibility of psychiatry as far as future treatment is concerned. This might mean that a seriously disturbed child should be admitted to an in-patient psychiatric unit or should receive specialised intensive psychiatric treatment as an out-patient. A requirement that psychiatric treatment be undertaken can be included as a condition of a supervision order. However, just as assessment is a multi-disciplinary process it must equally be recognised that the process of treating and managing the case also involves team work. Even in those very disturbed cases where psychiatry must make the major contribution to treatment other disciplines are also involved. There are very many cases however where there is no psychiatric disorder as such to be given specific treatment. This does not mean that the psychiatrist has nothing to contribute to the continued management of such cases. If treatment is a multi-disciplinary process carried on by a team, then the psychiatrist has his place in such a team. His rôle may be a fairly direct one, seeing the child for individual interviews or in taking part in group work, or in working with the families of the young people while the actual treatment of the latter is carried on by someone else. In other cases the rôle of the psychiatrist in the team may be less direct, namely that of being a support to those who are in direct contact with the case.

Particularly in regard to the treatment of young people in residential institutions this is the most important task that the psychiatrist can carry out. When visiting such institutions on a regular basis, the psychiatrist will be asked to assess some of the more obviously disturbed cases in the institution and to make recommendations on their management. He may also be involved in some on-going therapy with these cases. In general however the most useful rôle that he can play in the institution is that of taking part in discussion of cases with the staff, helping the latter to understand the underlying nature of the problems, helping them to interpret different patterns of behaviour and so encouraging them to utilise situations in a therapeutic and positive rather than in a harmful and negative way. Perhaps one of the most difficult tasks that human beings are called upon to do is to work day in day out in a residential institution for disturbed and delinquent young people. The demands put upon the staff of such institutions are very considerable and often they have had little preliminary training for this work. The psychiatrist has therefore an extremely important rôle to play in helping and supporting such staff.

The forms of treatment most likely to be offered to the young person referred to the psychiatrist after a children's hearing are individual and group psychotherapy. The nature of these is often misunderstood by laymen, and it must be admitted that psychiatrists themselves have not always been particularly helpful in making their methods better understood. As far as individual psychotherapy is concerned, perhaps the most important feature is the gradual building up of a relationship of trust with the child and the family. Within this relationship defensiveness can be reduced, a sense of security engendered, and underlying problems and tensions brought to the surface and explored. It is not a matter, for the psychiatrist, of isolating some crucial childhood event which, once uncovered, both explains and magically eliminates the problem which has brought the patient to treatment. Rather he is concerned to unravel the significance of a set of problems, in the context of the patient's life-history and present circumstances, to encourage self-awareness, to enhance self-esteem and to mobilise the patient's inner resources for self-help.

Individual psychotherapy, however, though very valuable in selected cases, does not have a major contribution to make in the psychiatric treatment of young delinquents. Group therapy on the other hand has considerably more to offer. Delinquency so often arises from a failure to establish satisfactory social relationships that it seems logical to use the social interaction of a small group as a medium of treatment. Group therapy involves a series of meetings of a small group of 'patients', usually of the same age-group and with a common problem. It is the group members themselves who decide what to discuss, with the therapist remaining as far as possible in the background, intervening only to guide and interpret the discussion at suitable points. The discussion of private and emotionally significant subjects is encouraged, and it is important to maintain a permissive atmosphere in which aggressive attitudes and mutual criticism can be openly expressed and openly examined. The group as a whole gradually acquires a certain identity of its own and provides a supportive framework for individual members. The aim of the therapist is the difficult one of unobtrusively using the group situation so that individual members achieve greater insight into other people's problems and into their own, and can be guided towards less egocentric and more socially constructive patterns of behaviour. In the particular form of group therapy known as psycho-drama, the patient presents dramatised episodes from his life, helped by a cast selected from other patients and members of staff. In trying to bring the characters to life he must to some extent identify himself with them and may consequently come to see them and himself with greater objectivity. This insight can be deepened by the open discussion which follows the 'performance' and by the summing-up, in which the therapist draws out the implications of the experience.

Group therapy as described above, though more generally useful with disturbed young delinquents than individual psychotherapy, is nevertheless a process in which verbal expression plays a very important part and tends therefore to require a reaonable level of intelligence and verbal ability. For the many adolescent delinquents who are below average intelligence and have limited capacity for verbal self-expression, group therapy of this kind does not have a great deal to offer. Such young people can only respond to therapy in groups where the group is centred around activity. Many types of activity are appropriate, including handwork, metal work, clay modelling and art. In activity group therapy with the younger age range art therapy groups have been found extremely productive, art being a valuable medium of expression for the adolescent who is too old to express himself through play, but not old enough nor sufficiently verbal to express himself in words. The older adolescents require more loosely structured groups in which there is not only a choice of activity offered but a choice of therapeutic personnel running the group, with whom the individuals can begin to relate. Such group therapy with the older adolescent age range tends to resemble ordinary youth club activity, but it differs in working with smaller and more highly selected groups, groups of people who are very disturbed and often unpredictable in their behaviour. It has therefore to be run by skilled therapists drawn from the disciplines of psychiatry, social work, psychology, nursing and occupational therapy.

The principal aim of this chapter has been to show that there are important areas of overlap between the concerns of panel members and those of psychiatrists. It is not and should never be the business of the psychiatric services to take over responsibility for young people in trouble, or even to see children's hearings simply as a source of patients. There are however many ways, both formal and informal, in which psychiatrists can contribute constructively to the work of the juvenile justice system; for this to be possible it is essential that there should be a clear understanding of both the potential and the limitations of contemporary psychiatric practice.

REFERENCES

1. Rutter, M., Tizard, J. and Whitmore, K. (1970), *Education, Health and Behaviour*. Longman.
2. Graham, P. and Rutter, M. (1973), Psychiatric Disorder in the Young Adolescent: A Follow-up Study. *Proc. R. Soc. Med.*, **66**, 1226–1229.
3. Leslie, Shirley A. (1974), Psychiatric Disorder in the Young Adolescents of an Industrial Town. *Brit. J. Psychiat.*, **125**, 113–124.
4. Masterson, J. F. (1970), *The Psychiatric Dilemma of Adolescence*. Churchill.
5. Rutter, M., Graham, P., Chadwick, O. F. D. and Yule, W. (1976), Adolescent Turmoil: Fact or Fiction? *J. Child Psychol. Psychiat.*, **17**, 35–36.
6. Haldane, J. D. (1972), How to use Child Psychiatry. *Brit. Med. J.*, **3**, 520–522.
7. Child Psychiatry Section, Scottish Division, Royal College of Psychiatrists (1974), *Psychiatric Services for Children, Adolescents and their Parents*.

18

INTERMEDIATE TREATMENT

GEOFF APLIN

IN RECENT YEARS social workers have become increasingly conscious of the shortcomings of the services they can offer directly to children in need. For the most part these services have taken two forms: individual supervision or counselling where a child meets with one social worker while continuing to live at home; and residential care where the child is removed from home, usually for a substantial period of time. For some children, individual supervision is the most appropriate approach to meet the child's need, particularly where there is no adult who fulfils the dual parental functions of care and direction. However it is questionable whether the widespread practice of providing a short meeting in the office of a supervising social worker on a weekly or fortnightly basis can adequately meet his needs. A similar argument can be put forward in the case of residential care. Undoubtedly the home situation of many children can be seen to exacerbate rather than ameliorate the child's problems. Indifference to the well-being of the child, endless family conflicts, and the deliberate scapegoating of children are but a few of the many reasons suggesting that a child's interests would be best served if he were removed from home. However, it is far from clear that all children who are taken into residential care suffer from home situations which in themselves justify their removal. Frequently, such a decision is taken because individual supervision has failed to yield any appreciable results. The persistent truant continues to stay away from school, the child with a record of petty crime continues and perhaps increases these activities. For such children there is little evidence to suggest that such a drastic step as removal from home provides a solution to their difficulties. If anything, removal from the local community causes additional problems for the child for not only must he cope with breaking the links with his family, but in time, he is faced with the difficult task of building them all over again.

Faced with these difficulties, many supervising social workers have taken pains to make supervision more effective. Some have substituted activities for the traditional talking sessions. Others have varied their meeting place, choosing to meet, for example, in a park or disco. Others again have developed group supervision, sometimes confining this to children on supervision and sometimes including their friends. These variations have not always proved successful and it is rare to find a social work agency which has adopted, on a continuing basis, an alternative to the more traditional one-to-one supervision format. However, the widespread search for alternatives undoubtedly contributed to the proposal in the White Paper 'Children in Trouble'[1] that local authority social services departments should develop services for children intermediate between supervision in the home and committal to care.

The legal framework for intermediate treatment

The term 'intermediate treatment' does not appear in either the Children and Young Persons Act (1969) or the Social Work (Scotland) Act 1968. It has been borrowed from the White Paper 'Children in Trouble' to embrace some of the proposals for new approaches to the supervision of children which appear in these Acts.

Section 12(2) of the Children and Young Persons Act (1969) enables the court to include in a supervision order a requirement that the child or young person under 14 or between 14 and 17 found in need of care or control shall comply with any of three directions given to him by his supervisor, namely: (i) to live at a specified place for a specified length of time, (ii) to participate in specified activities, and (iii) to report to a specified person when required. These special requirements can take two forms:

(a) *that a child should live for a single period at a place specified by the supervisor for up to 90 days. This direction has to be given within twelve months of it being entered on the supervision order. The single period rule means that if a child is directed to attend a seven-day camp, he cannot be required to attend additional camps, and the remaining 83 days will be lost;*

(b) *that the child shall comply with the direction given from time to time by the supervising officer. Such an arrangement may last for three years with a maximum of thirty days taking place each year. It is most common for supervising officers to request this second requirement as this allows a greater degree of flexibility.*

In addition to specifying conditions for alternative approaches to supervision, the 1969 Act recognised that it would be necessary to identify appropriate residential and community-based facilities to which children might be directed. Section 19 required that Children's Regional Planning Committees, joint committees formed by groups of local authorities, should draw up a list of all facilities which might be appropriately used for this purpose. It also specified that a supervisor shall not give a direction under section 12(2) if it involves facilities which are not included in the schedule drawn up under section 19, each of which has to be approved by the Secretary of State.

With these conditions for supervision, and plans for a network of additional facilities, the 1969 Act provided a clearly defined legal framework for the development of intermediate treatment in England and Wales. By contrast, no precise legal framework of this kind exists in Scotland. Here, intermediate treatment has developed under section 12 of the 1968 Social Work (Scotland) Act which states – 'It shall be the duty of every local authority to promote social welfare by making available advice, guidance and assistance on such a scale as may be appropriate for that area by securing or arranging for the provision of such residential and other establishments as they may consider suitable and adequate. . . .'

This has allowed Scottish social work departments greater freedom to conceive and promote intermediate treatment facilities. It also allows greater freedom in the choice of children who may participate. 'Any child (under 18) requiring assistance in kind . . . may be taken into care or referred to a children's hearing where such assistance appears to the local authority likely to diminish the need.' Children's panels, for their part may write in a condition of attendance at an intermediate treatment facility, although this may not continue without review for more than one year.

Early developments

The Regional Committees set up under the 1969 Act published their lists of intermediate treatment facilities early in 1973. Many were of formidable length. For the most part they included youth organisations and recreational facilities which were already established in the different regions, and this highlighted the absence of clear guidelines for the task. By implication, scout troops, handicraft clubs or swimming clubs, when combined with individual supervision, could provide the necessary 'treatment' to meet the needs of the children referred to them. For some, this assumption was correct. For those who could abide by rules, who could accept authority figures, who could collaborate with others, but for some reason, perhaps shyness, needed that final push, such organisations were entirely appropriate. However, many of the children who might be considered as strong candidates, had deliberately turned their backs on such organisations. Others had already proved themselves too disruptive and had been banned from the very organisations which were now being proposed as intermediate treatment resources. It was against this confused background that the first intermediate treatment officer appointments were made. It would fall to them to make sense of the situation.

Local authorities have varied widely in the priority they have given to intermediate treatment. By no means all saw the need for special appointments. Indeed, in Scotland, only one such appointment was made. Where appointments were made, freedom of action was in some cases curtailed, leaving the officer to make the best use he could of the existing list. However, in a number of authorities the shortage of local resources which could provide support and help to young people with social and emotional difficulties has been recognised, and the officer has been encouraged to draw up plans to meet the problem. Where this situation obtains three options seem to be open to him. First, he could build links with existing youth organisations with a view to modifying existing practices or collaborating in new ventures. Second, he could explore possibilities of collaborating with education authorities, particularly around the problem of truancy. Third, he could propose special projects to be initiated by the social services department.

The making of links with youth and community services would seem a logical development. Frequently the child on supervision is known to the local youth leader. However, if he is already a club member, continued membership under the same conditions is unlikely to meet his needs. If he has decided against membership or has been excluded from the club, the same argument would apply. Links with youth leaders mean in practice that something additional to routine membership is called for. This he is not often free to provide. He has the interests of the majority of his members to consider. They look to him to see that the club runs smoothly. If he makes allowances for a disruptive youngster he might incur the disfavour of his regular members and he has to weigh this very carefully. At the present time it would appear that only a minority of youth centre wardens would be prepared to contemplate any special provision for young people on supervision. Where this is undertaken, only limited numbers can be considered, and the exercise calls for a responsibe membership. Bacon[2] cites an example where two boys on supervision were referred to a youth leader by their probation officer. His immediate recourse was to seek the support of his members' committee to help the boys settle in. The subsequent interest and support which this committee provided to these new entrants was no more than any entrant might receive but was sufficient to lead to their active and continued involvement.

While links with conventional youth clubs are often difficult to establish, a much more ready response has come from those engaged in specialised and unattached youth work. The street corner worker and the adventure playground leader share these same clients and are often happy to collaborate in an intermediate treatment scheme, although the element of compulsion in the English system raises some problems for them. Few such workers have offered intermediate treatment on a formal basis for this reason. One notable exception is the Youth Development Trust[3] which has undertaken a carefully evaluated programme in which they have provided groupwork to children referred by Manchester Social Services Department.

At a time when youth services are beginning to explore ways of sharing intermediate treatment with social services departments, there seems to be little evidence that links are being established with education departments. Schools traditionally have tended to seek solutions to their problems either within the school or at least within the range of resources provided by the education department. At one time the growth of 'free schools' suggested a greater willingness to take account of the child in his total community. Such were ideal resources for intermediate treatment. However, their recent decline in numbers is everyone's loss.[4]

A further resource developed by education departments outside the school has been the truancy centre. This has its counterpart in the special unit within the school. Recent thinking appears to be shifting in favour of the school based unit, but one notable example of collaboration between education and social services survives in the form of the Islington Family Service Unit Intermediate Treatment Centre.[5] This Centre provides alternative schooling to a small number of children who subsequently return to their day school.

The third option open to the intermediate treatment officer, namely that social services departments should develop their own programmes, is the one which has seen the greatest activity. Examination of the pattern as it has developed reveals little consistency in either perceived objectives or the methods employed to carry them out. Different reports of work in progress reflect these different expectations. It is intensive supervision. It is a method of helping deviants to conform. It is concerned with prevention – prevention of court appearances, prevention of re-offending, prevention of being taken into care. It is a groupwork approach to social work with children in difficulty. It is concerned to provide for those who are not attracted to, or who are deterred from, participating in existing community facilities. It is concerned to provide for all those young people at risk in the community.

The majority of these statements identify young people appearing before juvenile courts because of offences committed or failure to respond to supervision as the primary target group. However, this cannot be implied from all. Those who propose that intermediate treatment should be provided for all those at risk in the community embrace not merely the delinquent but any child in need of care. This reflects a shift away from an emphasis on children in trouble to the spirit of the 1963 Children and Young Persons Act which gave wide powers to what were then children's departments to prevent children whatever their age being taken into care.

This difference in emphasis has been reflected in the variety of resources developed under the umbrella of intermediate treatment. Perhaps the most common approach has been for a group of social workers to band together to take a group of children on supervision camping. This might be a one-off event or might run to a number of camps. Some have been hastily conceived and others have been planned with considerable care.[6] Another approach has been the provision of a series of weekly group meetings for children on supervision.[7] Here again, the clarity of objectives and the skill with which these have been put into practice have varied widely. At the other end of the spectrum, specialist intermediate treatment centres have been established. Among these may be numbered a 24-hour community resource centre,[8] and a ninety-day residential treatment centre.[9]

These are but a few of the host of resources which claim to provide intermediate treatment. Some have sufficient permanence to be added to regional lists, but a great many are short-lived efforts developing out of the initiative of one or more members of a social work team, and it is likely that *ad hoc* activity of this kind will continue until firmer guidelines for the development of services and the standard of practice expected in them are provided.

Bringing order to intermediate treatment thinking

With such a plethora of resources now claiming to provide intermediate treatment, systematic thinking is called for which can provide a sense of order. At present, intermediate treatment would appear to function as a kind of licence to experiment, but to do so without taking account of other facilities which are or might be available. Ideally the intermediate treatment officer should be able to call on a wide range of resources, and to match them to the varying needs of children. But what form should this range of resources take?

The first attempt at a conceptual design for intermediate treatment was undertaken by Paley and Thorpe.[10] These authors examine and compare a variety of intermediate treatment projects. From their findings they create a framework within which different examples of work of this kind may be placed, and their particular functions highlighted. With such a framework, or continuum of care as they describe it, it should be possible to identify the range of resources necessary to ensure adequate provision for all children at risk in a given geographical area.

At one end of their continuum of care they place 'basic and universal provisions'. These include provisions available to all children such as schools, youth clubs and other recreational facilities. These facilities are seen in no way as part of treatment. Rather, it is to these that it would be hoped the children would return after treatment. At the other end of the continuum they place community homes, List D schools and borstals. Between these two poles they describe eight possible facilities each purporting to provide more intensive treatment than the one which preceded it. For example, they begin with youth facilities used on a referral basis, move on to specialist youth clubs catering for the delinquent and disadvantaged child, and proceed through a series of proposals for local treatment groups to short-term care and day care.

As a discussion document their list has considerable merit. It draws attention to the need to provide an orderly range of facilities. It also recognises that a single facility may be inadequate to provide for the needs of any one individual and that the planning of a meaningful treatment programme might require such an individual to move from a more intensive to a less intensive facility before he could settle comfortably in the range of basic and universal provisions.

While no direct application of the Paley and Thorpe model has been made, considerable thought has been given to the range of resources which are needed to complete an adequate continuum of care. One important approach to this problem has been made by Roger Dove[11] who conducted a survey of all social workers in the Highland Region to determine the needs of the children for whom they were responsible and how they might best be met. For the purpose of this survey, he drew up a list of facilities which might be included. A shortened version of this list appears here:

(1) *One-to-one supervision.*

(2) *Conventional youth organisations with special provision for children with mild social and emotional difficulties. In such organisations he envisages support and counselling might be provided by volunteers.*

(3) *Local treatment groups. These would meet on a weekly basis and would not necessarily be confined to children on supervision. Group programmes would evolve around activity, and groups would be run by social workers with groupwork skills.*

(4) *Intermediate treatment centres. Such centres tend to employ several staff. They occupy their own premises, and usually serve a wide area. In addition to a variety of evening programmes for children and young people, some centres provide day care facilities such as alternative schooling. Others provide a refuge for children in crisis. In addition, these centres can serve as a central resource offering support and in some cases accommodation for neighbourhood programmes.*

(5) *Five-day care centres. Centres of this kind cater for small groups of children who either receive education in the centre or at the local school. They are seen as most beneficial for persistent truants and for some who have been excluded from school.*

(6) *Short-term residential treatment. Here the model proposed is a period of 30 days away from home during which time the young people are helped to understand their previous life situation. Such arrangements will only be effective where thorough after-care is available.*[12]

(7) *Hostel accommodation. This would take a form similar to probation hostels although in addition to normal residential hostel facilities, supervision and counselling would be made available. Such a provision would be required for young people who are about to start work.*

(8) *Foster care. Here he differentiates professional from traditional fostering, arguing that only a small proportion of traditional foster parents can cope with difficult and disturbed children.*

(9) *Family group homes.*

(10) *Residential care in List D and List G schools.*

This list has the advantage of placing intermediate treatment in context. The range of provisions from conventional youth organisations with special provision to hostel accommodation may be regarded as intermediate between supervision in the home and care away from home. This list is of particular importance in the fact that it grew from the need to draw up plans to provide comprehensive social work services for children at risk. It does not pretend to be exhaustive, but rather to contribute to the debate on the range of social work services that should be provided for children and young people and the place of intermediate treatment in this total provision.

Is the term 'treatment' appropriate?

When the term 'intermediate treatment' was first introduced, there was some scepticism about its appropriateness. The problem was compounded when the Regional Planning Committees published their lists. Because these lists emphasised youth organisations and recreational facilities, a number of writers began to explore the possibility of more suitable terminology. Flexible care, and intermediate care were among the alternatives suggested.

This early scepticism has continued. In the eyes of many social workers, panel members and juvenile magistrates, intermediate treatment has become identified as recreation, particularly recreation in the open air. This association is not unreasonable. Recreation does play a large part in most intermediate treatment projects, but increasingly this is becoming a means to an end rather than an end in itself. If the real potential of intermediate treatment is to be developed, then the term treatment may serve to provide direction. Treatment in a medical sense implies the application of well-tried remedies to diagnosed medical problems. These remedies have been developed out of careful research and study. Such resources are, as yet, not available to intermediate treatment practitioners. Our capacity to determine the needs of any young persons is limited; similarly, the methods employed to provide for these needs are at an early stage of development. What is called for is a willingness to experiment and a readiness to learn from the experiment. This combined with a genuine 'feel' for children and young people offers a clear direction for intermediate treatment.

This matter may be profitably examined with the aid of two examples.

An Intermediate Treatment Centre[13]

Panmure House, a large detached property situated in the centre of Edinburgh, was opened in 1974 as an experimental centre designed to explore different ways of working with young people at risk. The centre is generously funded and well equipped. It is staffed by a team of workers drawn from social work, community work and teaching, all of whom are committed to high standards of practice. In order to maintain rigorous standards, regular time is set aside each week to review aims and to define methods of work. These deliberations are overseen by a professional advisory group. Consideration is also given to the well-being of the team who meet together with a consultant in a sensitivity session each week.

In an experimental centre of this kind, programmes are constantly evolving. Despite this the original plan of work through the week has seen little change. It involves work with children from 4 p.m. to 9.30 p.m. from Monday to Thursday with Fridays being given over to programme development, referral of new members, a review of the progress of existing members and staff sensitivity training.

Any child coming to the centre is assigned to a mixed group of eight or nine members. This group, together with two other groups, comprise a régime. The centre operates two régimes, the older 15–17 year-olds meeting on Mondays and Wednesdays, while the younger, 13–15 year-olds, meet on Tuesdays and Thursdays. Each group has its permanent leader and can draw upon volunteers and students for additional support.

Unless a group is making a trip out of the centre it will share a similar programme to others in its régime. Certain activities occur at specific times. A meal is served at 4.15 p.m., arts and crafts are available between 5 p.m. and 7.30 p.m. and at the same time a programme of social education is provided. This includes films, slide shows and visiting speakers, and deals with such topics as violence, drug abuse and sex education. At 7.30 p.m. the small groups meet for talk sessions which deal with matters of importance to the group members both in the centre and in their daily living. At 9.00 p.m. there is a community meeting. In contrast to the small group meeting this is largely although not exclusively devoted to issues of importance to the whole community.

Few demands are made on the young people during their time at the centre. Attendance is voluntary but certain expectations are made part of an initial understanding before they arrive. These are that they come at the beginning of a session and stay to the end, and that they attend their small group meeting. These conditions apart, if the formal programme does not appeal there are a host of things to do: TV, pool, a juke box or just talk. Should a young person wish to talk to an adult, invariably there is one at hand ready to listen.

Initially it was anticipated that a member would remain at the centre for approximately six months, but subsequently, it was decided that each child should monitor his own progress jointly with his group leader. Six months remains the upper limit but now he will be expected to attend for a minimum of three months, any additional time being fixed by negotiation. Throughout this time the child continues on statutory or voluntary supervision.

While evening programmes have changed little, the centre itself is evolving additional components. Over the first year the staff became increasingly concerned about the number of young people coming to the centre who were either excluded from or refusing to attend school. This led to an approach to the Education Authority which agreed to fund a small day unit for such children. Currently this is staffed by two teachers who provide a varied educational programme for a small group of children of mixed ability.

A Neighbourhood Intermediate Treatment Programme

In 1975 three children's panel members approached the Quality of Life Project in Dunbartonshire to ask if they would fund an intermediate treatment project in the Vale of Leven. When the application was approved they immediately brought together a working party to establish objectives, and to draw up outline plans which would ensure adequate support for the worker. The objective was defined as the need to explore the function of a specialist intermediate treatment group worker in the community. At the outset it was agreed with the social work department that priority must be given to building links with the local area team. As far as support for the worker was concerned, it was foreseen that two needs would have to be met. He would require the approval and support of local people who were professionally concerned with children. He would also require consultation and supervision to ensure that the project developed systematically and that high standards of practice were maintained.

The worker took up his appointment in September 1975, and was given accommodation in the offices of the local social work team. He was invited to participate fully with the team and attend their meetings. Accommodation for group meetings initially proved a problem and the possibility of a specially designed portakabin or play bus was explored. The matter was resolved when two adjacent apartments in a housing development were made available for the use of the groups.

It was decided that the majority of the worker's time would be given over to a programme of groupwork counselling.[14] This is a method which reinforces and amplifies the experience of the child in the group through systematic individual counselling. To do this effectively, two workers are required, usually a man and a woman worker together to provide father and mother figures to the group. A single group can be extremely demanding of time and at first it was assumed that two groups of eight children would be as many as the project could serve. However, it has subsequently been possible to show that where teachers and other skilled volunteers are available, additional groups may be run, provided time allows the worker to offer them regular supervision. The present pattern involves three groups – two for boys, one for girls. In no group is there more than an 18-month difference in age. One group is run by volunteers, the other two by the worker and social work students taking a special option in groupwork. Each group meets on a different night in the week. Groups contain children on supervision and their friends. A separate social worker fulfils the statutory supervision.

The programme brings worker and child together at least twice a week over a maximum period of six months. The regular pattern of counselling and group meetings is augmented on at least three occasions during the life of the group by periods of residential living. Each group begins life with a long weekend and will use subsequent time away as focal points in the group programme. Each weekly evening session lasts for three hours. Much of the time is given over to activities planned in counselling sessions. In addition there are two business meetings, the first being primarily concerned with plans for the evening, the second being given over to issues which are important to the children. In the early life of the group, discussion is devoted largely to matters within the group be it a choice of menu or rôles for the sharing of activities or the resolution of fights. Later, attention turns to broader issues in the lives of the children such as friendship, school attendance, or the sort of job they hope to find.

These examples illustrate two different approaches to 'treating' children through intermediate treatment. Although the physical setting of each is quite different, the actual aims are very similar. They may be described broadly as being ' . . . to improve social functioning and coping with social problems'.[15] The primary aim is not to control delinquency although such a result is to be hoped for. The primary aim rather is to see each individual young person's world through his own eyes and share with him in discovering whether his way of coping is the best possible way for him.

Just as aims are similar, so the means to achieve these aims have a number of similarities. Relationships are at the centre of each treatment programme. Initially, the relationship between group worker and child is of great importance. In both examples, the restrictions of a formal supervisory relationship have been stripped away to allow the maximum ease of contact. Many of the young people concerned have become accustomed to the idea that adults, and in a lot of cases peers think ill of them. For this reason, every effort has to be made to convince them that they are accepted in their own right.

At the outset the worker approaches the child in an uncritical accepting way. As time goes on, so the relationship begins to assume a sense of direction with the worker beginning to explore ways in which they can communicate together. Inevitably this task follows a different pattern in each setting. In the centre it can be shared with a variety of adults while in the neighbourhood programme the counselling time provides regular opportunities to develop these skills.

The small group is a fundamental part of this process of relationships. In the neighbourhood programme, it is the total treatment community. In the centre it is the individual child's primary reference group. In both settings the small group plays a major part in helping the child to make sense of the way in which he can use the treatment experience. Other small group members can offer friendship which, for the lonely child, can be of enormous importance. However, they can offer much more than this. They can offer opinions and experience. However hard an adult tries to talk to a child on his level, his age and breadth of experience must affect the communication. For the children it is different. They are part of the peer culture and are aware of prevailing attitudes to theft, truancy, critical parents and the multifarious issues with which pre-adolescents and adolescents have to wrestle. If the other children can be drawn in to help any individual member, provided the worker handles the discussion with sensitivity, a great deal can be achieved.

This process can be illustrated by a further example. It relates to a boys' group which had been meeting twice a week for six months. Over this time business meetings had gradually moved from generalities to specific issues which concerned them. The task focus for these small group meetings was made interesting by a range of techniques including brain storming (a technique whereby ideas are summarised on cards and are arranged on a board by the group as a visual stimulus to group discussion), games and rôle play. Up to the time in question the worker had played a very active leadership rôle in the group. Now with Eric's review meeting with the panel due in three days, it was he who informed the group:

'We're going to have a panel tonight. I want to know what I'm going to say and you lot have got to help me.' (His remark was made to everyone.) It seemed he hadn't forewarned anyone because there was a shocked silence. He then pulled a piece of paper out of his pocket and began to allocate rôles to everyone. I [the worker] was to be myself.

There was some horseplay but the group accepted the idea with little fuss and were quickly involved in the rôle play. I had expected that as the boys warmed to the task, they would create caricatures of the rôles they were playing, but this didn't happen. All were absorbed by the fact that Eric, a notorious truant, had decided to go back to school 'to work for some "O" levels'.

The following day the worker met Eric to draft his report for the supervising social worker. It proved to be a fruitful meeting:

Eric showed an eagerness I've never seen before. In the past he had either been morose and uncommunicative, or responded to discussion in an extremely superficial way. This time he virtually dictated my report for me.

Is treatment an appropriate term? Well, yes and no. Undoubtedly its association with the high standards of diagnosis and treatment to be found in medical practice can offer a sense of direction, but perhaps this is the extent of its usefulness. Few practitioners are at ease with the term. For the great majority, intermediate treatment is a shared experience with the child that has more to do with learning and growing than with getting well.

A real or an illusory resource?

It has been shown that intermediate treatment means different things to different people, both in terms of the range of activities it can embrace, and in terms of the results it hopes to achieve. To some practitioners, it is taking kids on the hills for the day. To others it is a groupwork programme prepared meticulously and followed systematically. To some policy makers it is a resource provided entirely by youth and recreational services. To a handful, it is a whole range of resources, some provided by educational services, some by youth services, and some by social workers themselves. Against this background, it would not be accurate to suggest that it is an effective or real resource. In practice it is a great many different resources, a proportion of which can be shown to be potentially valuable additions to the resources already available to panels and courts.

It is early days to assert that any intermediate treatment programme is effective. Few have been running for any length of time. Fewer still have been subjected to any systematic evaluation. At this stage in development one can only assess potential effectiveness. This raises such questions as: are there clear objectives, is there a realistic plan of action, and are staff available with the necessary skills to pursue these objectives? Both examples cited in the previous section were chosen deliberately because they can be shown to have established objectives, carefully planned programmes of experience, and in the absence of any thorough going training programme to prepare practitioners for work of this kind, each has secured in-service training as a means of extending and promoting skill. In addition, neither team of workers has any illusions about the quality of service they are providing. Both recognise that they are engaged in an experiment which must be carefully and continually monitored. For a long time to come this spirit of inquiry will be an essential ingredient of any innovation in social work services for children and young people.

Intermediate treatment is an important idea. It opens the door to a range of resources which can in time provide more effective social work services for children and young people. Such services could, if they are planned carefully and run efficiently, substantially reduce the List D school population, as well as improve the services already provided for children living in their own homes. As yet, there is little evidence that policy makers recognise this potential. For the most part, intermediate treatment is not planned in relation to other services. Such an initial step is essential if its potential is to be realised. There are few straws in the wind. However, it is encouraging that one English Social Services Department has committed itself to the systematic development of intermediate treatment by appointing a specialist group worker to each of its social work teams.[16] By doing so it is demonstrating that intermediate treatment can become an integral part of the basic range of social work services for children and young people. It is to be hoped that others may soon follow this example.

REFERENCES

1. *Children in Trouble* (1968), Cmnd. 3601, HMSO.
2. Bacon, M. (1975), *Intermediate Treatment*, Summit NYBC.
3. Roberts, C. and Davies, M. (1975). *The Wythenshawe Intermediate Treatment Project*. Mimeo. National Youth Bureau Library, 234.
    Also Naftalin, I. (1975), *Working Papers on the Wythenshawe Project*. Mimeo. National Youth Bureau Library, 235.
4. Newell, P. (1975), A Free School Now. *New Society*, 15 May.
5. Islington Family Service Unit (1974), *Intermediate Treatment Centre Report 1973/74*. F.S.U. Publications.
6. Thorpe, D. (1973), Three Kinds of Intermediate Treatment. *Social Work Today*, **3**, 24.
7. Coleman, D. (1974), *A Study of an Intermediate Treatment Project*. D.S.W.A. Dissertation, University of Glasgow.
8. Norman, J. (1975), 870 House. *Youth Social Work*, **2**, 2.
9. Morris, P. (1975), Open Air Treatment. *Community Care*, 4 June.
10. Paley, J. and Thorpe, D. (1974), *Children: Handle with Care*, NYBC.
11. Dove, R. (1975), *A Study of Intermediate Treatment Requirements*. Mimeo, Highland Regional Social Work Department.
12. Donohue, E. (1975), Short Term Residential Care. *Youth Social Work*, **2**, 1.
13. Demarco, L. (1975), *Panmure House – One Approach to I.T. and Our Kids*. Mimeo. National Youth Bureau Library, 237.
14. Aplin, G. and Bamber, R. (1973), Groupwork Counselling: The Case for a Specialist Provision in Intermediate Treatment. *Social Work Today*, **3**, 22.
15. Whittaker, J. K. (1974), *Social Treatment: An Approach to Interpersonal Helping*. Aldine Atherton.
16. Boddy, J. (1975), *Intermediate Treatment Papers*. Mimeo, Nottinghamshire Social Services Department.

Section V

CRITICAL PERSPECTIVES

IN ORDER to assess a system of juvenile justice we may isolate each of its components and each of its linkages with other services, and scrutinise them closely one by one. But a system can and should also be viewed as a whole, and its distinctive configuration examined critically from a number of perspectives. From the standpoint of moral philosophy, there are crucial questions to be raised concerning the values which inform the system and which legitimate the decisions taken in its name. These questions involve a characterisation of the system, in terms not only of its expressly stated objectives but also of its implicit goals, and should also entail an examination of the relevant ways in which the system under review differs from its competitors. When, as in the case of children's hearings, the system is one which seeks to keep legal formalities to a minimum in the interests of unhampered communication, it is also pertinent to enquire whether there is any danger that a casual attitude towards legal procedures and safeguards, however well-intentioned, may have the effect of eroding basic civil rights. And in an era in which the expectations aroused by the reform and reconstruction of services so often crumble into disappointment and frustration, it is of great interest to examine the changing pattern of juvenile justice in Scotland in the light of shifting attitudes and recurrent problems in the management of delinquency across the Atlantic. Finally, the hearings system may be seen through the eyes not of detached academic observers but of those members of the community continuously associated with its operation – the members of children's panels whose stable belief in the long-term social worth of their enterprise is a necessary condition of its continued existence, let alone of its growth and improvement.

19

THE UNDERLYING PRINCIPLES:
A PHILOSOPHICAL COMMENT

DAVID WATSON

ANY REPORT recommending changes in legislation 'may be felt to raise practical problems, involving major changes of organisation and machinery, of such magnitude as to be unworkable in the conceivable future'.[1] Since the inception in 1971 of the children's panels recommended in the Kilbrandon Report, public debate of the changes has focussed on such practical matters. As a result certain moral views about the general aims of systems of juvenile justice, which further entail views about the capacities of children and the responsibilities of parents, each discussed at some length in the Kilbrandon Report, have been ignored.

In failing to discuss these views of course we do the Report an injustice. More seriously, it seems to me, we deprive ourselves of information which is central to understanding the hearings system. We may be able to describe the 'New Alternative' but we won't be able to justify it. We won't be able to say how its justification differs from that of the juvenile court system.

It will be a conclusion of my discussion that, though similar in some respects, the hearings system manifests a different view of what kind of disposals in general are morally justified from that manifested by the preceding system. Of course, the writers of the Report thought that they were recommending a 'New Alternative'. They see the change as from a punitive to a non-punitive system, though they admit that others might not see it this way: 'it would . . . be unrealistic to imagine that cases will not continue in which public measures for a child's protection and future welfare will still be seen as amounting to compulsion and punishment' (para 57 Kilbrandon Report – all references to numbered paragraphs hereafter are to paragraphs of this Report). I shall argue that in many cases the others see it as it is. The disposals of hearings are like those of juvenile courts in sometimes including punishment. What's new about the alternative is not that it excludes punishment.

The Report's presumptions about and discussion of the degree of responsibility of which children in general are capable (paras. 55ff) and its discussion of parental responsibilities (paras. 17ff) must be matters for future discussion.

I begin with, and will give most space to, a discussion of juvenile offenders and punishment, but this will lead to some discussion, if not enough, of treatment and of children in need of care or protection. This chapter then is a discussion of what the Report calls 'the underlying principles' of the hearings system. We have neglected them too long. But we must begin with the preceding juvenile court system.

The underlying principles of the juvenile court system

It is important at the outset to have some grasp of the difference between a definition and a justification. Amongst other things, a definition tells us the correct use of a word so that, if the word is a name, we are put in a position to identify things named by that word. Broadly following Professor Anthony Flew[2] we may suggest five conditions satisfied by a standard case to which the the word 'punishment' would correctly be applied:

1. *it must be an intended unpleasantness to the victim;*

2. *it must be for an offence (actual or supposed);*

3. *it must be of the offender (actual or supposed);*

4. *it must be carried out by personal agencies (i.e. not merely the natural consequences of an action);*

5. *it must be imposed by authority (actual or supposed), conferred by the system of rules against which the offence has been committed.*

The word 'punishment', in its primary sense, is correctly used to describe a situation satisfying these five conditions; any such situation is punishment. Thus, though telling us how to identify things of a certain sort, definition is essentially a linguistic matter. Throughout this chapter 'punishment' will be used as just defined, except in discussion of paragraph 54 of the Kilbrandon Report when I argue that the Report does not use the word in this sense with important consequences.

Justification is essentially a moral matter. A justification tells us why something morally ought to occur or be as it is. Let me elicit the justifications which according to the Report underly that part of the juvenile court system concerned with offenders as opposed to children in need of 'care and protection'.

The Report argues that 'the shortcomings which cause dissatisfaction within the present juvenile court system . . . seem to us to arise essentially from the fact that they seek to combine the characteristics of a court of criminal law with those of a specialised agency for the treatment of juvenile offenders, proceeding on a preventive and educational principle' (para. 71).

The point is, the Report continues, that in a court of criminal law the offence is viewed 'simply as an act in isolation' and its potential seriousness judged 'simply by the ready-made standard offered by the range of sanctions which the law (and thus society at large) attaches to the particular class of offences which it exemplifies' (para. 71).

That a court of criminal law views an offence as an act in isolation is true only of the proof stage of proceedings. At a later stage previous offences and other circumstances are regarded as relevant. (This is to some extent conceded in paras. 35, 36 and 52.) However, the important point is that there is an offence and a corresponding limited range of socially approved sanctions.

On 'a preventive and educational principle' on the other hand, 'the offence, while the essential basis of judicial action, has significance only as a pointer to the need for intervention' (para. 71). There is an offence and in principle an unlimited range of forms of intervention among which it is hoped will be found at least one corresponding to the needs indicated by the offence.

These two features of the juvenile court system are strictly not compatible and occur in an uneasy alliance in that system because two distinct moral points of view underlie it, one providing a justification for one feature or set of features, and the other providing a justification for the other feature or set of features. The moral points of view in question concern punishment, and have traditionally been called, respectively, *retributivist* and *consequentialist*. Broadly, the retributivist view is that punishment is justified by breaches of law, while the consequentialist holds that punishment is justified if it produces the best consequences. Thus the retributivist makes the punishment fit the crime, while the consequentialist makes the punishment fit the criminal.

I want now to bring out some important differences between these two views about when punishment is morally justified, in order to show why a system of juvenile justice which attempted to combine features justified in these different ways would leave many dissatisfied.

(a) On the retributivist view, responsibility for an offence is a necessary condition[3] of justified punishment. Only someone choosing to do one thing rather than another, and in circumstances allowing him to choose, can in the relevant sense be responsible for an offence and justifiably punished. Of course, in various circumstances, responsibility may be reduced, and on this view the punishment merited correspondingly reduced.

Speaking of juvenile courts, the Report says, 'it is evident that the system of criminal prosecution assumes a high degree of personal responsibility – of choice in doing right and wrong, and that doing wrong – where this involves the commission of an act recognised by law as a criminal offence – merits punishment. In the ultimate, this might seem to imply that every crime detected ought to be followed by criminal proceedings so that the offender can receive the punishment he deserves. Although in practice this consequence does not invariably follow, it is the case that, where prosecution does follow, the possible legal consequences demand the most stringent safeguards to ensure that the innocent are not punished' (para. 51).

This quoted passage highlights a feature of the juvenile court system resting on the retributivist requirement of responsibility. 'The innocent' who must not be punished are precisely those not responsible for the offence.

On the consequentialist view, responsibility for an offence is *not* a necessary condition of justified punishment. The consequentialist is *interested in* the responsibility of the offender, but only as one of the many factors relevant in guiding him towards the intervention most likely to produce the best consequences.

'The common law, while assuming the criminal responsibility of juveniles, accepts that youth may be a mitigating factor. This appears to be a recognition of the varying moral and intellectual capacity of children. ... Statute law imports the 'welfare' of the child as a major consideration ... penal measures being imposed for his welfare ... as by a father on the basis, "it's for your own good" ...' (para. 55). It was a feature of the juvenile court system then, to presume children less capable of responsibility, but nevertheless sometimes to punish them 'in their own interest'. Further, offenders and non-offenders alike might receive 'special measures of education and training' which placed the emphasis on discipline (cf. para. 13).

Responsibility for an offence, then, was not a necessary condition of punishment. Nor was it more than one of many relevant factors in cases where some responsibility was presumed. The true significance of the offence 'could be judged only on a thorough assessment of the circumstances, and only on that basis could the child's needs be decided and his further training taken in hand with any realistic prospect of success' (para. 59).

(b) On the retributivist view the punishment, to be justified, must correspond to the *offence* punished. The sense in which a punishment can 'fit the crime' is not always clear, but the following points may help. The prevailing public morality provides us with the idea that some offences are more immoral, evil, wicked or 'serious' in themselves than others; for example, rape than shoplifting. The same public morality also provides us with the idea that some punishments are more 'serious' in being more unpleasant in themselves than others; for example, two months detention than a £20 fine. To inflict two months detention on an innocent man would be a greater injustice than to deprive him of £20, other things being equal; and the former is the more *severe* punishment if inflicted on an offender. To match these scales of 'seriousness' is to make the punishment fit the crime.

As we have seen, the Report asserts that the seriousness of an offence was judged in the juvenile courts 'simply by the ready-made standard offered by the range of sanctions which the law (and thus society at large) attaches to the particular class of offences which it exemplifies' (para. 71). Here again is a feature justified on retributivist grounds.

On the consequentialist view, the punishment must correspond to the *offender*.* And this too was a feature of juvenile court practice. 'There were cases in which, where an offence had been committed by a child, no very drastic steps appeared to be justified on the basis of the offence itself. But these included cases in which, looking to the whole background, it might be that the child's

---

* This is, of course, a simplification. If the consequentialist aims to produce the best consequences for the offender, the assertion needs little supplementation. But, as Andrew Lockyer has pointed out to me, if the aim is to produce the best consequences for others, and the consequentialist adopts the strategy of deterrence, the punishment may pay little or no attention to characteristics of the offender, and much more to characteristics of those he aims to deter by punishing the offender.

quite minor delinquency was simply a symptom of personal or environmental difficulties, so that, for the prevention of more serious offences and for the future protection of society as much as in the child's own interests, more sustained measures of supervision were . . . called for' (para. 13).

This paragraph brings to light a further feature of the juvenile court system worth noting. I have so far said only that on the consequentialist view, to be justified, punishment must produce the best consequences. But we must ask, best for whom? It may be that the consequences best for society at large are not best for the individual offender. In each case punishment should, for the consequentialist, correspond to characteristics of the individual and his background which led to the offence, but our answer to the present question determines *which* characteristics are given attention.

If the consequentialist aims to produce the best consequences for society, and doesn't presume to know better than society at large what is best for society, he will produce, or at least aim to produce, the consequences society at large wants. In general this will be sufficient change in the offender to prevent recurrence of the offence, and as little other (social) change as possible.

If he aims to produce the best consequences for the individual offender, and doesn't presume to know better than the offender what is best for him, he will aim to produce the consequences the offender wants. In general this will be as little change in the offender as is consonant with non-recurrence of the offence, and as much other (social) change as is necessary.

The last quoted paragraph suggests that the juvenile courts aimed at the best consequences both for society and for the individual offender, and hints, I think, that where both cannot be achieved, the former should take priority.

Here are some other relevant points of difference between the retributivist and consequentialist views about when punishment is morally justified, and which again were reflected in features of the juvenile court system.

(c) On the consequentialist view, the best consequences are usually to be achieved by means of deterrence or reform. Deterrence obviously typically requires change in the offender, attempting to prevent recurrence of the offence by giving him reason to fear repetition, or by causing in him a non-rational aversion to such offences.* It might, however, require little or no change in the offender, but considerable other change. For example, one might deter repetition of offences involving under-age drinking not by punishing such drinkers severely, but by giving adults selling alcoholic beverages to children reason to fear – by imposing heavy fines on any adult caught so doing.

Reform more clearly can vary in where it requires change. It may require transformation of the offender's character, or of the relevant parts of his environment.

---

* John Grant informs me that criminologists generally use 'deterrence' to refer just to putting off *others* and 'prevention' to putting off the offender *himself*. In this chapter I use 'deterrence' to include both. In discussion, Andrew Lockyer drew my attention to a further distinction which might be drawn between forms of 'prevention' in the criminologists' sense. We may prevent by the means mentioned in my text or by denying the offender the opportunity to repeat the offence, e.g. by locking him up. This third form of 'prevention' could of course also be a third form of 'deterrence' in the criminologists' sense, if we locked up potential offenders.

The juvenile courts employed both consequentialist strategies. Sentencing 'has, certainly in more recent times, increasingly had regard not simply to fitting the punishment to the crime, but to the future. Sentencing looks to the future in that considerations of deterrence are or may be present, both in relation to the offender and to others, and in that the principle of educating and reforming the criminal has in more modern times received increasing attention' (para. 52).

The retributivist does not accept that such strategies can be justified. As Immanuel Kant put it, 'judicial punishment . . . of the criminal . . . must at all times be inflicted on him for no other reason than *because he has acted criminally*. A man can never be treated simply as a means of realising the views of another man.'[4]

As we have seen, if the consequentialist aims to produce the best consequences for the offender, deterrence and reform strategies may not be 'means for realising the views of *another* man'. Even so the retributivist cannot adopt them. For him punishment is justified by and only by breaches of law. Possible future offences have not been committed, and so cannot merit punishment.

(d) The retributivist, as we have seen, focusses on the *offence*. He wants to know whether the offender was responsible for it and what punishment is merited by it, whatever the consequences of its application. There is no danger, then, of the retributivist view yielding anything other than a system of *punishment*. The consequentialist, on the other hand, though dealing only with cases involving an offence, focusses on the *offender*. As we have seen, his attempts to deter or reform may demand little of the offender. In such cases we may be inclined to say that the consequentialist is not in fact *punishing* the offender. In these cases the offence really is merely a pointer to the need for other action.

In defining 'punishment' at the beginning of this section I said that one condition to be satisfied was that it must be for an offence (actual or supposed). In the present kind of case this condition is fulfilled. What is done is done for an offence. However, this does not entail that what is done is a punishment. There are other conditions to be satisfied. One might respond to an offence with indulgence. One important feature of punishment is that it must be an intended unpleasantness to the victim. My present point is that when the best consequences are produced without pain for the offender, at least when he aims to produce the consequences best for the individual, the consequentialist will not *punish*. These cases might perhaps be described as cases involving 'compulsory care' though there will be few, if any, cases of this kind in a society whose members value liberty. Compulsion implies loss of liberty, and in such a society such a loss will usually be painful for the offender. The juvenile court system is such that some cases of this kind might arise, and of course the system of children's hearings is one in which all cases are claimed to be of this kind. I shall later argue that this is not so, but for the moment I simply want to show how the consequentialist can drift from punishment of the offender towards care, by omitting to inflict intended unpleasantness on him.

In any case, it should at least be clear by now that that part of the juvenile court system dealing with offenders was an amalgam of features reflecting, and justified by, two distinct moral points of view. Retributivism and consequentialism, and the conflict between them, are manifested in features of that system.

A New Alternative

I began the preceding section of this chapter stressing the importance of the distinction between a definition and a justification. Thereafter most of my discussion was about the manifestation of conflicting values in the juvenile court system. I now turn to paragraph 54 of the Report. I shall argue in a moment that this paragraph has strongly influenced our conception of the hearings system. I shall also argue that since in that paragraph the writers of the Report confuse definition and justification, we have been misled. We have been led to say that children's hearings (as described in the Report) cannot punish, and to say that the hearings system is a non-punitive radical departure from the juvenile court system. Both claims are false. But first let me summarise paragraph 54:

1. *punishment is restricted to proved offenders, whereas treatment may be given to merely potential delinquents;*

2. *punishment cannot be extended far beyond the individual offender, while treatment usefully may;*

3. *punishment must fit the crime, whereas treatment fits the needs of the offender;*

4. *punishment by its nature is 'once for all', whereas treatment can be modified to yield better results.*

If we look again at the definition of 'punishment' given in the preceding section we can see that, as part of a *definition*, what is said about punishment in paragraph 54 is somewhat different. Perhaps the first two points made in paragraph 54 correspond to conditions 2 and 3 of the earlier definition, but this is not true of points three and four. Following points which appear to be put forward as part of the definition of 'punishment', point 3 reflects the retributivist's view of when punishment is morally justified – when it corresponds to the offence. Again point 4 reflects the retributivist's view that to be morally justified a punishment must correspond to the offence. For that reason 'the criminal is entitled to ask that the judge should decide his punishment on the information available at the time of his conviction, and once the judge has weighed out the appropriate punishment, there are no good grounds for its alteration, since the acts which merited it have been done and cannot alter' (para. 54(4)).

Even point 2 is explained by introducing retributivism. 'Punishment cannot be extended far beyond the individual offender, since no other person has the degree of guilt for the offence which would be acceptable as a prerequisite for punishment' (para. 54(2)). This explanation reflects the retributivist view that *responsibility* is a necessary condition of justified punishment.

In this way paragraph 54 confuses definition and justification. To be precise, it asks us to call 'punishment' only punishment which can be justified on retributivist grounds, the rest we should call 'treatment'. If we follow this lead we will claim that any consequentialist disposals, whether made by the juvenile courts or the children's hearings, are necessarily not punishment but treatment.

We should not follow this lead because it involves confusion of definition and justification. Let me now try to clarify how the claim it encourages arises and why it is false.

On the first point, we may distinguish two uses of 'treatment'. In its wider use 'treatment' can be used to signify any response to an offence justified from the consequentialist point of view. In this use 'treatment' can include punishment in the sense defined in my preceding section. This is the sense in which the consequentialist disposals of the juvenile courts were concerned with the treatment of juvenile offenders. In its narrower use 'treatment' does not include but is opposed to punishment as I defined it. This is the label we would use to identify means other than punishment used by the juvenile courts or children's hearings to achieve the best consequences.

Given the opposition of treatment and punishment in paragraph 54, we naturally presume 'treatment' to be used in its narrower sense. In fact this is not so. As we have seen, in that paragraph treatment is opposed to punishment which can be justified on retributivist grounds. In this use it can thus include punishment which can be justified on consequentialist grounds. If we take what is in fact the wider use to be the narrower use, we end up describing *all* disposals justified on consequentialist grounds as 'treatment'.

On the second point, for the consequentialist actions are right in so far as they tend to promote the best consequences, wrong as they tend to produce the reverse.[5] Punishment would be morally wrong on this criterion if it did not tend in a particular case or in general to promote the best consequences.* When the best consequences are achieved by means other than punishment as I have defined it, punishment will be abandoned in favour of 'treatment' in the narrower sense. But, and this is why the claim encouraged by paragraph 54 is false, if the best consequences are achieved by punishment (as I have defined it), the consequentialist will punish willingly.

It is false to say that consequentialist disposals are necessarily not punishment but treatment because, as a matter of theory, consequentialism does not preclude punishment. It would thus also be a mistake to presume the consequentialist disposals of the juvenile courts to be necessarily non-punitive. Some consequentialist juvenile court disposals could have been punishment rather than treatment. And of course, given our definition, in fact some were. Clearly most deterrent fines were punishment.

---

*Of course, general tendencies might not occur in a particular case. This leaves room for two sorts of consequentialism – one saying that punishment is wrong in this particular case if it does not tend to promote the best consequences in this particular case, another saying that it is right in this particular case even if it does not tend to promote the best consequences in this particular case, provided it promotes the best consequences in most cases. Cf. J. J. C. Smart, 'Extreme and Restricted Utilitarianism' in P. Foot (ed.), *Theories of Ethics*, Oxford, 1967.

Thus paragraph 54 misleads us about the consequentialist disposals of the juvenile courts. Let me now explain its encouragement of the false claim that hearings as described in the Report cannot punish. We will then be in a position to see that the hearings are not a non-punitive departure from the juvenile court system.

The children's panel is described as an agency 'empowered to consider measures of treatment . . . its sole function being the consideration and application of training measures . . . appropriate to the needs of the individual child . . . for as long a period as was judged to be necessary . . . the agency would have the widest discretion to vary or terminate the measures initially applied, and where appropriate substitute others' (para. 72).

Such an agency is clearly conceived as operating within a framework justified on consequentialist grounds. It is concerned to match disposal to the offender both initially and subsequently. We are told that its consequentialist disposals will be 'measures of treatment'. Given the opposition of treatment and punishment in paragraph 54, we are encouraged to presume 'treatment' there and thereafter to be used in the narrower sense. So the 'measures of treatment' dispensed by hearings, if they are correctly described, cannot include punishment.

As we have seen, however, consequentialism does not preclude punishment and if all the possible disposals of a consequentialist system were to be labelled 'measures of treatment', 'treatment' would be being used in the wider sense which includes punishment as I defined it. Further, in fact in paragraph 54 'treatment' is opposed only to punishment which can be justified on retributivist grounds. 'Treatment' there and thereafter in discussion of the disposals of hearings, may thus include punishment which is justified on consequentialist grounds. 'Measures of treatment' dispensed by hearings, if they are correctly described, can include punishment. And of course, given our definition of punishment, many disposals of hearings include punishment. Every child does not find the same features of a disposal unpleasant, and the same child may find different features unpleasant at different times. On present arrangements every hearing disposal in cases involving offences satisfies conditions 2–5. Condition 1 is satisfied whenever the disposal intentionally includes an element the child is known to find unpleasant. Any requirement, for example, that removes a juvenile offender from home against his wishes and which it is known will cause him some distress, is to that extent punitive.

Since hearings can and do punish, they cannot be a departure from the juvenile court system by being, unlike that system, wholly non-punitive. Further, the writers of the Report themselves stress their desire for continuity of 'basis of approach'. Speaking of juvenile court disposals they say 'the principle underlying the present range of treatment measures is . . . primarily an educational one (para. 35) . . . if then the existing arrangements are nevertheless unsatisfactory, this does not seem to us to point to some new and totally different basis of approach, but rather to a consideration of the points at which the present machinery fails to give full effect to the educational principle on which the existing treatment measures in general purport to be based' (para. 36).

The hearings system is not *totally* different from the juvenile court system, because all its disposals, like some of the latter's disposals, can only be justified on consequentialist grounds. Consequentialism is the continuity in the 'basis of approach'.

So what's new? Clearly a reduction in the influence of retributivism. The decline of retributivism inevitably means a decline in the amount of attention paid to any offence. The degree of responsibility for any offence is less important, measures of treatment cease necessarily to correspond to any offence, and indeed it is no longer necessary to have committed an offence to be subject to unpleasant measures of treatment.

On this last point, the hearings system draws no great distinction between offenders and children in need of care and protection. Section 32(2) of Part III of the subsequent Social Work (Scotland) Act 1968, classes children in both categories as 'in need of compulsory measures of care'. The Act set up a system accepting the claim of Kilbrandon's witnesses 'that in terms of the child's actual needs, the legal distinction betwen juvenile offenders and children in need of care or protection was – looking to the underlying realities – very often of little practical significance' (para. 13). Given that in most areas, the same juvenile court dealt with juvenile offenders and juveniles in need of care and protection alike (para. 46), superficially there has been little change. However, when offenders and children in need of care or protection are dealt with by the same agency and very often dealt with in the same way, since – looking to the under-lying realities – the offence 'has significance only as a pointer to the need for intervention' (para. 71), then it isn't important that an offence was committed. Some other pointer might do.

We have seen that hearings can punish. In disposing of offenders and non-offenders in like manner it seems then that they sometimes punish non-offenders. This need not worry the consequentialist. However, this is not a strictly correct description of unpleasant disposals of non-offenders. On the definition of punishment I gave earlier, punishment must be for an offence (actual or supposed), and in these cases this condition is not satisfied. Strictly, in these cases hearings do not *punish* non-offenders, but they do deliberately inflict unpleasant measures on them. This a retributivist would find objectionable, and the decline of retributivism is marked by its toleration.[6] Or rather, since this was also tolerated by the juvenile court system, the decline of retributivism is marked not by its toleration but by its toleration without qualm.

Two points might be borne in mind here. First, the intended unpleasantness may not be all that is intended, and indeed only an accidental feature of the disposal. Second, it is difficult to imagine any system avoiding such intended unpleasantness to those in need of care or protection. In some cases at least the subject will find the disposal, say removal from home, unpleasant. At least, any *paternalistic* system will have difficulty avoiding this problem. But 'children's rights' are a subject for another day.

In recommending the New Alternative the Report suggests 'the desirability of separating clearly the two issues of (a) adjudication of the allegation issue, and (b) consideration of the measures to be applied' (para. 72). Of course such a change does not itself entail a move to disposals justified only on consequentialist grounds. Even so, if these two issues are dealt with at separate stages of the hearing process there will be less encouragement to focus on the offence and the offender's responsibility for it when it comes to consideration of the measures to be applied. It is in this way that the first issue can colour the second, by reminding us of retributivist values. The separation recommended is then another mark of the decline of retributivism and leaves the field clear for consequentialist disposals.

I said earlier that the decline of retributivism was marked by the new system's toleration without qualm of deliberately inflicting unpleasant measures on non-offenders. In paragraph 70, the writers of the Report endorse the view that the initial basis for action in relation to juvenile *offenders*, i.e. the offence, 'be established beyond doubt by stringent and testing procedures'. They accept that 'fairly sustained measures of education and training ... thorough and searching enquiry into the whole surrounding circumstances including the child's home background' are not warranted otherwise. Since such measures are also applied to juvenile non-offenders, the writers of the Report might have found here a reason not to tolerate deliberately inflicting unpleasant measures on non-offenders without qualm.

In any case, the passage shows that the Report and its New Alternative are not totally committed to consequentialism. Some hesitation appears too in paragraph 76. Some measures of treatment 'may be represented as unwarranted interference in the liberty of the individual'. However, in the first kind of case 'if the child denied the act in question, action by the agency would be stayed, and the case would immediately be referred to the sheriff court' and in the second kind of case appeal might be made to the sheriff court. Both limitations on the system's consequentialism further recommend themselves to retributivists in the context of the recommendation that the referral of cases to the panels should be in the hands of an officer with a legal qualification (para. 98). At least as regards offenders, this would increase the probability of the initial basis for action being beyond doubt an offence. Where this recommendation is not strictly followed, as at present in Strathclyde, the decline of retributivism is again marked. If it is not important that an *offence* has been committed, it is not necessary to employ reporters qualified to identify cases which will stand up in court. As regards non-offenders, of course, any punishment is contrary to retributivism, but scope for appeal to the sheriff court may serve.

A consequentialist 'New Alternative' as we have seen, though it might be punitive, unlike a retributivist system, need not be punitive. It is less likely to be punitive if at least two conditions are satisfied. First, if the consequences pursued are those best for the individual referred, as judged by that individual, as opposed to those best for society at large or judged best for the individual by society at large. If the child sees the disposal as a means to *his* ends he is less likely to find that means unpleasant, or at least the unpleasantness of the means will be offset by the pleasantness of the end. The 1968 Act instructs the hearing to do what is in the best interests of the child (see for example 43(1)) and Rule 17(2)(d) of the Children's Hearings (Scotland) Rules 1971 obliges it, if possible, to discover what the child wants or to attempt genuinely to persuade the child that what the hearing wants, if this is different, is best for him. The Act and this Rule facilitate non-punitive disposals. It also helps the system avoid, to some extent at least, a common retributivist criticism of such consequentialist systems. That is, that their disposals are instruments of social control. 'Measures of treatment' in the best interests of society may show no respect for individual autonomy, aiming simply to produce a well-behaved and uncritical population.

Second, disposals are less likely to be punitive if sufficient alternative means of achieving the best consequences are available. It seems to me that the recurring debate about resources available to the hearings system to some extent reflects the wish for non-punitive means of disposal. Though I share that wish, it is perhaps worth noting that it has perhaps been fired by paragraph 54, which describes punishment in such a way as to misleadingly imply that hearings can't punish.

Thus the 'New Alternative' has continuity with the juvenile courts in that its disposals are to be justified on *consequentialist* grounds. It is a departure in that not just some, but all its disposals are to be justified in this way. The retreat of retributivism is marked by the decreasing importance of the offence and of the distinction between offenders and children in need of care or protection. It is not non-punitive but in certain circumstances, being concerned with what is in the best interests of the child, it is less likely to be punitive than the juvenile court system.

The Report argues that much of the dissatisfaction with the juvenile court system which led to the institution of hearings stemmed from its attempt to combine features justified by conflicting moral viewpoints. We have seen that the New Alternative attempts to remove the conflict and consequent dissatis-faction by strengthening features justified by consequentialism, and removing or giving less prominence to features justified by or encouraging retributivism. Even so, the writers of the Report comment 'we do not believe that this apparent conflict of aim can ever be wholly eradicated' (para. 57). This is hardly surprising for the conflict rests on widely held genuine differences of moral belief. My purpose in this chapter has been to show the main differences between these moral beliefs, their relation to the juvenile court and hearings systems, and their significance in encouraging and shaping the change from one to the other. All this should also facilitate debate about the *moral justifications* for the present hearings system, present practice and any recommended changes, as I said at the beginning, an aspect too little considered.

I will conclude with an example to illustrate such a debate in context. At present supervision orders are supposed to correspond to the needs of the child. Suppose the child has been referred for an offence. Given the kind of cor-respondence recommended, the order will often be quite out of proportion to the offence. For example, a child might be placed on supervision *initially* for one year for a minor offence such as a breach of the peace or shoplifting, if the social background report shows sufficient deprivation. From the retributivist point of view this is an unwarranted interference with individual liberty. To be required to do as a supervising officer demands for so long with a probable extension of the period if *he* thinks it best, is an unjust imposition for such a minor infringement of the law. Further, the retributivist might argue, the much vaunted flexibility of the consequentialist 'New Alternative' is in fact no more than a licence to subject an individual to 'measures of treatment' until conformity, or the age of 18. Hearing disposals on the whole aim to make the individual and his family behave in socially acceptable ways in their present environment. Though they may make residential requirements, hearings have no power to make long-term environmental changes for the individual, of house or school or income, for example. In cases in which this is what would *help* the individual, the hearings insist that behaviour improve without this help, and this brings out the priority of conformity. Far from being a system designed to further the best interests of the child, the range of disposals available shows that in fact it is designed to further the best interests of others. And in the move to thoroughgoing consequentialism, retributivist limitations on 'measures of treatment' by which this can be achieved, have been removed. The consequentialist might disagree.

REFERENCES

1. Children and Young Persons. Scotland (1964), Cmnd. 2306, HMSO (Kilbrandon Report).
2. Flew, A. (1969), The Justification of Punishment, *in*: H. B. Acton (ed.), *The Philosophy of Punishment*. London, Macmillan.
3. Wallace, G. and Walker, A. D. M. (1970), *The Definition of Morality*, p. 2, n. 1. London, Methuen.
4. Kant, Immanuel, *Die Metaphysick der Sitten*.
5. Mill, J. S. (1861), *Utilitarianism*. Ed. Mary Warnock (1962), Fontana.
6. Fox, Sanford J. (1975), The Scottish Panels: An American Viewpoint on Children's Right to Punishment. *J. of the Law Soc. of Scotland*, vol. 20, no. 3.

20

PROTECTING THE RIGHTS OF THE CHILD*

JOHN P. GRANT

CONCERN is frequently expressed in legal circles at the adequacy of the safe-guards for the rights of the child in the children's hearings system. We must accept the fact that under the children's hearings system more children are being sent to residential establishments than under the juvenile court system and that more children are being placed under supervision than before April 1971. It is axiomatic that any system that has the power to deprive a child of his liberty or to impose any sanction on him, however benevolent or positive the intention of that sanction, must have regard to the rights of the child.

Expressions of concern about the legal safeguards in the children's hearings system can be grouped under three main heads:

1. *that children may be 'pulled off the streets' without having committed an offence or satisfied any of the other grounds of referral;*

2. *that children may be subjected to the jurisdiction of children's hearings, and the possible consequences emanating therefrom, without that jurisdiction being tested in a court using the normal rules of evidence;*

3. *that the decisions of children's hearings may be improperly arrived at, for example by proceeding on facts which are not established in a court and which may not even be divulged to the family.*

In examining each of these heads, it is essential to look at the totality of protection afforded to the child. The children's hearings system derives primarily from Part III of the Social Work (Scotland) Act 1968, a statute that has, with some justification, been described as difficult to interpret, for the person interpreting cannot, in the words of one commentator, 'make intelligible that which is unintelligible nor complete those deadly lacunae'. The bare bones of this Act have been clothed with a number of statutory instruments, the most important for present purposes being the Children's Hearings (Scotland) Rules 1971.

* This is an abridged version of an article that appeared in 1975 *Juridical Review* 209.

Yet the Act and the Rules do not, between them, exhaust the framework within which children's hearings operate. These legislative measures contain both gaps and ambiguities, and practices have evolved to bridge the gaps and circumvent the ambiguities. It would be quite futile to search for uniform national practices and it is no exaggeration to say that practices have tended – and will continue – to be as many and varied as the number of children's hearings.

Pulling children off the streets

The essence of this fear is a misconception of the preventive nature of the children's hearings system, which has been interpreted by some as authorising a children's hearing to make a decision about a child who has not committed an offence (or satisfied any of the other conditions specified in section 32(2) of the Act) and appears before a hearing simply because he seems to need care.

A child can appear before a children's hearing only if:

(a) *one of the eight conditions set out in section 32 of the Act is satisfied (Act, secs. 32(2) and 42); and*

(b) *the reporter is convinced that the child may be in need of compulsory measures of care (Act, sec. 39(3)).*

At the initial stages both these matters are determined by the reporter and whether or not children will be 'pulled off the streets' depends on the way the reporter interprets both his rôle and the facts of cases before him.

While the Act makes no mention of the reporter's attitude to the offence or the other grounds of referral, he must obviously satisfy himself that there is a *prima facie* case to answer. So, for the child offender, the reporter would satisfy himself that there is sufficient evidence to indicate guilt; for, should the child deny the offence grounds at a subsequent hearing, the reporter may be directed to attempt to establish the grounds before the Sheriff. However, at the initial investigation stage the reporter will rely to large measure on the police report, and he will not take precognitions from witnesses unless and until he is directed by the children's hearing to go to the Sheriff.

The reporter must also satisfy himself that the child may be in need of compulsory measures of care. If he considers that no measures of care are necessary then he is required by the Act to do nothing; if he considers that voluntary measures of care are appropriate he may institute them; it is only where the reporter considers that the child requires measures of care on a compulsory basis that he is entitled to refer the child to a children's hearing.

Because of the quasi-judicial nature of the work that a reporter is required to do, one might expect legal qualifications to be a prerequisite to appointment. The reporter must decide if a child may be in need of compulsory measures of care on the basis of information passed to him and of his own initial investigation; if the child or his parents do not accept the grounds of referral, the reporter must prepare and present the case to put before the sheriff; and the reporter will appear in any appeal by the child or his parents against the decision of a children's hearing. Despite the fact that the Kilbrandon Committee (para. 102)[1] considered it important that reporters should be legally qualified, no formal qualifications are required of applicants for posts of reporter and, while the legal profession was at one time the major professional group represented among reporters, nowadays most reporters and their assistants have no formal legal training.

It can be argued that a lack of legal training can influence a reporter's attitude to his work. Some reporters may see it as their function to get children whom they think to be in need of care before a children's hearing, without undue regard as to whether the child satisfies any of the conditions specified in the Act for conferring jurisdiction on a children's hearing. This approach places the cart well and truly before the horse, and, in the context of a juridical structure that can result in the deprivation of liberty, is dangerous in the extreme. Of course, the fact that the office of reporter is filled by a qualified lawyer will not necessarily prevent this problem arising, but it must surely minimise its incidence.

The nub of the matter is that, whatever his training and qualifications, the reporter is not subject to any external control over his activities. The closest equivalent to the office of reporter is that of procurator-fiscal, who is appointed by the Lord Advocate to institute and conduct criminal proceedings in the sheriff court and district court subject to general and particular control by the Lord Advocate. While the importance of keeping the reporter independent of his paymaster, the local authority, is emphasised by the interposition of the Secretary of State in the appointment and dismissal of a reporter, there is no provision for an agency to exercise a supervisory function in relation to re- porters. And just as there is no supervisory agency, so there is no advisory agency to which reporters can turn for expert and technical advice. Such advice as reporters receive comes inevitably from Social Work Services Group, an independent group within the Scottish Education Department. But Social Work Services Group is by and large unable to provide the kind of advice that reporters require, having neither the expertise in, nor experience of, the issues that trouble reporters. Further, Social Work Services Group is the agency to which many parts of the social work structure turn for advice and guidance; in addition to guiding reporters, it advises the Government, social work departments and children's panels and hearings. There is, therefore, the pos- sibility that Social Work Services Group might find itself asked to advise both sides disputing a point of procedure or practice under the Act.

It is less than satisfactory that reporters are subject to no external control and have no direct access to independent advice. Both these defects could be remedied by placing reporters within the Crown Office framework, like the procurator-fiscal service, thus subjecting reporters to general and particular constraints, directions and supervision; and at the same time enabling them to obtain advice and assistance on points of law and procedure.

There is no suggestion that to date reporters have acted in such a way as to make the establishment of external control a matter of urgency. No evidence exists to show that reporters perform their duties with anything less than acceptable standards of expedition, fairness and conformity to the law. The contention that reporters, lacking the tradition of the procurator-fiscal service, in some way fall short of the standards of that service, is untenable. Reporters are a responsible, professional group and such successes as the children's hearings system has enjoyed in its five years of operation are in no small measure attributable to the work of reporters. Nonetheless, the desirability of exercising some supervision over the work of officials performing quasi-judicial functions is obvious.

The jurisdiction of hearings

The Kilbrandon Committee (para. 75) was at pains to emphasise that ... 'there is no question of taking juvenile offenders outwith the ambit of the law. Under these proposals ... juvenile offenders would be dealt with not by criminal procedure, but by a special agency on whom this specialised jurisdiction would be conferred by law'. It is implicit in the proposals made by Lord Kilbrandon and his colleagues, and given legislative form in the Social Work (Scotland) Act 1968, that there will be no substantial diminution of, or departure from, the normal rights accorded by law to an accused person. In view of the fact that children are less able to assert their own rights than adults, it may be appropriate to assess whether there is in fact *any* diminution of, or departure from, the normal rights of the accused.

The general law of arrest applies to children as to other suspected persons, with the exception that a child should only be detained in custody for the most pressing reasons, as for example where he is suspected of a serious offence or is unusually recalcitrant, and, if so detained, should not be kept at a police station or jail. Personal searches of children, such as fingerprinting or photographing, which were matters of considerable concern at the time the Social Work (Scotland) Bill was passing through the House of Commons, have been severely restricted. Thus, in theory, both are to be used in as few cases as possible, only in respect of older children and, where possible, in the presence of the parents.

One of the cardinal rules of criminal procedure is that an accused person should be given sufficient notice of the charge against him to enable him to take advice and prepare a defence. For the vast majority of children's hearings, including those concerned with final disposal of a child's case, the child and his parents must be given not less than seven clear days notice (Rules 7 and 8). Thus, while the period of notice may appear adequate, whether a defence can, in fact, be prepared depends on two further factors: the adequacy of the specification of the grounds in the notice, and access to professional advice.

The Children's Hearings Rules require that the notice indicate the specific condition upon which the case is proceeding and state the facts on the basis of which it is sought to show that that condition is satisfied (Rule 15). In respect of offence grounds, the degree of specification required is the same as that required in a complaint from the procurator-fiscal, so that there can be no room for the suggestion that the law permits inadequate specification in the grounds of referral: the child will know the reason for his appearance before a children's hearing with a similar degree of specification as an offender.

There is, of course, little point in providing ample notice and adequate specification if the individual is unable to understand the essence of what is alleged against him, and has no access to professional advice. In Scotland, an accused person may, depending on his means, be entitled to free legal advice before his appearance in court and legal aid to represent him there.

The child and his parents are entitled to bring a representative to a children's hearing (Rule 11), but the absence of provision for the granting of legal aid at a hearing largely removes the possibility of that representative being a lawyer. The underlying philosophy of Part III of the Social Work (Scotland) Act is that children 'in trouble' are taken out of the court setting and dealt with by lay sentencing tribunals who have no rôle in determining innocence or guilt, but proceed on what may be termed an 'agreed referral'. It can therefore be argued that there is little a lawyer could do at a children's hearing: there are no issues of innocence or guilt; and a plea in mitigation is irrelevant where the aim is to focus on the total problems of the child in his environment, and not merely on the specific grounds of referral. However, there is much force in the counter-argument that a competent lawyer could be of great assistance in advising the child whether or not to accept the grounds of referral and in marshalling and presenting the child's case to a children's hearing.

From the point of view of protecting the rights of the child, the most important preliminary safeguard is the provision of professional advice on the essence of the allegation made in the grounds of referral and on the consequences of acceptance or non-acceptance of these grounds. At present there is little positive help offered to the child: neither the leaflet 'To tell you about the children's hearing' which must be sent to the child and his parents prior to a children's hearing (Rules – Forms 1, 2A and 2B), nor such advice as a social worker may give, is sufficient to provide the type of guidance needed. Nothing less than expert legal advice will suffice, and such advice falls within the '£25 scheme' introduced by the Legal Advice and Assistance Act 1972. It now rests with those operating the children's hearings system to give positive encouragement to families to seek legal advice before a children's hearing. This could be done by amending the notes appended to the forms used by reporters to notify children of children's hearings; or by incorporating reference to legal advice in the leaflet 'To tell you about the children's hearing'. At any rate the present position is not wholly satisfactory and many children may not be receiving the guidance they need to prepare them for a children's hearing.

No child should be pressured or 'duped' into accepting the grounds of referral at a children's hearing. Before a hearing can proceed to consider a child's case, the grounds must be explained to, and understood by, the child and accepted by him and one of his parents (Act, sec. 42 (1), (2) and (7)).

It is not enough for the chairman of the children's hearing to 'put' or read the grounds of referral to the family: the Act requires that they be explained (Act, sec. 42(1)). No guidance is given to the chairman as to what constitutes an explanation of the grounds and, sadly, there is no express provision in the

Act or Rules equivalent to the requirement in the prosecution of children that 'the court shall explain to the child the substance of the charge in simple language suitable to his age and understanding . . .'. Nonetheless, this formula must be read into section 42 of the Social Work (Scotland) Act 1968: the Act does require an explanation of the grounds that the child is capable of understanding and has, in fact, understood. So the chairman is required to explain the essence of what is alleged against a child. But how, one might ask, is a lay chairman to explain the essence of, say, reset or housebreaking with intent to malicious mischief or breach of the peace? The practice has developed in some areas for the chairman of the children's hearing to ask the reporter to explain the grounds of referral. While the Act makes no mention of the chairman delegating this function, it is obviously more in tune with the spirit of the Act that the reporter give an adequate explanation of the substance of the grounds of referral than that the chairman should either read the grounds to the family or hazard his own explanation of what is alleged. But even this expedient does not take us completely out of the woods when one bears in mind that most reporters have no formal legal education.

Another threat to the rights of the child can occur in the way in which the child's acceptance or non-acceptance of the grounds is sought, and in this respect three potentially dangerous situations can be identified.

In the first place, if the child does not accept the grounds the hearing may either send the matter to the Sheriff to have the grounds tested or discharge the referral (Act, sec. 42(2)(c)). It is quite possible that these alternatives may be explained to the child in such a way as to make it apparent that, should the grounds not be accepted, the case *will* be sent to the Sheriff. This type of pressure is illegitimate, but there is little that can be done by legislative action to prevent it, especially since the family will already know from the leaflet 'To tell you about the children's hearing' that this is a possibility. One must trust to the impartiality and good sense of the chairman of the children's hearing to avoid undue emphasis on the possible application to the Sheriff.

Secondly, the child may, in response to the chairman's explanation of the grounds of referral, make admissions that do not constitute a full acceptance of the grounds of referral. The danger here is that the chairman might take it upon himself to question the child about the events in such a way that the child is interrogated, and this is wholly unacceptable. There is, however, a narrow dividing line between on the one hand obtaining a 'confession' by interrogation, and on the other hand seeking by simple and neutral questions to elucidate the child's response to the grounds of referral. Again, much will depend upon the impartiality and good sense of the chairman of the children's hearing.

The third area of difficulty arises in relation to the amendment of the grounds of referral. The sad fact is that the 1968 Act made no provision for amendment or adjustment of the grounds of referral. The Children's Hearings Rules require that a child be given seven days notice of the hearing and of the reason for the hearing (Rules 7 and 15), and the amendment of the grounds or the addition of grounds within that seven-day period contravenes the Rules.

Some reporters take the view that it is permissible to amend the grounds of referral or to add new grounds of referral within this seven-day period as long as the child and his parents consent to, and sign, a minute of waiver. They argue that the amendment or addition of grounds is convenient both from the reporter's point of view, which it obviously is, and also from the family's point of view, in saving them another appearance before a children's hearing, which it may also be. Yet this is a dangerous and indefensible practice. The Act and Rules permit no amendment of grounds and require a period of notice. That period of notice is designed to enable the family to consider the situation in which they find themselves, to take advice and to prepare themselves. The amendment or addition of grounds deprives the family of a substantial element of the protection afforded by the children's hearings system.

It has been suggested that children in need of compulsory measures of care on the ground that they have committed offences should be referred to the procurator-fiscal by the reporter so that they can be taken to court and thereby given the advantages of the legal safeguards attendant on criminal procedure, as well as of legal aid and advice. There is nothing fundamentally wrong with the present methods of testing the jurisdiction of children's hearing that could justify at this time any modification of the philosophy of the children's hearings system and of the Act and Rules. The Kilbrandon Committee estimated that something like 95% of all children brought before children's hearings would accept the grounds (para. 73). In fact, statistics to date show that just under 90% of children accept the grounds of referral. It would only be where this percentage fell dramatically to, say, 70% – or where the procedures and practices of children's hearings could be shown to offer little protection to the rights of the child offender – that this proposal to refer to the procurator-fiscal might have to be given serious consideration.

Great importance was attached by the Kilbrandon Committee to the right of appeal to the courts from decisions of children's hearings (paras. 111–117). The Social Work (Scotland) Act 1968 allows the child or his parents – and not the reporter or the social work department – to appeal to the Sheriff against 'any decision of a children's hearing' (Act, sec. 49). Further appeal lies on a point of law or irregularity of procedure to the Court of Session (Act, sec. 50). So the child can challenge the grounds where they are in breach of the formal statutory requirements on, for example, authentication and period of notice, or where they are irrelevant or lacking in specification. The child can challenge a disposal arrived at through an irregularity of procedure as, for example, where a parent is excluded against his will, or the child is pressured into accepting the grounds of referral, or the views of the child are not sought. The child can challenge facts wrongly considered as, for example, where the decision is taken on a fact not disclosed to the family. The child can challenge an unreasonable or unsupportable decision as to disposal, as, for example, where he considers it too severe.

The Sheriff is enjoined to allow the appeal if he is satisfied that the decision of the children's hearing is not justified 'in all the circumstances of the case' (Act, sec. 49(5)). In making this determination, the Sheriff is provided with a copy of the reasons that the children's hearing gave for its decision. The Sheriff's function is to test the decision *and* the reasons for it against the facts of the case.

A children's hearing, it now seems clear, must not simply give reasons, but must give adequate reasons: they must narrate not simply 'what' was done or 'how' it was done, but 'why' it was done. One children's hearing gave as the reasons for its decision the following:

> Taking all the advice and all the recommendations available into consideration the hearing agreed, after taking into account the full discussion of the hearing itself, that the best possible way of helping this child was to allow her to remain in [a children's home].

On appeal in this case, *K.* v. *Finlayson*, the Sheriff rightly considered that these reasons were wholly inadequate saying, 'insofar as this is a statement of anything at all, it is a statement of the procedures adopted by the hearing in coming to its decision. It cannot by any stretch of interpretation, or indeed imagination, be construed as giving a single *reason* for the decision.'[2]

There has been debate among Sheriffs on their rôle in appeals from the decisions of children's hearings. Some hold that their function is to review the whole case and to come to their own decision on the most appropriate disposal for the child. Others maintain that the Sheriff should interfere with the decision of a children's hearing only where he is convinced that some error has been made or some important factor has not been taken into account.

In the only reported decision on this point to date, *D.* v. *Sinclair*, the Sheriff adhered to the latter view, stating that 'a Sheriff should not interfere with the determination simply because he felt another form of treatment would be preferable. Accordingly, I consider the Sheriff should not allow an appeal unless there was some flaw in the procedure adopted by the hearing or he is satisfied that the hearing had not given proper consideration to some factor in the case'.[3]

So, should defects occur in procedure or a wrong decision be reached there is a means of redress by appeal to the courts. There have, however, been very few appeals, and there is a strong case for ensuring that the chairman of the children's hearing informs the family specifically and directly of their right of appeal (as in fact Rule 17(4)(f) requires) and that this information be reinforced by mention in the copy of the supervision requirement sent to the family after the children's hearing.

Decisions improperly reached

There is a belief that children's hearings tend to be lax in their procedures. This belief is reinforced by the broad aim of the hearings system of holding an informal and frank discussion of a child's circumstances and, particularly, by Rule 9(1), which states that, save where the procedure is laid down in these Rules, 'the procedure at a children's hearing shall be such as the chairman shall in his discretion determine'. That there may be laxity in procedure is undisputable; that the laxity may, on occasions, be serious is probable. But any laxity that violates the rights of the child can arise only through imperfect appreciation or application of the procedural standards set by the Act and the Rules, and as such is appealable to the Sheriff.

The chairman of the children's hearing is not a completely free agent in determining procedure. Thus, his apparent discretion in procedural matters is fettered by a number of specific statutory requirements: he must identify the child and ascertain the child's age (Act, sec. 55); he must ensure that the number of people present is kept to a minimum, while at the same time permitting the presence of those who have a right to attend (Act, sec. 35(2) and (3) and Rule 12), and he must explain the purpose of the hearing to the family (Rules 17(1) and 19(2). Further he must explain the grounds of referral to the child (Act, sec. 42(1)); he must ascertain whether they are understood and accepted by the child (Act, sec. 42(2) and (7)); he must ascertain whether the grounds are accepted by one of the parents (Act, sec. 42(2)). He must chair the discussion on the merits of the case, and the children's hearing must, under his direction, consider the grounds of referral (Act, sec. 43(1)) and any report made available to the hearing (Act, sec. 43(1) and Rules 17(2) and 19(3), discuss the case with the child, his parents and any representative (Rules 17(2) and 19(3)), and endeavour to obtain the view of the child and the parents on the best disposal of the case (Rules 17(2) and 19(3)). The chairman must inform the family of the substance of any reports before the hearing (Rules 17(3) and 19(4)); he must inform the family and any representative of the decision of the hearing (Rule 17(4)), and the reasons for that decision (Rule 17(4)); he must inform the family and any representative of the right to appeal to the Sheriff (Rule 17(4)), and of their right to receive a written copy of the reasons for the hearing's decision (Rule 17(4)). As these matters afford no discretion, and as they exhaust the situations in which the rights of the child are most at risk, it is fair to say that the Act and the Rules afford adequate protection in the hearing situation.

In relation to procedure, particular concern has been expressed about the account taken of facts in social background reports. The Rules do not require that these reports be made available to the family or any representative, though the *substance* of all reports before the hearing must be communicated to the family 'if it appears to [the chairman] that this is material to the manner in which the case of the child should be disposed of and that its disclosure would not be detrimental to the interests of the child' (Rules 17(3) and 19(4)). Failure to disclose facts in a report where they are material to the decision of the hearing would render that decision liable to be set aside on appeal. Similarly, children's hearings must, and it is submitted do, take a narrow view of non-disclosure on the grounds that disclosure would be detrimental to the interests of the child. Again, this is a question that can be regulated by the courts on appeal.

Much has been made of the decision in the case of *K. v. Finlayson*. The case concerned an appeal from the decision of an Edinburgh children's hearing to commit a child to a children's home. The gross inadequacy of the reasons given by the hearing for its decision, which have been discussed already, would, in themselves, have been sufficient to justify the Sheriff in setting aside the hearing's decision. The Sheriff appears to have been compelled by the arguments put before her to consider the appeal on another ground, that is, whether a children's hearing must take its decision on the basis only of facts accepted by the family or established by the Sheriff, or whether it can take into account other facts as well.

Sheriff Sinclair concluded that the hearing must have regard only to the grounds of referral, and she said that, on the basis of natural justice, it was 'nonsense . . . to say that the hearing is then entitled to take into account any other matter whatsoever that they choose, including grounds which were not placed before the parent'. It may be that the learned Sheriff expressed herself infelicitously, for it is absurd to suggest that a children's hearing is restricted to considering the grounds, accepted or established, and nothing else.

The essence of the children's hearings system is that once a hearing has jurisdiction in respect of a child by the acceptance or establishment of the grounds of referral, it is empowered to examine the child's whole circumstances in arriving at a decision in the child's best interest. The Kilbrandon Committee were reluctant to lay down any rigid framework for the procedure at a children's hearing but did emphasise the importance of 'full, free and unhurried discussion' (para. 109). The White Paper, *Social Work and the Community*, suggested the procedure to be followed at a children's hearing once the grounds are accepted or established: 'The panel will go on to consider background reports on the child, the advice of the social work department and of any specialists consulted. They will discuss the whole circumstances with the child and his parents, and in the light of the discussion will reach a decision on the treatment or training which the child should have' (para. 66).[4]

The Act itself provides ample evidence that discussion is not restricted simply to the grounds of referral. Section 43 makes it clear that the grounds relate to the initial question of jurisdiction, and once jurisdiction is established, the children's hearing can consider the social background report and 'such other relevant information as may be available to them'.

However, the decision in *K. v Finlayson* emphasised the importance of the disclosure of all material facts. The chairman of the children's hearing is obliged to disclose to the family the substance of all reports. The parents have a right to be present at all stages of a children's hearing considering the case of their child (Act, sec. 41(1)); the failure of parents to attend the children's hearing can render them liable to a fine. The child will invariably be present except where the hearing is satisfied that it would be detrimental to his interests to attend (Act, sec. 40(1) and (2)); the attendance of the child can be secured by warrant. So the legislation provides as best it can for the attendance of the child and his parents throughout a children's hearing – save in exceptional circumstances – and for the disclosure to the family of the substance of all reports including, of course, all allegations made against him. Thereby, the family will have an opportunity to challenge allegations and to put their point of view.

REFERENCES

1. Children and Young Persons. Scotland (1964), Cmnd. 2306, HMSO (Kilbrandon Report).
2. *K. v Finlayson* (1974), *Scots Law Times* (Sheriff Court), 51.
3. *D. v Sinclair* (1973), *Scots Law Times* (Sheriff Court), 47.
4. Social Work and the Community (1966), Cmnd. 3065, HMSO (White Paper).

21

JUVENILE JUSTICE REFORM: SOME AMERICAN-SCOTTISH COMPARISONS

SANFORD J. FOX

AT about the same time that the Kilbrandon Report appeared there was also important change taking place in the juvenile justice system in America. In both countries a central issue in the debate over how to improve the system involved re-examining the relative importance of rules of law on the one hand, and powers of discretion on the other. The question was whether what happened to children alleged to be in trouble with the law was to be determined by reference to fixed legal principles or by the judgement of some official who, although required by law to pay attention to some matters (child welfare) and not to others (child punishment), was nonetheless free to reach a decision in particular cases that one could hardly declare to be legally wrong. Another way of describing the rôle of this discretion would be to say that there were hardly any sets of facts concerning delinquent children which would give rise to a legal right to a particular decision. Contrast this, for example, with the rule of law that says that in thus and so circumstances a person has a right to legal aid, or to cross-question his accuser, or to have his denial of the charge listened to in court. Where the underlying circumstances are present, no official has discretion to withdraw these rights. Mandatory prison sentences provide another clear contrast.

According to Kilbrandon, there was little problem in Scotland concerning either the scope of discretionary power over children, or about the manner in which it was exercised. A central difficulty was that the use of discretion to reach decisions about the welfare of young offenders was that it was too intimately tied to the inflexibility of the legal rules of criminal procedure. It was simply a bad mix to vest the same tribunal with the responsibility to administer the somewhat rigid criminal law and the duty to reach discretionary decisions about individual children. And so Parliament decreed a divorce between these two and custody of the discretion about disposal was awarded to the children's hearings.

In America there was indeed a problem concerning the scope and exercise of discretion. By the early 1960's it had become apparent that in American juvenile courts discretion had achieved a near complete dominance over law. Whereas in Scotland there was little doubt that the courts were following the rules of law before the discretionary stage of disposal was reached, the claim that no such thing was transpiring in our juvenile courts was becoming strident. Studies and individual experiences had demonstrated that frequently children were told far too little about why they had been brought to court, their opportunities to deny charges – even when this had been adequately explained to them – were severely handicapped by the overpowering belief by juvenile court judges and their staffs that they could do some good for children and that it was, therefore, quite unimportant whether the particular charges were or were not true. The presentation of witnesses for the child, searching cross-questioning of witnesses against him, intelligent exploration of the significance of the evidence brought forward by both sides – these all suffered largely because the child (and his parents) were left to their own skills and courage in demanding and exercising the judicial rights that centuries of Anglo-American history had demonstrated to be necessary for an impartial and fair search for truth. Few of the families that found themselves in American juvenile courts could afford to retain their own attorney to assert their rights and the idea of a legal advisor provided at public expense was extremely popular.

The situation that existed in traditional juvenile courts in America might best be illustrated by describing a children's hearing I observed on my first visit to Scotland in 1971, only two months after Part III of the Act had come into force. A young boy age 10 had been referred to the hearing for theft of some copper piping. He had denied that he had stolen anything to the police and to the social worker who had come to his home prior to the hearing. The reports before the hearing showed that he had been apprehended along with other boys immediately following a break into a place where the piping was stored. It was not clear whether he was in actual possession of the stolen things when he was caught. The boy's story, repeated to police, social worker, and then hearing, was that he had urged his companions not to engage in the theft and that his only fault was in not leaving the scene when the others dashed in to take the piping. The reports also indicated, however, that the boy was living with his mother and a step-father, and that there was a great deal of tension, hostility and unhappiness in the relationship with the step-father. When asked whether he accepted the grounds of referral, the boy repeated the narration he had given earlier. The hearing then engaged in a line of questioning that included: 'But you knew they were going to do it, didn't you?' and 'You could have run away, couldn't you?' and 'You were involved in this thing then, weren't you?' and, finally, 'You therefore accept the grounds of referral, don't you?' This followed, of course, by 'Aye'.

I think that as a matter of Scottish criminal law, there is probably no offence committed by virtue of knowledge that another will engage in criminal conduct and mere presence at the scene of the other's crime, at least when the crime is relatively minor as this one was. But obviously the problem was not that the boy was coerced into accepting that he had committed a crime that did not exist under the law. It was that he was coerced at all into accepting the hearing's authority over him. Later discussions with the members of the hearing confirmed what appeared to be happening. They knew of the troubles the boy was having at the time, they thought they could help, and that was all that counted. I should add that this is the only instance I have observed of illegal coercion in a children's hearing and I have, since 1971, seen no reason to generalise from it. But discretion to decide on what sort of help children in trouble were to be provided has been translated into discretion to disregard the law.

The well intentioned overpowering of the law by discretion was seen as an epidemic in America. Telling the judges that their *raison d'être* was to help children was causing them to forget that they were judges and not social workers. The central thrust of American juvenile justice reform in the sixties was, therefore, to expel discretion and motive-to-help from where it did not belong and to revitalise those phases of the juvenile justice process where decisions were to be made by reference to rules of law. It would not be inaccurate to describe this reform as an effort to move the American system to the point where Kilbrandon had found the Scottish system – faithful adherence to law by the same tribunal that had disposal discretion as well. Conversely, the Social Work (Scotland) Act, by establishing a corps of volunteer officials whose responsibilities included some observance of rules of law, but whose remit was almost entirely to provide help, ran some risk of repeating the American mistake. In other words, while there was little concern that the Sheriffs had neglected their legal duties, would the panels manage the same devotion to law?

It may well be wondered why, even if rules of law were being so frequently disregarded in American juvenile courts, this was considered to be such a central problem, in light of the fact that these rules were largely irrelevant for most of the children. Kilbrandon had rightly observed that for almost all the children under discussion the rules of criminal procedure were not important since they pleaded guilty and demanded no trial in which these rules would be applied; the same was, and is, true in America. Only a small proportion of children charged with offences dispute the facts and proceed to a trial. In America, as in Scotland, the problem was what to do with the children who acknowledge their accountability, and who should decide what should be done? There are, I think, two reasons why the American reforms, although so much a matter of the tail wagging the dog, were vigorously pursued nonetheless. One is that, as the 'piping-pinching' case described above illustrates, there is a legal right not to be coerced into being one of the children about whom the problem is one of disposal, and that right is easily ignored. In this respect it is simply not true that legal issues are of no importance to the bulk of the children in the system. While this is so, I think it is largely a hindsight rationalisation and that it played, at most, a minor rôle in propelling the American reforms down the road of securing legal rights for children.

Far more important is the fact that because large numbers of the children in American juvenile courts were (and still are) blacks and other minorities, and were (and still are) from families at the lower end of the economic ladder, the reform of juvenile justice got caught up in the Civil Rights movement and in the War on Poverty. Both of these social and political developments expressed themselves in many ways, not the least of which was the demand for allocation of a larger proportion of national wealth for the deprived classes. But the claim for legal rights – based in my view on a serious overestimate of the power of legal principle to produce rapid social change – was in the forefront of the insistence on a better life for the poor and the minorities. It would have been an intolerable anomaly for adults to have gained access to the law as a means for achieving economic independence and social autonomy, while their own children remained deprived of fundamental legal protections when their liberty and independence were at stake in juvenile courts. And so, rather than focus on whether juvenile courts were capable of using their discretionary disposal powers in an appropriate fashion, as did Kilbrandon, Americans concentrated on forcing juvenile courts to confine their discretion and administer rules of law.

There was, moreover, some precedent for this. Here and there in the 1950's courts had already begun to vest juvenile court children with some of the legal rights normally provided by rules of criminal procedure. This gained great momentum in the early 1960's as New York and California came forward with sweeping overhauls of their legislation concerning delinquent children and mandated that juvenile court procedure resemble more closely the conduct of a criminal trial. Central to these developments was the requirement that poor children be provided a lawyer at public expense, unless they declared that they did not want one. By 1967 the Supreme Court of the United States had stepped in and declared that fundamental legal rights for these children were immutable requirements of the federal constitution, meaning that neither the state legislatures nor other courts had any choice but to grant these rights. The privilege against self-incrimination, the right to an adequate notice of charges, the right to confront accusers – these and other rights came quickly to be part of what was required in the juvenile justice process. Most importantly, the expectation that these rights could be enforced was based on what was considered to be the most basic right of all . . . the right to have a lawyer.

These changes in the legal environment of juvenile justice in America have been hailed by some as landmark achievements; others have bitterly decried them as constituting a destructive inroad on the power of society to help delinquent children; another group sees the whole thing as quite an irrelevant turn of events in a system whose problems are entirely a matter of inadequate resources. And everyone is right. There is an important, though concededly non-utilitarian, value in according children the dignity of not being required to incriminate themselves and in otherwise recognising them as autonomous beings who are not merely pawns in the adult game of crime prevention. In this sense, the legal rights movement has, in fact, been a landmark accomplishment. Furthermore, there is little doubt that the exercise of legal rights has imposed a barrier between some children and efforts by the adult world to do something good for them; the frustrated helpers are also right. And it is demonstrably true as well that these rights have done little to remedy the resource starvation of the system. Not only have these rights been impotent to bring new resources to the system, they have also been incapable of preventing an era of general economic depression from taking back resources that had already been committed. These latter weaknesses have tended to erode the whole legal rights achievement itself as well, for it turns out that lawyers for the poor have to be paid for and they need to be seen as one of the required systematic resources. The lawyers are, for this reason, in as much of a short supply as all the other resources and without them the enforcement of other legal rights has regressed to an earlier era of gross neglect.

To an American who must regretfully acknowledge these failures of a a decade of reform to change very much, developments in Scotland over the past five years are of more than passing interest. Here reference is made to the persistent complaint about the endemic shortage of resources for children, and the inability of the hearings to command the services and treatments called for by the needs of the children that come before them. It may be, of course, that there can never be 'enough', and that the attitude of hearing members and others similarly disturbed by the resources problem do not take sufficient account of what increases there have, in fact, been. Since 1972, for example, at least 17 new children's homes are reported as having opened while about a dozen more are under construction – all of which is aimed at providing around 500 new places. It appears as well that approximately 70 new places will be provided in List D schools. But these are absolute figures and they may not tell whether there is sufficient service when one takes account of the number of children in need. If this is so, and if the grand design of the children's hearings system is to bring service and resources to children, then the parallel with the American experience regarding legal rights appears striking.

Have we both been chasing rainbows?

No more than we usually do. First some comment about the American habit of rainbow chasing, then more tentative observations about the panels. The American juvenile justice system is just about 150 years old, having first come into being with the establishment of the New York House of Refuge in 1826 as an alternative to incarcerating juvenile offenders in the adult prison. There has, since then, hardly been a period of peace and quiet, a period unmarked by efforts to reform this reform and then to reform the reform that had reformed the reform. Are the large congregate institutions like the New York House better than small ones? Is moral education superior to vocational education for delinquent children? Maybe we should forget about all that and concentrate on trying to provide parent substitutes and replicate the 'good' family life. When should children be apprenticed out? Where? What is the rôle of religion in all this? Whose religion? These and other questions were debated hotly by nineteenth-century reformers and reform followed upon reform, rainbow after rainbow. Our present century, with the arrival of the juvenile court in 1899, has been no different. The initial reliance on volunteer probation staff proved unsatisfactory and was followed by publicly paid probation officers. Municipally based juvenile courts were followed by a pattern of country-wide courts, followed by claims for the virtues of a state-wide court. Reliance on therapeutic discussions between judge and child was replaced by therapeutic sessions with a psychiatrist, replaced by a therapeutic session with a peer group, replaced by destroying the therapeutic reform schools, and so on. The hope that law and lawyers would do some good was, as I have suggested, nurtured by an interface of the juvenile justice system with other post-war developments in America, but it also springs from a tradition of perpetual reform that may be a fundamental feature of American culture. There is, therefore, cause for neither alarm nor despair in learning that we have to look in new directions for means of coping with our juvenile justice problems. We find ourselves required to ask new questions instead of seeking better answers to the old ones. My own suggestions, for example, involve that we cease asking how to make treatment more effective and begin thinking how to construct a fair and humane system that does not care overly much about treatment.[1]

In doing this, I think we can profit greatly from the Scottish experience, in two respects primarily. One is by creating a panel-type organisation that would exploit the demonstrated ability of the Scottish hearings to achieve a high level of communication in conflict situations. There are many, perhaps the bulk of juvenile justice cases, where achieving some understanding by each side of the problems underlying the child and between child and school might be dealt with this way, and it would make sense as well to place cases where the child is in conflict with society on account of a minor offence into this system. But on account of considerations of fairness to the child and in recognition of a more or less permanent shortage of resources, it might be well to deny any such American panels the power to compel anyone to do anything more than to appear and participate. In such a scheme, the analogy to the American model of a compulsory, but not binding, arbitration may be apt.

There are, however, far more fundamental matters that need to be resolved in the current round of reform in American juvenile justice. They arise because a major component of the present difficulty in America is the problem of the violent juvenile.

What appears to be of major importance is a more modest definition of progress, prompted by recall of the observation by President Johnson's Commission on Law Enforcement and Administration of Justice in 1967 regarding the inability of the American juvenile court to achieve the goals that had been set for it: '... failure is most striking when hopes are highest'. In part, the issue of failure intrudes at all on account of unrealistically high hopes about our ability to change attitudes and behaviour patterns, even regarding children. At stake now in America is the question of whether serious criminals, young and old, are merely good people waiting for the proper inspiration to come along to cause them to shed their false facade of wickedness, or whether there really are wicked people. Professor James Q. Wilson, for example, in referring to the failure again of programmes that followed from the recommendations of the President's commission has noted:

> Since the days of the crime commission we have learned a great deal, more than we are prepared to admit. Perhaps we fear to admit it because of a new-found modesty about the foundations of our knowledge, but

perhaps also because the implications of that knowledge suggest an unflattering view of man. Intellectuals, although they often dislike the common person as an individual, do not wish to be caught saying uncomplimentary things about humankind. Nevertheless, some persons will shun crime even if we do nothing to deter them, others will seek it out even if we do everything to reform them. Wicked people exist. Nothing avails except to set them apart from innocent people. And many people, neither wicked nor innocent, but watchful, dissembling, and calculating of their opportunities, ponder our reaction to wickedness as a cue to what they might profitably do. We have trifled with the wicked, made sport of the innocent, and encouraged the calculators. Justice suffers, and so do we all.[2]

Such an outlook counsels that with serious delinquents the need is for control and public protection; that resources need to be devoted to this end and taken away from programmes designed primarily to deal with minor delinquencies and children whose conflicts involve no criminal conduct at all. Since a system of priorities of this sort can only be mandated by legislation, it appears that we are about to enter on a national debate in which proponents of this, and the sharply opposing more traditional view about using the justice system as a case-finding service to provide services to children in need, will seek public support designed to influence the legislative process one way or another. This time, we appear to have a choice of rainbows.

An assessment of the Scottish reforms of the 1960's must start off, of course, with an acknowledgement that the 'highest hopes' were far more complex than are described by an expectation that more resources would find their way to delinquent children. Allison Morris, for example, has noted that portions of the Kilbrandon report imply that 'by moving from a court to a tribunal and by replacing punishment with treatment, it becomes possible to treat not only the child referred to the hearing but also the family of the child and the potential delinquent'.[3] This suggests that the hopes were still higher, for the reform can be seen not only as a matter of more resources, but more resources for more people. On the other hand, however, the report also notes that 'Broadly, . . . we recommend that those classes of children who are at present subject to the jurisdiction of the juvenile courts should in future be dealt with by the juvenile panels' (para. 92). Perhaps it was not contemplated that the target population would really be expanded.

The same sort of ambivalence can be seen regarding whether a purpose of the new system is to prevent delinquency, or merely to control it; whether delinquent conduct is always a symptom of maladjustment or is sometimes (often?) a normal and episodic event in childhood; whether the causes of delinquency are within the control of courts or panels, or are beyond the reach of the justice system. Rainbows abound, and for that reason an assessment of the five years of the panel system is far more complex than an evaluation of the American effort (once unravelled from the civil rights and war on poverty issues) to bring law and lawyers to the justice system. Whether there has been success or failure depends on what goals are selected for achievement. Importantly, this choice is not dictated by logic but by philosophy. The reduction of delinquency by the rehabilitation of delinquent youth, for example, is a rational goal only if one makes assumptions about the malleability of human nature; whether the target population is large or small depends on what relative importance one assigns to the control of criminal conduct as compared with the importance of providing services on a broad scale; and what is society's responsibility to children? Is it larger or smaller than its responsibility to its older citizens or to the next generation? What is the ultimate justification for intervening in other people's lives? The Kilbrandon Report called attention to this when it posed the question,

> It must finally be a matter of judgement how far, in relation to juveniles and their parents, the application of an educative principle in this way would in fact and in practice represent an appreciable inroad into personal and family life, amounting to loss of liberty or freedom from interference such as to be unacceptable in our society.

It was, of course, the judgement of Parliament that was invited, and this was expressed in passage of the Act. But the question of values cannot be avoided if purpose is now to be compared to accomplishment. It is important to know what the experience of the past five years has been; but it is probably equally as important to know what that experience teaches in terms of the choice of goals for the future.

REFERENCES

1. Fox, Sanford J. (1975), The Scottish Panels: An American Viewpoint on Children's Right to Punishment. *J. Law Soc. Scot.*, March.
2. Wilson, James Q. (1975), *Thinking About Crime*, p. 209. Basic Books.
3. Morris, Allison (1974), Scottish Juvenile Justice: A Critique, in: R. Hood (ed.), *Crime, Criminology and Public Policy*, p. 237. The Free Press.

22

PANEL MEMBERSHIP:
REFLECTIONS ON EXPERIENCE

1. MARGARET DOBIE

TO BE a member of the children's panel is to feel sometimes like a member of the Spanish Inquisition and at others like an Aunt Sally in a fairground. It is to see a great deal of failure but seldom recognisable success. It is to believe that a true concern for children and a willingness to study their needs and problems are the best qualifications for making decisions about those children who are in some kind of difficulty. In other words, it is more a matter of qualities than qualifications and the right qualities are to be found in all sections of the community, regardless of age, sex or education.

The feeling of being a Spanish Inquisitor comes from having to make decisions that unpleasant things should happen to other people for their own good. Historically speaking, probably more crimes have been perpetrated from this motive than have resulted from genuine malevolence and sometimes a panel member can feel sickened by what he feels to be a 'this hurts me more than it hurts you' attitude. He may even envy the Spanish Inquisitor his certainty that the pain inflicted was going to save the soul of the victim from eternal damnation: the price we pay for 'enlightenment' is loss of certainty and we can never feel sure that removing a child from a 'bad' home environment to a 'good' institution will enable him to grow into a better person. To lose certainty is not necessarily to lose faith, however, and we can find the courage to continue so long as we have faith in the hearings system as an expression of the right attitude towards dealing with children in trouble.

If the private, unhappy face of the panel member is that of a Spanish Inquisitor, the public unhappy face is that of an Aunt Sally at a fairground. He gets into this unhappy situation in the following way. He may have a general desire to help children in trouble and when he looks round to see who is most in need of his help he may decide that, although the physically and mentally handicapped are in much need, there is already an army of kindly people sympathetic to their needs: but he knows that children who have grown up without normal care and affection are also handicapped, and are not always so sure of a sympathetic ear. Nobody dreams of blaming a boy who has a deformed foot for not being able to do gymnastics. The boy is excused for his disability and given the normal love and care which every child needs; he can grow into a fine man who can live a normal life in almost every way and be a good father to his children. But many people do blame a child who is born into a situation where he is not wanted and who grows up unable to love and care about other people. Caring for others is something which must be learned and there are some children who never get a chance to learn it. They are therefore handicapped emotionally and require help rather than further punishment.

He decides, therefore, to volunteer for the children's panel. He shoots the (rather slow) rapids of applying and being selected and goes on to his training. The training gives him further insight into the effects of deprivation on children and reinforces his conviction that this is work he wants to do. He visits residential establishments and hears lectures by psychologists, psychiatrists, lawyers and policemen until, by the end, he almost doubts his own or anybody else's adequacy for the task. However, he reassures himself that his rôle is limited to that of decision-maker and all the work of diagnosis and treatment will be carried out by the professionals. Imagine his dismay when he finds that, although he is making the decisions, as agreed in his unwritten, unspoken contract, in many cases these decisions are not being carried out. The diagnosis is made, the decisions are made, but there the matter may end, because there are not the resources in the form of residential places and social workers' hours to give the child the care he needs. The hearing is then akin to a charade. When the panel member finds that he is being attacked because the children's hearings system is not dealing adequately with children in trouble, he wonders if his appointment is in truth to the position of an Aunt Sally. He is exposed prominently (the names of panel members are displayed in post offices and public libraries) and people are throwing criticism at him such as 'you're soft', 'you're just a lot of do-gooders', 'you haven't any teeth'. Not only the general public but the police, the legal profession and even the Bench join in this barrage and the panel member is helpless in the face of it. The criticism is aimed mainly at the lack of resources which he is powerless to change, but this is not clear to critics or public and he feels he has been set up to receive the full impact of the missiles and no official voice is speaking up to explain the truth. He sometimes thinks that hearings are confusing the issue and making it appear that something is being done, screening from the public the fact that very little is being done for children in trouble, less perhaps than ever before. In the old days of punishment, at least some notice was taken of the child who did wrong and there is an argument which says that some attention, even of the wrong kind, is better than none.

So here we have a picture of panel members with two unhappy faces, but they do have a third and happy face. Most panel members are people who feel they are deeply and usefully involved in the problems of their community. They rejoice in the fellowship of the panel itself and the contact it brings with people in all the fields of caring for children. These include social workers, police, teachers and staff in residential establishments. They are left, however, with a number of problems which they must solve for themselves as these are inherent in the system and will still exist even when adequate resources are available.

Firstly, there is the punishment/treatment paradox. The hearing is striving to reach a decision which will be in the best interests of the child but, because of the element of compulsion which is implicit, the child sees it as containing at least an element of punishment. Social workers and police continue to talk in terms of 'giving him another chance' and 'warnings'. It is difficult to see how a police warning can be meaningful unless there is a possibility of some future punishment. So we have a long way to go before we are rid of this attitude. There is the additional possibility that the fact of having been under supervision might be used to the child's disadvantage. This can interfere with a decision to put him on supervision because of lack of parental care rather than because of offending on the part of the child. If the chips are already loaded against a youngster, nobody wants to load them still further by giving him a bad reputation. Until public opinion sees a supervision requirement as something designed purely to help a child and in no way reflecting bad morals, the panel member is going to be faced with this dilemma. It is basic to the thinking in the Social Work (Scotland) Act that children in need of care and protection should be treated in the same way as children who have committed offences. But public opinion has not yet caught up with this legislation. The picture the public has of the child's parents as bingo playing, hard drinking, overpaid spendthrifts is seldom the picture seen by panel members. More often, there is one parent only, living on social security and with a mountain of problems. It is possible that even the most ardent flogger might pause before deciding that all that was required was swift and sure retribution. And in the case of affluent but non-caring parents, it may well be in the best interests of the child that he should be taken into the care of the State, and it is up to the machinery of the State to see to it that the parents contribute to the cost of this care. Any attempt to introduce fining or direct punitive measures against child or parent would destroy the integrity of a hearing.

Secondly, there is the problem of compromising between the formality required by a quasi-judicial process and the informality of a hearing which will allow a child and his parents to express their feelings. Many panel members find this a difficult reconciliation. A frightened child and his anxious, apprehensive parents come into the room. The chairman tries to put them at their ease by a friendly manner and a relaxed atmosphere, but the checking of personal data and the establishing of the grounds for referral make this difficult. Again, at the end of the hearing, when perhaps an empathy has grown up between family and members, the chairman has certain formal duties to perform. He may feel that advising the family of their right to appeal, when a decision has been reached by a full discussion and agreement among all concerned, introduces a contradictory note. This compromise can be achieved and frequently is, but it is not easy and requires skill.

This leads on to the third paradox which has to be resolved. The panel member must be an amateur, an ordinary member of the public, with no special qualifications other than an interest in and concern for children. Yet he is also required to exhibit considerable skill of a sophisticated nature. He is expected to understand and even interpret the law at times, to safeguard the legal interests of the child and to diagnose his social and personal needs. He may be endowed with the right personal qualities, but feel that the task is too much for him intellectually. Let him be consoled by the thought that the task is one to which experts of different kinds have applied themselves all down the ages and it can be seen by the state of our society today how unsuccessful they have been. Let him be confident too that with his concern, humility and humanity he is as likely as anybody else to succeed. He is not after all being asked to undertake the diagnosis or treatment himself. He is being asked to look at a number of opinions and facts about the child provided by experts – social workers, teachers, psychiatrists, psychologists – to see what they add up to and to see if the composite picture matches up to the child in front of him. There can be several different views of a child and his behaviour, and at a hearing they are all brought together. He will follow the recommendations of the experts unless they are contradictory or he has a reason for disagreeing with them. A feeling of inadequacy is often expressed by panel members, especially perhaps by those without professional qualifications. Can there be any better qualification than understanding from experience the social stresses and strains to which a child is subject? The person whose interest is based on theoretical knowledge alone cannot always communicate so well with a child as the person who shares at at least some of his difficulties. The intelligent, concerned panel member who lives in the same community as the child, and who has the principles of the Social Work (Scotland) Act at heart, is probably the ideal panel member. It is a pity that there are not more of them. The idea that being a panel member requires academic skill which must be learned would be better dispelled, so that more non-professional men and women might volunteer.

Another area of conflicting loyalties is 'the best interests of the child' versus 'the interests of society', in other words, how much antisocial behaviour should be tolerated. The 1968 Act states clearly that the only criterion for decision-making is 'the best interests of the child' and the panel member may have to risk at times being accused of being manipulative if he wishes to have regard to the protection of society. He will have to say 'it is not in this child's best interests for him to be allowed to continue to indulge in antisocial behaviour'. A certain amount of delinquency is tolerated by society in other spheres, e.g. when shops display their goods in such a way as to make shop-lifting easy, they consider the commercial gain to be had from this type of display justifies the loss they will have to bear. In other words, they tolerate some stealing. Sometimes a child goes through a delinquent phase and it may be in that child's best interests, and in the long run society's, that a certain amount of delinquency should be tolerated. The balance must be reached by the conscience of the hearing.

Finally, the panel member has somehow to reconcile the relaxed, friendly atmosphere of a good hearing with the element of compulsion which must emerge, and which must be acknowledged implicitly throughout. The hearing is not a democratic meeting of equals, discussing the child's best interests from equal standpoints, because at the end one section is going to impose a decision on another section and a third, the social worker, is going to have to carry it out, whether or not he agrees with it. Furthermore, the decision is backed by the full force of the law. The panel member has to face up to the responsibility of his powers or others will not recognise the powers that he has and will think that a decision by a hearing is less binding than a decision by a court. This would do a great disservice to children and would mean, contrary to Kilbrandon, that they were being dealt with outside the ambit of the law, instead of by a special agency with its full backing. This authoritarian aspect of his rôle may trouble the panel member but his conclusion must be the reflection that the whole procedure is in the best interests of the child and anything he does should be measured only by that yardstick.

To sum up, the panel member very often finds himself involved in consideration of problems much wider than the immediate difficulties of one child. He sees the causes of delinquency and child neglect hopelessly intertwined with all the other social evils such as poverty, unemployment, drunkenness and sexual promiscuity and he sees that, whatever else the children's hearings system may do, it is not going to cure all those ills. He might, however, see himself as being in at the birth of a new social era. Physically man seems to have evolved as far as he usefully can. With the help of his technology, he can adapt to his environment better than any other animal, but unless he can find a way of solving his social conflicts, from child battering through juvenile delinquency to adult violence and international warfare, he is in immediate and real danger of becoming extinct. To be on the children's panel is to look at society in microcosm. It is sometimes not a pleasant sight and sometimes, as yet another sad little procession shuffles in before a hearing, the panel member may find it almost too painful to contemplate; the parents, too inadequate to manage their own lives let alone those of their children, and the child, bewildered, but defiant, trying to make a life for himself in a social jungle. Added to this suffering is the suffering the child may have inflicted on some innocent member of the community. The awful, pathetic messiness of it is all too plain and the members of hearings are forced to look at it, knowing that resources which might help the child are unlikely to be available. But this is where the hope lies. Many hundreds of ordinary people know now, as never before, the nature of social deprivation and its consequences in terms of social conflict and they are not going to retire hurt from the encounter. Everywhere they are putting what pressure they can on government, regional and central, to provide resources and to spend money where it will have the most effect.

Panel members now find themselves in a position from which they can profoundly influence the community's way of dealing with its problems and they are not going to miss this opportunity.

2. MAEVE MCDONALD

EVERY PANEL MEMBER is quite clear that his primary duty is to reach a decision, together with his colleagues, as to the course of action which will benefit the child appearing before the hearing. In the past five years however it has become quite apparent that the general public has a completely different view. Panel members are expected to eliminate or at least to reduce the incidence of juvenile crime. Time and time again, we have been criticised in the press, on radio and on television for failing to deal satisfactorily with delinquents. These uninformed and misdirected criticisms have done positive harm to the system; potential volunteers have been dissuaded from offering their services and those already active have been discouraged. Many people in our society take on voluntary work, and there is no doubt as to the value of their efforts. Most of those who give willingly of their time expect little in return but it would be fair to say that they have a right to obtain some degree of satisfaction from what they do. Sadly, too many panel members are deprived of this reward.

There can be few people interested in the system who are unaware of the tragic lack of the matching field organisation necessary to implement the decision of a children's hearing. Many areas are desperately short of social workers, assessment facilities are inadequate or non-existent, suitable residential places are not available, suitable foster parents cannot be found, and so on. None of us was serving very long before becoming conscious of the unsatisfactory situation in which we are expected to operate. Nonetheless, I am constantly heartened when I meet newly appointed panel members. In spite of all these difficulties, significant numbers of concerned people of high calibre continue to volunteer.

It is the responsibility of the local Children's Panel Advisory Committee – the CPAC – to select new members. This is no easy task. What are the criteria they should use? There has been a long and continuing debate on the suitability v. representativeness issue. In other words, should the CPAC select a volunteer because he, as an individual, is potentially a good panel member or because his inclusion in a given area panel will contribute to that panel being recognised as an accurate reflection of the local community? I have no doubt where I stand on this issue: the personal qualities of the individual are all-important. Whereas I can acknowledge the dangers of panel members appearing remote from the families with whom they come in contact, the ability to appreciate other people's feelings and to establish constructive communication soon breaks down class barriers which are often more apparent than real.

The selection process, which consists of individual and group interviews, is followed by a period of pre-service training. Unfortunately, the interval between making application and commencing training has often proved to be long and frustrating. Positive efforts must be made by local and regional CPACs and the Social Work Services Group to speed up their procedures. When delays do occur it would be helpful if the prospective – and serving – panel members were informed.

The pre-service training programmes have attracted – and continue to attract – a great deal of criticism. This is as it should be. Constructive criticism has been sought, welcomed and acted upon. The present pre-service training bears no resemblance to that of five years ago. Formal lectures by university and local authority staff have been replaced by small tutor groups chaired by an experienced panel member. New members are given the opportunity of meeting and learning from those working in the system. It is a measure of the increasing confidence and expertise of panel members that some have been able to take the responsibility of introducing their newly appointed colleagues to the system.

During this period of training, which usually lasts about three months, a new member quickly learns that, if the system is to work effectively, good relationships, based on mutual respect, must be established between the part-time lay panel members and the full-time professionals. This is most obviously true in the case of the reporter to the children's panel. There is no other member of the system with whom a panel member will have more contact. It has been quite noticeable that, over the last five years, panel members have become less dependent on the reporter in the hearing situation. In the early days, it was probably inevitable that we looked to the professional for advice about procedural rules and points of law. But if a family is to have confidence in the people who are taking a decision affecting the life of their child, it is vitally important that the panel members have full knowledge and control of the situation. At least some of the credit for this development must be given to those reporters who have given their time and support to the training of panel members.

In Glasgow, we have always been most fortunate to enjoy the full support of the reporter's department for area panel meetings. Every area chairman has been more than grateful for the prompt and cheerful assistance given by the office staff in typing and sending out letters to panel members and visiting speakers. Area meetings are normally held in the department which has always been made available on request. The reporters usually attend these meetings as a member of the area, demonstrating that there is no divide between the lay members and the professionals.

One of the ways in which panel members have earned the respect of all the professionals with whom they work has been by the extent to which the confidential nature of their reports has been honoured. I well remember the concern which was voiced when it was proposed that detailed social background reports, school, psychological, medical and psychiatric reports should be sent to lay panel members. Happily, all the doubts have proved to be without foundation. Throughout the country panel members have proved that they can be relied upon to protect the interests of the families who come before hearings.

The social worker's background report is normally the main source of information which the panel members receive before the hearing. From this and other assessments each of the panel members can decide upon the topics he wishes to explore with the family. During the hearing, however, the panel member must be alert and sensitive to pick up any signals – verbal or non-verbal

– which may indicate the areas which the child or parents consider to be important. Together with the social worker and the reporter, the panel members must try to establish a full, frank and open discussion so that a decision acceptable to everyone present may emerge from the hearing. This is not easily achieved. Much scorn is poured on the 'cosy chats' which are supposed to be characteristic of children's hearings. My experience is that many families are under a noticeable degree of stress when they are introduced. Panel members have to develop considerable skills to overcome such barriers as silence, reticence, fear or aggression.

Despite the best efforts of all concerned, we do sometimes find ourselves in considerable difficulties. There are a few families who simply refuse to co-operate with what we are trying to do. In these circumstances we have to admit that we have no appropriate measures to deal with such attitudes. But even more frustrating is the situation where we are convinced – and the family agrees – that a supervision requirement could be of benefit to the child and the social worker explains that the resource is not available – be it suitable staff or a residential place. Every panel member in this part of the country appreciates the serious shortages in the social work department but to what extent do we tailor our decisions to meet the present unsatisfactory circumstances? This all-too-familiar problem is one which forcibly indicates to the panel member that his responsibilities are not restricted to the hearing room. We must do what we can to improve the resources which are available to us.

At the same time I am firmly convinced that the resources we do have are not being used as effectively as possible. It seems to me absolutely necessary that each time a supervision requirement is made – be this at home or in some residential establishment – the expectations of the hearing must be clearly spelled out. The nature of the service which is being offered by the social work department should be described in as much detail as possible. Here I should emphasise that I am more concerned with the quality as distinct from the quantity of the social work involvement. It is not surprising to find that panel members are watching with great interest the developments which are taking place in 'intermediate treatment'. As yet, this interest is purely academic as this resource is not directly available to the hearings. Panel members are pressing that this situation is only temporary.

We are also looking to the day schools with increasing expectations. With improved staffing it is hoped that primary and guidance staff will continue to improve their service to children in need and to those who come before hearings. There can be little doubt that this last year has seen a greatly increased contact between guidance staff and panel members. The benefits of such meetings are rapidly becoming obvious. Each group has a growing appreciation of the other's task, the importance which is attached to school reports is being recognised and the quality of the reports has markedly improved. Certainly all panel members are convinced that close co-operation between the education and social work departments holds the key to many of the problems The appointment of more school social workers is the dream of many panel members.

Being a panel member is a time-consuming business – a fact not clearly spelled out by the Children's Panel Advisory Committee when they recruit new members. At least two or three times a month, four hearings will take up a whole morning, or afternoon or most of an evening. Some hours are necessary to familiarise ourselves with the reports. We must do more. It is quite irresponsible of any panel member to be a party to a decision to remove a child from home if he does not have a clear idea of the type of establishment to which that child is being committed. We must conscientiously visit assessment centres, List D schools, children's homes and hostels. We must make every effort to meet and get to know the people who work with the children – social workers, teachers, police, youth leaders. The time devoted to making such contacts is always well spent. Information so gathered can be put to good use to establish the communication which is so vital in the hearings.

In-service training is, to me, a most important part of the work of a panel member. Commitment to such meetings should, I think, be emphasised at the selection stage. Again Children's Panel Advisory Committees have not been making this sufficiently clear to the people they interview. We must continue to learn while we are in service as panel members. Training does not turn us into semi-professionals but should help us to heighten our sensitivity to the problems we encounter in the hearing room.

In the four years I have been a panel member I have become increasingly conscious of the degree to which the children's panel has been an exercise in community education. This exercise is just beginning. As we gain experience, panel members form valid opinions about the needs of children in trouble. Opportunities are provided at in-service training and at local area meetings for us to discuss and formulate our ideas in the light of our unique and privileged experience. Some of our more politically minded colleagues take upon themselves the responsibility of communicating our views to those in the appropriate positions of authority. Through the hearings system many of us have learned a great deal about how our society is organised and have applied pressure to local officials with varying degrees of success. This last year has, however, been a particularly frustrating one. Local authorities are, of course, faced with serious financial problems but that should not prevent us, as panel members, from pressing that the needs of the children who appear before us are met. In a situation where resources are scarce it is vitally important that those which are available are deployed correctly. It is surely no bad thing that a large number of people have been made aware – at first hand – of the problems of our children and that those in positions of responsibility should be thoroughly questioned by informed members of the public as to their priorities and actions.

Possible changes in the legislation relating to the powers and procedures of children's hearings are now under active consideration. It is right that members of children's panels are being consulted. Just as in the hearings, where panel members are faced with achieving a difficult balance between identifying the needs of the individual child and reflecting the values of the community, we shall have to be careful to preserve the enlightened ideas in the Social Work (Scotland) Act 1968 whilst admitting that some new measures are needed to meet the present situation.

23

ACHIEVEMENTS, ISSUES AND PROSPECTS

F. M. MARTIN AND KATHLEEN MURRAY

IF towards the end of the 1960's some United Nations official, expert in comparative social statistics, had been asked to compile a short list of countries in which an original and forward-looking system of juvenile justice was likely to become firmly rooted, it is unlikely that he would have ranked Scotland high among his priorities. Questioned specifically about Scotland, he would have referred to that country's excessive propensity to seek 'institutional' solutions to social problems, with law-breakers disproportionately often committed to prison, the mentally ill to in-patient care, the mentally retarded to hospital, deprived children to residential homes. He would no doubt also have drawn attention to the persistence in Scottish life of many illiberal and even punitive trends: the greater emphasis on formal discipline and the acceptance of corporal punishment in schools, the failure to reform either the law of divorce or the law relating to homosexuality in line with changes accepted in England. The signs in Scotland, the international observer would almost certainly have concluded, were anything but propitious.

It is pleasant to record that this hypothetical adviser would have been mistaken. Perhaps the most important achievement of the children's hearings system is quite simply that it has survived. It has experienced many difficulties and encountered much criticism, and is likely to continue to do so in the future. But there are no serious proposals to replace it with any alternative; while it is becoming increasingly apparent that the system is putting down roots, developing a capacity for self-examination and organic growth, and attracting international interest. It is a striking feature of Scottish juvenile justice that its inner tensions and inconsistencies are explicit and unhidden, and its very honesty tends to invite criticism from both extremes, from repressive disciplinarians and from those who find any form of social control intolerable. These criticisms usually tell us more about those who express them than about the system against which they are directed; but to members of children's panels, who generally have a much clearer awareness of the system's failings and limitations, they are a constant source of pain. And yet for all the lack of obvious public approbation, and in spite of the inevitable frustrations when the services required to support the work of children's hearings are so often inadequate both quantitatively and qualitatively, panel members maintain a continuing commitment and are even able to attract an ample flow of new recruits. When the Dumfries and Galloway Region has six vacancies on its children's panel and more than 50 applications, or when Tayside, with 12 vacancies, is able to select from 150 candidates for unpaid service, it is evident that Scottish culture is far from unitary, and that there are within the community veins of disinterested social concern which our system of juvenile justice has been uniquely successful in tapping.

Mutual support plays an important part in maintaining the morale of panel members; so too does training. As professional educators we may perhaps be biassed on this score, but we would argue that both preliminary and in-service training contribute vitally to the sharpening of skills and the broadening of awareness. Imaginative training makes it possible for practical experience to be reviewed, evaluated and shared. It can also do a great deal to counter any tendency to inwardness and parochialism, by ensuring a flow of contributions from outside the area or outside the system, introducing panel members to new developments in theory or practice. Finally, training helps to reinforce the self-confidence and sense of independence of panel members. It would be highly unproductive if panel members were always at variance with social workers and reporters, but it would be a denial of the significance of the lay component in the system if the decisions reached at hearings invariably reflected the recommendations of the professionals. Through the integration of training and practical experience the voluntary workers are able to achieve a level of knowledge and discernment which justifies the expression of an independent viewpoint.

Our emphasis on the importance of training and of the evaluation of experience implies a view of the Scottish pattern of juvenile justice as having a potential for organic growth and evolution. Some of the imperfections of the pattern are, we would maintain, inescapable; any set of procedures for dealing with children who have broken the law must in our view necessarily involve a series of compromises if it is to survive, compromises which may be unacceptable to those for whom philosophical consistency is more important than viability. But others of its failings can be identified as such within the system's own terms of reference, and can in large measure be remedied. To a greater extent than some alternative models, the children's hearings system has both the capacity and the will to profit from the examination of its own performance.

The essence of what has been achieved so far is a very unusual – indeed, in the context of British justice, an unprecedented – separation of the process of disposition from that of adjudication. By removing from the courts of law the cases of the vast majority of young delinquents, it has been made possible for unhurried consideration to be given to what might be the most appropriate course of action for each individual child. Like most human undertakings, children's hearings sometimes fall short of their own ideals, but at their not infrequent best they are able to move away from the traditional segregation of the all-powerful authority figure remotely dispensing justice and the stigmatised delinquent, and to achieve a degree of communication and mutual understanding which personal impressions and the admittedly limited research evidence suggest is a good deal in advance of what is generally accomplished either elsewhere in the United Kingdom or in the United States. An opportunity is provided, to a degree never previously attainable, for collaboration between the various professional and voluntary agencies concerned with the provision of services for children. In addition, and in the longer term not least among the achievements of the system described in this book, there is its contribution to the slow enlightenment of public opinion. Members of children's panels, educated through their work in children's hearings to an awareness of the needs and problems of children and families, can form an articulate source of pressure for the social changes needed if those problems are ever to be alleviated, and can also both collectively and individually through their other rôles in society, diffuse this awareness outside their own ranks.

Many issues remain unresolved. Some of the most important of these, we have argued, involve conflicts or tensions within the system which we would not expect to be harmonised in the foreseeable future. Their existence should be seen not as a sign of an intolerable ideological impurity but as a source of strength. In our own society and in most broadly similar industrial societies, attitudes to juvenile delinquency are confused and contradictory. The picture would be complex enough if members of the community could be divided neatly into either a 'tough-minded' or control- and punishment-oriented category or a 'tender-minded' or care- and treatment-oriented group. We suggest however that in fact a rather large proportion of citizens embody both sets of attitudes in varying proportions. It seems an inevitable consequence that these ambivalences should be reflected in conflicting expectations confronting any system of juvenile justice. The principles and procedures of children's hearings in Scotland involve a striking degree of movement away from a simple 'crime and punishment' philosophy. But if the concern of the system were solely with 'treatment', if 'compulsory measures of care' were not defined in the 1968 Act as including 'protection, control and guidance' as well as treatment, it would not merely run ahead of general public opinion – as it already does, and should – but outdistance it to such an extent that it would have little or no chance of survival. The range of options available at any one time is not unlimited – and this applies to both ends of the spectrum of penal possibilities.

From this point of view the distinction between consequentialism and retributivism, for all its theoretical interest, seems to be of only limited relevance to current disputes over juvenile justice or other penological issues. We see retributivism as one component of attitudes towards delinquency, occupying a dominant position in some persons and an insignificant rôle in others, but only exceptionally accounting for the sum-total of an individual's attitudinal set. We are all consequentialists now, and have been for a long time. Disputes over penal policy have mainly been between different varieties of consequentialism, and have concerned the relative importance to be attached to such objectives as deterrence, moral reform, social rehabilitiation and psychological change – alternative and sometimes conflicting principles, but equally consequentialist.

If the adoption of retributivism as a guiding principle entails our having regard only to the characteristics of the offence and not at all to the characteristics of the offender, we should be discarding not merely the explicit emphasis of the hearings system on the individualisation of dispositions, but even the practice of virtually all judges in the overwhelming majority of cases, of differentiating between first offenders and those with criminal histories of varying lengths and degrees of seriousness. An attempt to make such a principle operative in the real world would we suspect give rise to a sense of injustice more profound and more pervasive than any generated by the vagaries of consequentialism in any of its varieties.

In addition to the constant problem of maintaining an acceptable balance of objectives in a pluralistic system, panel members have also to set their face against the peculiar moral hazards of what may be referred to as 'welfare totalitarianism.' Given a high degree of discretion in a system which attaches very great value to promoting the interests of the individual child, there is always a danger that in an excess of well-intentioned enthusiasm measures may be taken which are experienced as punitive or highly restrictive and which are manifestly disproportionate to the scale of the offence. Especially if taken outside the scope of a judicial system, such measures can make serious inroads on civil liberties and understandably provide converts to a belief in retributive justice and tariff systems of punishment. If this risk is ever run in children's hearings, it is not because the necessary safeguards are lacking. The legislation makes comprehensive provision for protecting the rights of children and their parents at every stage of the proceedings; should these be neglected panel members and their professional advisers are gravely at fault. It is of course an extremely difficult task to maintain a due regard for legally correct procedure while at the same time creating an atmosphere of informality which encourages open communication, and it would be surprising if there were never any temptation to take short cuts. Yet the reconciliation of the legal and the psychological requirements is essential for the satisfactory conduct of hearings; its full achievement reflects not only successful training and practical experience but also a considerable capacity for self-scrutiny and the retrospective analysis of performance.

For most panel members the most salient present-day issue is that of 'resources'. There is a widespread tendency to see the potential of the hearings system as having been frustrated both by an absolute shortage of the skills and facilities needed to implement the decisions reached at hearings and by the variable quality of those which are available. A good deal of scepticism has been expressed about social work supervision, and there has been criticism both of the lack of an adequate variety of types of residential accommodation and of the shortage of treatment facilities within the community. All of these problems are discussed in earlier chapters, and the arguments need not be recapitulated here. Perhaps it is worth adding that although the shortfall of provision is manifestly excessive and inexcusable, we are a long way from knowing what scale and pattern of services would be optimal. In order however to define the appropriate levels of provision and their mode of deployment, we should need to build up the kind of detailed research into service delivery and its consequences, the lack of which is at present a major handicap to systematic planning and even to intelligent discussion of the whole range of personal social services.

Finally, among the issues which have a bearing on the future of the hearings system, we would include the question of the relative significance of the many factors affecting the level of delinquency in the community. We do not think it important to counter the criticism to be found in some newspapers and in the public pronouncements of self-appointed defenders of law and order, to the effect that continuing high levels of delinquency clearly indicate the 'failure' of children's hearings, with the corollary that a reversion to highly punitive methods would solve all our problems. We would however suggest that the Kilbrandon Committee's views on causes of delinquency were not sufficiently balanced. The basic causes, it was argued, were not social and environmental but were rather to be sought in personal maladjustment. Environmental factors, it may be thought, were too lightly dismissed; and the dichotomy between psychological and sociological factors, here as in so much other literature, may be more apparent than real. The great majority of the children appearing before hearings are drawn disproportionately from areas of the greatest relative deprivation. This does not necessarily imply any simple and direct link between poverty and law-breaking. If we are ever to gain a balanced understanding of the causes of delinquency we have to understand the ways in which given social, economic and environmental circumstances affect the quality of family life and the relations between parents and children, and how these in their turn are influential in shaping the outlook and even the personalities of the children. If this view is acceptable, it follows that the anti-social behaviour which brings young people before the hearings is the most recent link in a whole chain of causal processes. It also follows that the work done with individual delinquents during and after the hearings cannot be sufficient in itself to bring about major changes in the overall level of delinquency in the community. To say this is in no way to diminish the value of such interventions, but only to argue that they must be supported by action on another plane to improve our social arrangements and to humanise our cities. Preventive social action is a good deal more difficult than optimistic reformers used to believe, but that does not mean that it is impossible.

One special aspect of this general problem of the interaction between individuals and social institutions deserves mention here. There is a danger that, like social work, the hearings may be used to tidy up the failures of society. It is dangerously easy for the personal social services and the juvenile justice system alike, sometimes unconsciously to collude with many agencies in our own society which help to generate or at any rate intensify social problems. One striking example is the whole question of truancy. There is a real hazard that schools might become excessively complacent and self-satisfied if truancy were defined simply as a problem of deviance. Such an attitude tends to discourage schools from looking much more closely and critically at their own teaching methods, their own curricula and their own responsibilities for failing to capture the interest and imagination of the children in their care. Instead of concentrating wholly on the management of delinquent behaviour, it may be helpful to look also at the system against which the behaviour is a reaction.

What prospects can we look to in the future? First, we would hope that the substantial measure of public support that children's hearings now enjoy will expand significantly. For reasons discussed above we would not expect a profound transformation in the short term, but rather assume that conflicting expectations and critical attitudes will be very much in evidence in the foreseeable future. Indeed, there are particular grounds for tempering optimism with caution at the present time, when liberal ideas and welfare philosophies are everywhere under attack. Nevertheless, it is not unreasonable to anticipate a gradual development of humane and informed attitudes towards children in trouble, with panel members playing an important contributory rôle. In particular we have begun, just begun, to enter into the inner world of the boy at the bottom of the heap, with limited personal endowment, with little or no parental encouragement, for whom the educational experience seems meaningless and irrelevant, a source only of failure and frustration, and for whom the expectation of work is the expectation of endless routine and subordination.

A more widespread understanding and acceptance of the philosophy that informs the children's hearings system might help to ensure that a broader cross-section of the public was recruited to panel membership. In identifying this as a desirable objective we would dissociate ourselves completely from the assertion that the largely middle-class composition of most children's panels is in some sense a guarantee of their incompetence. There is available at present a vocabulary of social abuse, a collection of words with lethal properties comparable to those of the arrows blown by the Amazonian Indians. 'Middle-class' is one of these poison-tipped epithets, although its use in a destructive sense is curiously restricted to television interviewers, university lecturers and others of unquestionably middle-class status. The criticism rests upon an untested and almost certainly false assumption – namely, that panel members who differ in social class from the children who come before them can neither 'understand their problems' nor communicate effectively with them. To hold such a view seriously it is necessary either to ignore the part played by insight, awareness and compassion in the conduct of children's hearings or to assume, against all the evidence, that such qualities are denied to people who happen to be teachers or ministers, secretaries or shopkeepers. Also implicit in this attitude is a crude and in many ways patronising view of social class differences in value – orientations, with 'the middle class' holding an exaggerated respect for law and order and the maintenance of restrained standards of behaviour and 'the working class' displaying tolerance of delinquency and impulse-gratification. Value systems are complex and multifarious, and there are marked variations within classes so broadly defined as well as between them. It would in the present context be particularly obtuse to underestimate the strength of dedication to the law-abiding ideal which persists among a majority of wage-earners and their families. Most of the available evidence on juvenile delinquents suggests that they tend to be drawn from the most disadvantaged strata of the working class and not with equal frequency from all parts of it. To suppose that working-class panel members would have some special bond with the children on the other side of the table is an illusion, even though it is one which may gratify middle-class romantics. The serious argument for broadening the basis of panel membership rests not on any pre-judgements of suitability but simply on the conviction that the children's panels represent a very important form of citizen participation and that like all voluntary movements it gains in strength by drawing upon as many sections of the community as possible.

The decision embodied first in the 1966 White Paper and subsequently in the Social Work (Scotland) Act to depart from the original Kilbrandon recommendation and incorporate supportive services for children's hearings within comprehensive local authority social work departments has meant, inevitably if unintentionally, that the effectiveness of the hearings system has depended heavily on the vicissitudes of the new service in general. The social work services, as an earlier chapter has argued, have from the beginning been inadequately supplied with capital, with personnel and with imagination, and have frequently failed to measure up to expectations. If the services made available to children's hearings have often been inadequate, so too have the services provided for the mentally ill, the physically disabled, the elderly. . . . It would not be unreasonable to hope for an inflow of resources such as would permit hearings to make decisions with a fair degree of confidence that they would be carried out. The problem is not merely one of scale however. There is an urgent need not only for a better deployment of appropriately trained social workers, but also for some attempt at the integration of the variety of specialist diagnostic and treatment services provided for children. No doubt it would be too much to hope for a multi-disciplinary service providing for the needs of a client group rather than a series of separate, specialist services each catering for one aspect of need – specifically, for a children's service rather than several fragments of medicine, education and social work; we take it for granted that doctors can only work in a health service, that all social workers must come under the command of the director of social work, that psychological services must be an appendage to education and staffed by former teachers – and the patterns of provision which emerge from our planning activities may differ greatly from the arrangements which would emerge if the needs of clients rather than of professions were the point of departure in the planning process. In the far-from-Utopian short term however, we might reasonably expect to achieve a unified assessment service for children appearing before hearings.

Lastly, we attach much importance to the prospect of a major contribution from research. Reporters to children's panels have very considerable discretionary powers, and the system can only benefit from a careful and objective examination of the interplay of the many factors which bear upon their decision-making. The disposals agreed upon at hearings arise from the weighing of information contained in reports, of subjective impressions gained in hearings, of judgements of the quality of services likely to be available; research, if sufficiently subtle, can illuminate the relative significance of the different components of the process. Such studies are best seen as collaborative ventures between research workers and professional and lay participants in the hearings system, a process of self-examination leading to greater awareness and enhanced competence. On a different plane, there is a need also for a monitoring of performance of the system as a whole, taking account of the after-histories of youngsters from the time they first come to the attention of the reporter. Such studies would not in any serious sense 'evaluate' social work supervision or intermediate treatment or residence in a List D school, but they could provide invaluable descriptive information on the consequences of alternative decisions. Research into children's hearings has so far, with only one or two exceptions, been on a very small scale and restricted to relatively peripheral issues. Five or six years after the inception of the system there is a powerful case for a major new initiative.

It was Felix Frankfurter, one of the most distinguished of American jurists, who remarked that the best single measure of a country's level of civilisation was its criminal code; nothing was more revealing about a society than the way it treated its own enemies. If this criterion can be applied to the treatment of juvenile offenders, we may say with confidence that the hearings system should be an authentic source of pride to the country in which it has become established.

SELECTED BIBLIOGRAPHY

Children and Young Persons. Scotland (1964)
    Cmnd. 2306 HMSO (Kilbrandon Report)
Social Work and the Community (1966)
    Cmnd. 3065 HMSO (White Paper)
Social Work (Scotland) Act 1968

BRUCE, NIGEL — 1975 — Children's hearings: a retrospect
Brit. J. Criminology 15, 4

BRUCE, N. & SPENCER, J. — 1973 — Children's hearings and the Scottish courts: some lessons from the case of Mary Cairns
The Year Book of Social Policy in Britain

FOX, SANFORD J. — 1974 — Juvenile Justice Reform: innovations in Scotland
American Criminal Law Review 12, 1

1974 — Evaluation of the system by an American observer
Int. J. Offender Therapy and Comparative Criminology 18, 3

1975 — The Scottish Panels: an American viewpoint on children's right to punishment
J. Law Soc. Scot. March

GALLACHER, JIM — 1974 — The children's hearing system: treatment or control?
Justice for Children Care Discussion Paper No. 2

GORDON, GERALD H. — 1972 — Renton and Brown
Criminal Procedure According to the Law of Scotland (4th ed.) pp. 412–447

1973 — Prosecuting Children: an assessment of the situation in the light of the 1968 Act
J. Law Soc. Scot. 18, 11

GRANT, JOHN P. — 1971 — Juvenile Justice: Part III of the Social Work (Scotland) Act 1968
The Juridical Review Part 2

1973 — Bridging gaps. Three cases on children's hearings
Scots Law Times (News) 190

1974 — More bridges, but more gaps. Two further decisions on children's hearings
Scots Law Times (News) 213

1974 — Children's hearings: some legal and practical difficulties
Justice for Children Care Discussion Paper No. 2

1974 — Model procedure for a children's hearing
Scots Law Times (News) 229

1975 The rehabilitation of offenders Act 1974 and children's hearings
J. Law Soc. Scot. April

1975 The legal safeguards for the rights of the child and parents in the children's hearing system
The Juridical Review Part 3

1976 Legal united 1, reporters association 2
J. Law Soc. Scot. February 1976

1976 The children's hearing system in Scotland: strengths and weaknesses
Irish Jurist

KELLY, ALISTAIR F. 1974 Children's Hearings
Int. J. Offender Therapy and Comparative Criminology 18, 3

MAPSTONE, ELIZABETH 1973 The selection of the children's panel for the county of Fife
Brit. J. Social Wk. 2, 4

MARTIN, F. M. 1976 Children's Hearings
New Society 12.2.76

MAY, DAVID 1971 Delinquency control and the treatment model: some implications of recent legislation
Brit. J. Criminology Vol. II pp. 359–370

MAY, D. & SMITH, G. 1970 Policy interpretation and the children's panels: a case study in social administration
J. Applied Social Studies Vol. 2

MORRIS, ALLISON 1972 Children's hearings in Scotland
Criminal Law Review 693

1974 Scottish juvenile justice – a critique
in *Crime, Criminology and Public Policy.*
Hood, R. (ed.)

1976 Juvenile justice: where next?
The Howard Journal Vol. 18

MURRAY, KATHLEEN 1974 Children's panel training: learning to change
Scot. J. Adult Educ. 1, 2

MURRAY, G. J. & ROWE, A. J. B. 1973 Children's panels: implications for the future
Policy & Politics 1, 4

PARSLOE, PHYLLIDA 1976 Social work and the justice model
Brit. J. Social Wk. 6, 1

RITCHIE, M. & MACK, J. 1975 *Police warnings.* University of Glasgow

ROWE, A. J. B. 1972 *Initial selection for children's panels in Scotland*
Bookstall Publications, London

1972 Children's hearings
New Society 2.3.72

SINCLAIR, ALASTAIR 1976 Whither reporters: the future of the profession of reporter to the children's panel
Social Work Today 7, 5

SMITH, G. S. & MAY, D. 1971 The appointment of the Aberdeen City children's panel
Brit. J. Social Wk. 1, 1

SPENCER, JOHN 1973 Juvenile justice – the demands of treatment
I.S.T.D.

WILSON, ANDREW 1974 Recent developments in social work
Int. J. Offender Therapy and Comparative Criminology 18, 3